STRINGBEAN

MUSIC IN AMERICAN LIFE

A list of books in the series appears at the end of this book.

STRINGBEAN

THE **LIFE** AND **MURDER** OF A COUNTRY MUSIC LEGEND

TAYLOR HAGOOD

UNIVERSITY OF ILLINOIS PRESS
Urbana, Chicago, and Springfield

Library of Congress Cataloging-in-Publication Data
Names: Hagood, Taylor, 1975– author.
Title: Stringbean : the life and murder of a country music legend /
    Taylor Hagood.
Description: Urbana : University of Illinois Press, 2023. | Series:
    Music in American life | Includes bibliographical references
    and index.
Identifiers: LCCN 2022040026 (print) | LCCN 2022040027
    (ebook) | ISBN 9780252044984 (cloth) | ISBN 9780252087110
    (paperback) | ISBN 9780252054167 (ebook)
Subjects: LCSH: Stringbean, 1915–1973. | Banjoists—Appalachian
    Region—Biography. | Murder victims—Tennessee. | Trials
    (Murder)—Tennessee.
Classification: LCC ML419.S828 H34 2023 (print) | LCC ML419.
    S828 (ebook) | DDC 787.8/8092—dc23/eng/20220824
LC record available at https://lccn.loc.gov/2022040026
LC ebook record available at https://lccn.loc.gov/2022040027

for the late Jesse and Helen McKenzie,
their son, Kevin,
and their daughter, Michelle, and her husband, John

CONTENTS

A NOTE ON NAMES

Stringbean's family historically has spelled the last name in a variety of ways, most often "Akemon." While I attempt to pinpoint when Stringbean began spelling it as "Akeman," in order to reduce confusion the name will be spelled "Akeman" throughout the book when referring to him. I use "David" and "Stringbean" as well as "String" strategically to try to capture the development of the Stringbean persona and how people knew and interacted with David Akeman as Stringbean. Stringbean's closest associates will be referred to often by first name in an effort to convey their informal, intimate connections with him and to capture the particular familiar and familial atmosphere fostered by the country music industry during Stringbean's lifetime. Stringbean's chief instrument I will refer to as the Vega No. 9: my presenting it as a living entity is not mere anthropomorphism but reflects the peculiar agency and sympathy of a resonant actant fashioned of wood, metal, and flesh. Finally, each chapter title is taken either from a Stringbean album or one of Stringbean's recorded song titles.

STRINGBEAN

SHORT LIFE AND TROUBLE

November 11, 1973

Grandpa Jones and his wife, Ramona, were up early on this cold Sunday morning while their teenage son, Mark, lay asleep upstairs. Grandpa loaded his suitcase and guns into the trunk of his Lincoln under a full moon.[1] The thermometer registered twenty-eight degrees, and a calm wind stirred here in Ridgetop, Tennessee, twenty miles north of Nashville. Grandpa was about to embark on a trip to Virginia, where he would hunt grouse with his old buddy Joe Wheeler.[2] Joining them would be Grandpa's best friend and neighbor, who lived on the other side of the hill here about a half mile up Baker Station Road. Grandpa had agreed to pick his friend up at six o'clock. Then he, Grandpa, would drive the entire way to Virginia.[3] His friend never drove.

Dawn's gray encroached on the darkness just above the hills as Grandpa hugged and kissed Ramona good-bye and got into the car. He had just reached age sixty last month but had been known as "Grandpa" for decades. The name had proved to be a great marketing move: rather than having to worry about outliving his billing, he just grew into his persona. Even before taking on the moniker, he had billed himself as "Marshall Jones, the Young Singer of Old Songs." Old times and old-time music were what he loved. And he shared these passions with the neighbor he now drove toward.

He and that neighbor shared many other similarities and passions as well. They both hailed from Kentucky. They had many mutual acquaintances in the country music industry. Their wives were best friends. The two families had even, at one point, lived on the same property. Like himself, his friend went by a stage name. But where Grandpa had shed false whiskers and wrinkles for real gray and marks of age, his friend's stage name described a lifelong physique. Standing more than six feet tall and extremely skinny, he embodied the handle country fans around the world knew him by:

Stringbean.

As Grandpa topped the hill, bringing Stringbean's small home into view, his eye caught something unusual. Stringbean always got up early and built a fire in the fireplace, so a plume of blue smoke should be hanging in the air. This morning, however, no smoke curled from the chimney.

Grandpa wondered if his friend was sleeping in.[4] But when he turned up the long dirt driveway to the house, he noticed something else. At first, he thought it was just a coat lying in the grass near the driveway about seventy-five yards away from the house, fifty away from the cattle gate.[5] When he got closer, he realized the coat encircled a person. He stopped the car, got out, and walked swiftly to the body.

It was Stringbean's wife, Estelle, crumpled facedown, covered in the morning's heavy frost.[6] Grandpa had seen dead human bodies during World War II when he was stationed in Germany, including a woman who had been shot in the neck five times. When he felt how cold Estelle was, he knew she was gone. Then he saw she had been shot in the back and the head.[7]

Terrible comprehension filled him. He rushed toward the house. "String! String!" His voice echoed around the surrounding hills.[8] On the front porch sat the case containing the Vega No. 9 Tubaphone five-string banjo Stringbean had played throughout his career. Grasping the storm-door handle, Grandpa found the front door open. He looked inside.

There, in front of the cold fireplace, where so often he had sat happily playing the banjo and smoking his pipe, lay Stringbean.[9]

*   *   *

"Somebody killed Stringbean!"

My grandmother Virginia Azalee Jackson Hagood erupted with the news she heard on radio station 650 WSM. She made her way around the house telling my grandfather and the kids still living at home as they dressed to head out for morning worship service here in Tullahoma, Tennessee.

My parents happened to be visiting that weekend and heard my grandmother deliver this shocking revelation in her husky voice. Although my mother was no country music fan, she recognized the name "Stringbean." It raised an image in her mind of a lean old man comically dressed in a long shirt and short pants playing the banjo and singing. With such a getup, he was hard *not to see*, especially at her in-laws' house when he appeared on the television program *Hee Haw*. Besides that, he occupied a place in the pantheon of country music heroes her mother-in-law regularly referred to in a running conversation. He was even known in the folk scene my mother and father loved.

The simple, heartbroken sentence my grandmother spoke that morning encapsulated everything about the persona she referred to, his murder, and the story yet to unfold. For true fans like Azalee, country music meant far more than an industry or just entertainment. Opry stars were practically kinfolks, and my grandmother grieved on a personal level when any of them came to harm. Already she had suffered through the deaths of Hank Williams and Patsy Cline.

Thousands of people in middle Tennessee experienced the same emotions that morning, wondering in outrage and bafflement, "Who would kill Stringbean and why?" Stringbean had never done anything but bring people joy, with his outlandish costume, his up-tempo songs, his jokes, his banjo playing, his comical "letters from home." Folks of all kinds liked him.

To so many like my grandmother, the murder felt like an assault not just on the music they loved but on the lifestyle that music represented. They had endured a decade's worth of assassinations, cultural revolution, and war in Vietnam. Before that, they had borne up under the crushing weight of the Great Depression and World War II. Through it all, the Grand Ole Opry had remained a Saturday-night constant that offered simple country fun during unsettling times. Yet these days, country music itself seemed to be changing more, with the growing outlaw-country movement and now the Opry actually preparing to move out of the iconic Ryman Auditorium.

Now Stringbean was dead, murdered.

The inexplicable nature of the Stringbean tragedy has never ceased. It remains profound, its pain beyond easy or adequate definition. The characters of this archetypal story vividly represent good and evil. But there is more than that. There is something in the Stringbean persona and the instrument he played. Something in the fact that he enjoyed fame and wealth yet chose to live with his wife in a tiny farmhouse and stick to the country ways of his youth. Something in his well-known love of taking whole days to drift down the Harpeth River fishing. Something in his way of saying he had a letter from home somewhere next to his heart, heart, heart.

The biography of Stringbean differs from most because it includes a substantial series of events *after* his murder. Most biographies end at the point of death, but this story does not even flag then. Much has been written about the investigation of the murders, and it often contains inaccuracies. The murder trial—one of the most sensational in Nashville history—constitutes yet another story. The events of the investigation and following juridical processes appear herein as they unfolded, and readers familiar with the often-told standard account of the murder and its aftermath may be surprised to find some unexpected questions and uneasy resolutions.

This book, then, offers a three-for-one: biography, true crime, and courtroom drama. These dimensions are all part of the Stringbean story, which is a vital one in the history of country music and American popular culture. With all that has been said or written about Stringbean's death, one might wonder whether his life has meaning beyond the fact of his murder. The answer is a resounding, "Absolutely, yes." Stringbean was a major multitalented star. He played the banjo in a distinct style that combined clawhammer with two-finger picking, and his Vega No. 9 banjo takes its place among the iconic instruments in country music history. As a singer, he had a gift for interpreting traditional and even new songs with originality and gusto while also writing his own. As a comedian, he brought a fine brand of dry-witted verbal humor that contrasted hilariously with his outrageous physical comedy, as his hand gestures and short-legged jig dances were unforgettable, while his catchphrases live on in people's memories now decades later. His murder fundamentally changed Nashville's conception of itself and led country stars to insulate themselves in ways not previously thought necessary. And the trial articulated and enacted a public spectacle of retribution that, over the course of the following decades, set the stage for a controversial redemption.

It is a sad irony that Stringbean's name appeared in more newspapers the week after his murder than ever in his lifetime. But, even had he not been killed, he would shine just as securely in the constellation of country stars as Grandpa, Roy Acuff, and Minnie Pearl. Like those stalwarts, Stringbean represented a bridge from the earliest days of the industry to its iteration at the time of his death. In fact, his experiences distinguished him. To Stringbean belonged the distinction of being Bill Monroe's first banjo player. He became the mentee of foundational Opry star Uncle Dave Macon. Stringbean performed at the Opry the night Hank Williams debuted, in the same segment of the show. As time progressed, younger stars adored him, especially fellow Kentuckian Loretta Lynn, who has so powerfully and authentically blended traditional sound with edgy contemporary topics. Along the way, fans and industry colleagues alike found themselves drawn to Stringbean's blend of aloof strangeness and open familiarity. Those people are part of his success and legacy; they actualize the Stringbean story and form a vital part of it.

Just as a banjo, like other instruments, resonates in sympathy with the sounds near it, so Stringbean both illuminated and was illuminated by the decades he lived through. He suffered the scars of economic depression and war while participating in the revolutionary media developments of radio and television. He was born the same year as Frank Sinatra and was the antithesis of banjoist and folksinger Pete Seeger; Stringbean's life interfaces with theirs in disconnected but mutually revealing ways. Meanwhile, throughout his life, Stringbean negotiated constant cultural change that accelerated in pace and immensity with each decade.

My hope is that this book not only presents these dimensions of the Stringbean story effectively but also captures and conveys something fundamental to country music and to the values Stringbean ascribed and spoke to. His blend of music and humor meant to bring people together in allegiance to simple, unplugged happiness. His persona is intimately tied to the banjo and its own life-affirming history and impact. In their personal lives, Stringbean and his wife chose to live according to Thoreau's principles of frugality and avoiding unnecessary noise.

Those values of Stringbean's arguably represent humanity at its best. And, while the story that follows features humanity also at its worst, in the end, Stringbean's example prevails as a hope and balm.

WAY BACK IN THE HILLS OF OLD KENTUCKY
1915-1935

LIVING A DREAM: 1942

In the summer of 1942, David "Stringbean" Akeman was living out his dream in a way few people ever get to do. He had just become a member of Bill Monroe's Blue Grass Boys, one of the hottest bands in hillbilly music.

Still in his twenties, David's face beamed fresh among those of the other band members riding to show dates in Bill's Hudson Country Club Eight with the bass fiddle strapped on top.[1] On the rare occasions when David smiled, his bad teeth marred his otherwise handsome face. But then the bad teeth somehow made him more endearing. That face and his physique bore a passing resemblance to the lanky film star Jimmy Stewart.

On a clear day, David might have seen the sunlight catch the ornate tower of the Tennessee state capitol building perched in Greek Revival splendor atop the high green hill in the middle of Nashville. Upon first arriving to the city, he probably could not have picked out the National Life and Accident Insurance Company's five-story, columned brown-gray cement building on the corner of Seventh and Union. But he would have known this company owned WSM, which aired the Grand Ole Opry. And now David himself played on that music program he had listened to for so long.

He—a poor boy from eastern Kentucky—had hit the biggest big time of all.

A KENTUCKY CHILDHOOD AND BANJO PLAYING: 1915–1927

There had been nothing particularly "big time" about David's home back in eastern Kentucky's Jackson County. Straddling the Appalachian Mountains and a high lift of sandstone geologists call the Pottsville Escarpment, the countryside *did* offer plenty of lovely views. Looming peaks and dramatic precipices formed shelves over which streams and rivers fell in spectacular cascades. The most unusual of these was Cumberland Falls, one of the few waterfalls in the world that produces a moonbow.[2] Not far from there yawned the famous "Cumberland Gap," where Daniel Boone in 1775 led the way from the east to help the settlement of the then new Kentucky and Tennessee Territories. This natural passageway was commemorated in a song of the same name, which David would one day record.

Aside from these few distinctions, however, Jackson County marked a remote spot in Kentucky and the nation. Unlike the wealthy "bluegrass" area around Lexington, with its pristine white fences slicing lush green fields where thoroughbreds grazed, Jackson County was home to folks who worked hard against unforgiving land. These people may not have been coughing toward the grave like their neighbors in the coal-rich parts of the state, but the steep slopes and rocky land posed a formidable array of challenges and dangers for timbering and cultivation.

James Akemon was one of these Jackson County people. He was born on November 25, 1878, in Crockettsville, Breathitt County (two counties east of Jackson), the youngest child of Polly and Alexander. Although Alexander spelled his last name as "Aikman" (and listed himself as "deaf") on the 1880 census, the name has most often been spelled "Akemon" by members of the family residing in the area then and now.[3] James married Alice Johnston in 1901 or 1902, possibly in Indiana. Alice was born January 2, 1882, in Buckhorn, Perry County, Kentucky, just south of Breathitt County. Their first child, Nora, was born in 1903, followed by another daughter, Elizabeth, whom they called "Lizzie," in 1907, and then a son, Luther, in 1908.[4] The couple may have lost an infant daughter, Polly, in 1910. By then, the family was established in Jackson County, with James laboring in the way he would list himself in census records from 1910 onward, "General Farming."

James owned his own farm in the area called Pond Creek. The family lived in a dogtrot-style home, a structure in which two cabins shared a single roof with a breezeway in between, where dogs could lie down or run through.[5] The farm itself was about forty acres and lay on Highway 30 between Tyner and Annville, two of the larger communities in the county. The largest was the county seat,

McKee. Some of the rural communities in this sparsely populated area bore especially colorful names. There was Parrot, which was also at times referred to as "Letter Box" because historically mail got delivered to a box nailed to a tree. Another community was Egypt, so named because one of the early families moving there saw themselves as exiled Israelites. Mummie was named not for its proximity to Egypt but because early settlers allegedly found a mummified body there. Strangely, a number of mummies have been discovered in Kentucky.

After giving birth to another boy they named Joseph in 1911, James and Alice welcomed David on June 17, 1915.[6] Alice and James naming their son "David" would be prophetic insofar as, like the Hebrew king in the Bible, this little boy would grow up to play an instrument and compose and sing songs. Incidentally, his national littermates that year included a handful destined to fame as major popular music figures. In New York was born Doris Fisher, writer of such standards as "You Always Hurt the One You Love" and "Put the Blame on Mame." Dayton, Ohio, saw the birth of the future great jazz composer Billy Strayhorn, while in Philadelphia was born Eleanora Fagan, whom the world knows as Billie Holiday. In Hoboken, New Jersey, in a difficult birth that would leave his face scarred for life, Francis Albert Sinatra made his first debut on the world stage.

David grew from an infant into a little boy sheltered far away from the warfare roiling the Western world. The sinking of the RMS *Lusitania* that helped precipitate the United States' declaring war on Germany occurred the month before his birth. His father, at age thirty-nine, filled out a draft card on September 12, 1918, when David was three. Much more real to the child than the war was the birth of his sister Sallie on June 6, 1917, followed by that of his brother Alfred on September 22, 1919. The Akemons' final child, Robert, was born on March 7, 1922, when David had perhaps learned enough reading, writing, and arithmetic to count down the days to his brother's birth.

Assuming he was like most students in rural Kentucky, he would have attended school regularly unless it interfered with farm duties. Already by this time, he may have been doing chores at home, imitating his father and Luther by carrying lighter loads, pushing cedar pegs into the ground to set young tobacco plants, learning to shell peas and shuck corn. He may already have begun to be acquainted with the Kentucky Wonder variety of string beans that would figure so importantly in his professional image. His brother Robert remembered him preferring string beans: "Our mother used to have green beans on [David's] birthday, and he'd always come and visit just to get there and to have some green beans. He loved 'em, them and that good old country ham."[7] The family was probably making some money at the time, benefiting from the postwar agricultural boom itself aided by the 1917 Food and Fuel Control Act, which had regulated prices and food consumption as part of the war effort.[8]

Although he would always love country living, David would gain a local reputation for laziness, showing more interest in the pastimes of his area. He loved fishing the most and would later wax poetic over it. His cousin Sam "Dood" Medlock took him fishing often, and the two also connected in their shared love of music.[9] It has been claimed that Dood helped raise David, which might be an early sign of distance that would exist between David and his father. As David grew a little bigger, he also came to enjoy hunting. "Hunting," for him, ranged from seeking ginseng to killing small game to the Kentucky/Appalachian version of the fox hunt. The latter differed from the hunts in the Tidewater of Virginia that preserved the pageantry of old England. Here in Kentucky, hunters set up camp and sent their hounds out through the hills, blowing horns to call to them. These horns blended with the dogs' cries to form a grand, brilliant, alacritous music. Such music would inspire the music of David and other Kentucky performers.

The main musical presence of David's life came in the form of his father's banjo playing. Whatever walls would arise between them later, early on his father playing the instrument formed a deep connection for the boy. Moreover, there was something about the instrument that touched and expressed David's core. It has been written that the essence of a banjo lies in its having "a rounded or oval body covered with an animal skin."[10] Essentially a stringed drum on a stick, it blends percussion and manipulated tone in an effect both foundationally, organically familiar and provocatively, mysteriously bizarre. Unlike a purely wooden or metal instrument, the banjo shares a profound nonvegetable connection with humans. Skin is skin is skin, and the banjo's power lies in the range of voice it imparts to vibrating flesh. Even in our moment, when artificial banjo heads greatly outnumber those made of (usually goat) skin, the twang of the banjo retains its ability to lay before us the paradox of our knowing ourselves intimately yet struggling to understand not just the depths of our own personalities but also the organs, veins, and bones beneath our skin that can be so alien to us.

That paradox of the banjo—its ability to capture familiarity and mystery simultaneously—would in time become key to forming "Stringbean" as a persona that invited people of all walks of life to join together and mingle. The invitation to commingle, and in a distinctly joyous nature, characterizes the history of the banjo's development. Its roots clutched in the soil of Africa, from where it was imported along with African people, food, language, and other aspects of culture. Even as enslaved people endured hardship, they fashioned instruments based on ones they had played in Africa. The instruments that made their way through the Caribbean and into what would become the United States sported various numbers of strings with a shorter drone. They produced a bright sound that could cheer even enslaved people, helping them through hard, grievous lives. By the time of David's youth, the banjo had morphed from signaling African American culture to being a centerpiece of Appalachian culture, entrenched as an instrument in the white community to be played in the kind of backward-looking "old-time" music they cherished.

Such old-time music took different forms. It derived from truly old tunes originally sung in the British Isles, such as "Barbara Allen" and "Mary of the Wild Moore," that Scots-Irish and English immigrants brought with them to the New World and handed down through the generations. Added to these very old songs were those composed throughout the nineteenth century. These included Stephen Foster's compositions, including "My Old Kentucky Home" and Louisville native William Shakespeare Hays's "The Little Old Log Cabin in the Lane." Mixed into this soup were a host of nineteenth-century and older religious songs such as "Amazing Grace" and "Softly and Tenderly." It is unclear what the Akemons' religious affiliation was or how deeply they engaged in religious life. But, living near one of the centers of the Second Great Awakening, the family likely had some degree of church involvement and would at the very least have been well acquainted with such songs. By the time of David's childhood, there were also "new old" songs, composed in similar style to the traditional ones. One of these was written by Kentuckian Dick Burnett in 1913, originally titled "Farewell Song" but now much better known as "Man of Constant Sorrow," featured in *O Brother, Where Art Thou.*[11]

This fund of music surrounded David, and he watched and listened closely whenever his father performed at either home, barn dances, or other venues. James almost certainly played in the clawhammer style, in which he would form his right hand in the same shape he would to hold a hammer and then strike the strings in a hammering motion. Sometimes this style was called "frailing" because it looked like the hand was flailing recklessly as it snapped the strings and even drummed the head. This style of play had descended from African techniques, bearing similarity to the "stroke" styles fashioned according to the 1800s minstrel shows and detailed in such instruction manuals as Thomas F. Briggs's 1855 booklet, *Briggs' Banjo Instructor.* Playing thusly, the musician dropped the right hand, the thumb striking the drone string. Then the hand rose back up quickly and hammered down again with the nail of the index or second finger brushing either a single string or the other four at once. The minstrel style called for tuning the banjo to a relatively low D chord, the songs slower paced, the resulting effect a plunky mix of sounds typically bright with a touch of melancholy. While Appalachian players also tuned to D, they often used other tunings for high-speed fiddle tunes.

That need for speed and the relative isolation of different regions in Appalachia gave rise to innumerable variations in style. While clawhammer generally formed the foundational approach, banjo players forged their own techniques and borrowed from one another to produce whatever sounds they sought to get out of the instrument. David likely heard plenty of other banjo players in the area using slightly different styles, sometimes of that region and sometimes of the individual's idiosyncrasies. Examples of such style variation across Appalachia include western North Carolina's Bascom Lamar Lunsford's up-brushing reverse-clawhammer style and Virginia's Moran Lee "Dock" Boggs channeling blues he learned from African American musicians.

The boy David observed the way the banjo brought happiness and movement into people's lives, spurring them to dance, spreading their lips into smiles, driving their hands to clap. The fiddle did this too, but the banjo brought a percussive, exotic drive that appealed to David more. Years later, Robert, related the family story that David "used to go around before he got a banjo and he would get an old shoebox and some of my mother's sewing thread, and thump around on it, and pick up one of those legs and flop on it like he was playing the banjo, and he'd say, 'Boy, you'll hear me over the air one of these days.'"[12] Robert paints a picture of a ham, a boy filled with the exotic energy the banjo ignites.

When he said his family would hear him "over the air," everyone knew David was talking about the Grand Ole Opry.[13] It was neither the first, the only, nor the most famous program of its kind at that point. Chicago's WLS had begun a program in 1924 called *The National Barn Dance*, featuring singers transplanted from southern Appalachia to work in the city's factories. *The Barn Dance* re-created the kinds of events James Akemon played. When the National Life and Accident Insurance Company created the 650 AM radio station for promotional purposes the next October, the company gave it the call letters WSM, which stood for "We Shield Millions." The station aired classical music at first but then sought to present old-time music for its rural, working-class clientele. In November, the station brought George D. Hay from Chicago to host a barn-dance show in Nashville.

Hay first broadcasted the *WSM Barn Dance* on November 28, 1925, when David was ten years old. Two years later, on December 10, 1927, Hay changed the name, famously telling the listeners, "For the past hour, we have been listening to music taken largely from Grand Opera. From now on, we will present the 'Grand Ole Opry.'" In a region where "polka dot" was pronounced "polky dot," the word "Opera" became "Opry." The modifier "ole" not only identified its old-time music focus but also conveyed a sense of down-home intimacy, endearment, and familiarity, none of which were generally associated with opera. WSM's 5,000 watts reached throughout Appalachia where David could listen. He joined plenty of children, including his also musically inclined brother Alfred, in dreaming about performing on this show that, for all they knew, had reached world fame.

David listened especially for one star whose voice and ringing banjo crackled out of the radio's speakers in white-hot exuberance: Uncle Dave Macon. Hay had introduced a fiddler named Uncle Jimmy Thompson and a month later brought on this new "Uncle." Dave Macon had come to professional entertainment later in life after twenty years of running the Macon Midway Mule and Mitchell Wagon Transportation Company in middle Tennessee. He had chosen to go out of business rather than give up using mules to drive an automotive truck. He turned instead to entertainment. Already, he had spent years riding on his wagon playing, singing, and joking to folks working in their fields or sitting on their front porches all along the route through the knobby hills as he transported goods from the railroad in Murfreesboro to Woodbury. A career singing and playing made sense. In fact, they formed only part of Uncle Dave's act and persona, for he would also dance a jig and then grab the banjo by the peghead end of the neck and sling and spin it around. More than anything else, he was an entertainer with a larger-than-life personality. For him, playing, singing, and joking all combined to provide an entertaining experience, no one element superseding that ultimate goal.

David Akeman could not actually see this magical man who shared the same first name and strikingly similar last name over the air, but he could envision Uncle Dave's antics as he listened to his singing, playing, and joking. He drank in the Opry star's style and internalized that principle of putting entertainment first. Years later, David reminisced about Uncle Dave, "He was always my favorite. He was my idol. I always listened to the Grand Ole Opry. We didn't have no radio, and I walked three or four miles up to a little store up there in Welchburg, you know, and they had Uncle Dave on. I wanted him to do the whole show because he was my idol." The store David spoke of actually was a part of the Welchburg post office that the postmaster, Amon Jackson, had converted into a grocery store. According to Jackson family memory, a young David often came to sit around the stove.[14] He wanted to be like his father and this man who would be his spiritual uncle, if not his literal one. What touched and drove David about Uncle Dave was his ability to create out of the fabric of his very soul an experience filled with authenticity. Uncle Dave's singing and banjo playing

were extensions of the magic of himself, not special because they were necessarily better than other people's playing and singing (often they were not) but
because they channeled the enormous energy of a human being spreading the
intrigue of human existence itself in its purest, most real forms.

HARD TIMES AND MUSICAL GROWTH: 1927–1934

David needed that joy and exuberance of Uncle Dave's, for as the hot days of
July 1927 screeched toward month's end, David's older brother Luther fell ill.
His exact symptoms are not known to be recorded, but he may have manifested
the telltale rose-colored spots on the chest that confirmed the diagnosis of
typhoid.[15] James and Alice were shorthanded in nursing their son, since Lizzie
was married and living in North Carolina and Nora had married and moved to
Newport, Kentucky. Joseph may already have gone to live with Nora.[16] Whatever
they tried to do to save Luther, the disease won. He died on August 2.

What the twelve-year-old David thought and felt about his brother dying he
never seems to have revealed on record. Even if he did not get along with his
brother, it is hard not to imagine that grief settled deep into his personality. It
has been suggested that David dropped out of school in the sixth grade to "work
for his father," but that is unlikely, since David would later list his highest grade
of achievement as the eighth.[17] Nevertheless, David would have needed to grow
up quick and bury his pain in order to pick up the slack left on the farm in the
wake of Luther's death and the absence of his already departed older sisters.
Robert's story about David's being a ham at an early age suggests that he had a
native gift for the dry wit that would later typify his persona. But, as with many
people with a talent for comedy, an underlying sadness may have played a role
in fueling that comedy.

There were other sources of pain as well, for the agricultural sector was suffering now. Rising taxes on farm property as well as in labor and transportation along with cost of living steadily ate into profits, creating a massive gap of
annual per capita income that by 1929 reached an extreme of nonagricultural
labor at $750 and farming labor at $273.[18] The Akemons were never a wealthy
family. The glamorous 1920s decade of flappers, diamond rings, sleek furs, and
fast cars hardly touched Jackson County. It was actually a Kentuckian, Thomas
Lyle Williams, who decided to market his sister's concoction of petroleum jelly,
coal dust, and burnt cork to darken her eyelids after her name, Maybel, and thus
create a line of products called Maybelline. But it is more likely that Jackson
County and the Akemons had little truck with such city goings-on. David had
learned Uncle Dave's lyrics "Please don't bob your hair, girls," a direct plea to

young ladies not to follow the flapper style but instead to follow the Lord's way of keeping their hair long.

The stock market crashed on October 29, 1929, and financial crisis quickly coursed through the country as banks began to fail, with 1,325 failing in 1930 and another 2,294 in 1931.[19] Added to these problems came the Hawley-Smoot Tariff Act in June 1930, which curtailed the export market, including agricultural products. The country sank into the Great Depression, and it was probably at this point that David did indeed drop out of school (he would have been in the eighth grade in 1929 if he started his schooling at age six). David and his family knew how to feed themselves, but the need to conserve resources grew sharper. He learned to live on fewer and smaller meals, his body toughening under the strain as he and his family felt the pressures of having to provide while at the mercy of weather, pests, and economic crisis. He later spoke of having to go out and kill blackbirds with sticks or slingshots to provide sustenance.[20]

David learned the hard lesson of not trusting a bank, the axiom grinding into his brain and leaving a permanent scar. There was empowerment in learning frugality, of saving what little there was to be had against the looming, glaring face of disaster. Although the changes for David may not have been so visibly dramatic as for the likes of F. Scott and Zelda Fitzgerald, his experience nevertheless was extreme enough to change him for the rest of his life. He would never, ever fully trust a bank again, and he would always keep cash close at hand.

In the midst of this crisis, however, David was developing his skill and relationship with the instrument that would be central to his life. It was in this momentous year, at age fourteen, that he obtained his first banjo. One account of this life-shaping acquisition had him trading for it with "a couple of chickens he had raised himself." Other variations specify the traded animals as being a banty hen and a banty rooster.[21] Stringbean later claimed that he actually built this banjo with a friend and later gave the friend the two chickens for his share in the instrument.[22] "Didn't have no frets. No frets at'-all," Stringbean said of that banjo years later.[23] In a different but related vein, Amon Jackson told his son Charles that David sold rabbit hides to save up money to buy his first banjo.[24] The story claims that David sold the hides by mail order out of the post office, which was apparently illegal at the time, so Amon helped him package them in a way that hid them from postal service authorities. While that story seems to contradict the one Stringbean himself told, it could be that Stringbean raised money in this way later to buy a factory-made banjo, thus making it his "first" banjo in that sense. If so, then that might have taken place several years after this time.

David's primary banjo instructor was James. As David later told an interviewer, his father taught him "what little I know."[25] David may have begun playing before he obtained his first banjo, and he may have picked up playing knowledge from others. For example, Amon and his wife, Druscilla, played dances in the area and kept a banjo and guitar in the Welchburg post office/store. Amon would tell of teaching David to play the banjo and say that the boy was so shy, he would stop playing when customers came in.[26] Another Jackson County resident, Denver Adams, would always claim *he* had taught David how to play.[27]

Whomever David learned from, that learning required him to put his mind and efforts toward new skills. He developed the muscle memory of the frailing actions of his right hand, which may have helped distract him from emotions gouging his heart. He learned the clawhammer rhythm often referred to as "bum-diddy," practicing until he could do it without thinking. He would have been slow at first, but gradually he would pick up speed until he could frail faster than he could think. As that clawhammering motion became second nature to him, he began to focus on using the fingers of his left hand to make notes. The strings formed painful indentations in his fingertips until the flesh began to harden into yellow flattened calluses. He learned how to hammer on, pull off, and slide on the strings, especially the lower ones as he began to blend melody with chords. Those chords differed according to the various tunings he learned. In time, he would come to prefer standard G tuning (g–D–G–B–D) but taken a step up to A (a–E–A–C#–E), which would better fit his singing range as well as being a typical key for fiddles. He also learned to tune that C# string up another step to D# to create the eerie, unresolved, distinct "mountain modal" tuning, especially when he played the old song "Pretty Polly."

Whether from his father, from other banjos player in the area, or out of his own innovation, David also learned two-finger picking.[28] Two-finger picking styles were practiced by players in North Carolina and eastern Kentucky.[29] Professional performers who employed such picking included Lily May Ledford (whose life would later play into David's), Roscoe Holcomb, Doc Watson, and even Ralph Stanley.[30] In this style, the thumb picked down and the index finger (sometimes the middle finger) picked up, often in alternating leads. The picking did not quite conform to the smooth rolls that typify three-finger picking. Some performers produced a steady stream of notes that closely resemble those, but this two-fingered approach could produce a wide range of rhythms and articulations. In time, David developed a personalized technique built on halting phrases rather than a smooth roll, similar to a style Virgil Anderson played.

We can get a direct glance into David playing the banjo in his adolescence from Bob Baker, a neighbor who went on to have his own career in music. Born a year after David, Baker explained:

He lived adjoining farms to my aunt and uncle up in Jackson County, near Bond town [Bond, Kentucky]. And on weekends, sometimes, you know, we was small, mother'd let us go over there and stay over the weekend with my aunt and uncle, and String would come over and we'd pick and sing for hours and hours at a time. My aunt and uncle both played the five-string banjos. They'd pick a lot with String. That'd tickle String when we'd come, you know, and play them guitars second behind their banjos and things. We'd play and sometimes there'd be a few gather in, and they'd dance a little bit, too.[31]

This playing was purely for enjoyment, but David was gaining experience and learning from these other banjo players while also learning to play along with other instruments.

Whatever pleasure David gained from playing the banjo, the problems of the country grew as job losses increased and poverty deepened. In the midst of the darkness, however, emerged heroism of various and sometimes surprising kinds. One of these came symbolically, on October 1, 1932, when Babe Ruth, in Game Three of the World Series against Chicago, made a gesture that reporter Joe Williams claimed was calling his next hit to center field. Ruth slammed the ball, hitting maybe the most famous home run ever. David did not see the hit, but he envisioned it and that gesture of calling the shot. Growing tall and wiry, he was athletic and showed particular ability in playing baseball. And everyone loved Babe Ruth, who had hit his *first* home run just a month before David was born. Ruth's home run-calling gesture resonated so powerfully with David he would later adopt something akin to it in his performances.

Someone who *did* see the hit that day was Franklin Delano Roosevelt. As he sat in the stands at Wrigley Field, Roosevelt himself was only a little more than a month away from seeing the beginning of himself becoming legendary as the longest-sitting and one of the most lauded presidents in U.S. history. The hard lessons of endurance and courage the country was learning he had himself already digested. Struck down by a paralytic disease believed to be polio just as the 1920s jazz party was starting, Roosevelt eventually retreated to rural Georgia, where he became familiar with rural southern people and folkways. There he learned a new strength and optimism that fitted him for his own legendary role in history.

If David made his way to listen to the radio at Amon's store along with the rest of the nation as Roosevelt was inaugurated on March 4, 1933, he may have felt despair and hope warring within him. The new president spoke with firm authority, saying that "the only thing we have to fear is fear itself" and explaining that the country will endure so long as it resists "nameless, unreasoning, un-justified terror which paralyzes needed efforts to convert retreat into advance."

Two months later, he established the Federal Emergency Relief Administration, which provided an immediate $500 million paid directly to the states as matching grants, although Kentucky initially did not do its part to raise local money to be matched and thus received the grant only once its FERA office came into conformity.[32] This program, along with the Federal Surplus Relief Corporation, included a provision that distributed food to the needy. The Akemons benefited from this food distribution, and David later said of receiving boxes of macaroni, "We even had it for breakfast. By God, it tasted like the best stuff that ever was."[33]

Another major program Roosevelt proposed early in 1933 that directly affected David was the Civilian Conservation Corps. Congress ratified the president's CCC proposal within ten days, and the first camp, NF-1, called Camp Roosevelt, opened in Luray, Virginia.[34] For men in rural areas struggling to make ends meet, this opportunity seemed like manna from heaven. The camps also stirred controversy. Some fretted over too much government involvement. Not a few objected that the camps would drain the federal treasury. Others worried that the camps would breed vice, as one woman put it in a short 1935 film: "The entire moral tone of our community will suffer from the C.C.C. camps. There'll be drunkenness and gambling. Our women will be constantly exploited. I beg our selectmen to prevent this catastrophe."[35] Some wondered if these camps were training an American fascist army.

David was one of the young men looking for work. Camps F-3 and F-2 opened in 1933 in Jackson County, and he probably went to one of those or possibly to one closer to Lexington.[36] He fitted the bill as an unemployed, unmarried male between the ages of eighteen and twenty-three, usually whose family was on local relief already. It has been suggested that David left home against his father's will, and if that is true it would have been a sign of growing friction between the two.[37] One hears rumbles to this day among older Jackson County residents about David's lazy side, preferring to play a banjo than to do work on the farm.[38] As one writer later put it, he "tried farming but the call of the banjo was louder than the soil." Angela Hacker, a Stringbean enthusiast and Jackson County resident, remembers her great-aunt Margaret Combs declaring, "Stringbean was too sorry to carry a block of coal in the house!" It is not hard to imagine David's father feeling abandoned at such a critical time, and he may even have feared for his son's striking out on his own, especially given the CCC camps' reputation for breeding vice. James may even have been horrified if he happened to read or hear of a notice in the *Lexington Leader* of a young man named Elmer Clark being shot near Somerset while "walking toward Stearns to enroll in the CCC" because he "refused to hand over to [his assailants] the banjo he was carrying."[39]

David probably entered the camp in 1934.[40] The first thing for a CCC camp enrollee to do was take a physical exam. If found wanting, he went through a period of training to get him in shape. Now fully grown and built like his father, David would have towered over most of the other young men and been a natural to take on, especially given his athleticism. The camp had a distinctly military flavor, with officers overseeing sections of twenty-five workers into which the camp of as many as two hundred were organized, and the enrollees were issued uniforms and lived in barracks. It was not long until a number of them began to see the camps as prisons and themselves as workers on chain gangs who had to eat prison-quality food. They were paid thirty dollars a month, with a compulsory allotment of twenty-two to twenty-five dollars a month to be sent to their families.[41]

Work in the camps took on various forms. The young men helped repair roads and bridges and build dams and lookout towers, which helped with controlling forest fires. Erosion control served as a major focus in the South, which meant planting the Japanese plant arrowroot, better known as kudzu, a vine able to grow at a tremendous rate that has by now reached legendary status. In eastern Kentucky, much effort was given to forest maintenance and protection, which meant planting trees, seed collection, and building nurseries.

The camps provided recreation too, including boxing and, more important to David, baseball. On hot summer days, he and his camp fellows would have gotten up games while the grasshoppers wheezed away in the woods, David maybe calling his own hits like the Great Bambino himself. That said, the military-like nature of the camp may not have been something David cared for, partly perhaps because, if his later experiences are any indication, his view of war may have been ambivalent at best.

Despite the crisis and CCC experience, David found time to develop his skills in playing the banjo. He played enough that a friend of his in the camp, Bruce Brockman, got to calling him "Dave Macon," seeing the similarity to the name "Dave Akeman."[42] By now, David was developing a facility with the instrument and was honing his sense of timing. His frailing right hand may already have been wearing a smooth place on the banjo head, and calluses on his left-hand fingertips were now likely set into thick leathern pads. He and the instrument would be marking one another physically as their spiritual and psychical relationship grew more intimate and inextricable. Already instrument and man may have been entwining as two living beings, not necessarily a specific banjo but "banjo" and the entity growing within David, an avatar that as yet had no name but was sprouting inside him and bound up with the entity of banjo-ness.

David was learning to play the tunes at local dances. It would later be said of this time in his life that success "came slowly and by way of hunger and discouragement."[43] Although he did not sing much if at all in public at this point, he was learning the lyrics about the Cumberland Gap as well as to the song that spoke of going up to Cripple Creek in a run to have a little fun. There was the song about little Liza Jane, invoking her name over and over again in the chorus as if the tones of the name itself conjured every wonderful glisten of her eyes, curl of her hair, aroma of her person, and sparkle of her character. And there was the old number about pretty Polly, in its strange modal key, which may have conjured images of David's grandmother (and a dead sister, if the family actually did lose a child of that name). That one would become a signature for him.

CONTEST AND DISCOVERY: 1935

As 1934 gave way to 1935, David continued to refine his playing as he looked for ways to gain greater exposure. One way to get publicity was to participate in one of the contests being held in Kentucky in 1935. On Friday, October 5, the "Old Fiddler's contest" took place in the Broughtontown schoolhouse, with Roy Denham and Robert Bourne winning first and second prizes, respectively, in banjo.[44] A "Radio Contest" was held in Perryville on March 15 also at the high school in an event sponsored by the Lexington radio station WLAP. The contest winner, Joseph Brookshire, would appear on WLAP at 3:00 p.m. a week from Saturday, perhaps playing and singing his winning number, "The Little Red Barn."[45] It was this kind of contest that could get you on the radio that would be especially useful, and it may have been while listening to WLAP that David learned of a contest specifically designed for banjo players to be held in none other than McKee in Jackson County.

The contest was being hosted by WLAP star Asa Martin. A native of Clark County, near Lexington, Asa had been raised by parents who harbored hopes of his becoming a medical doctor.[46] They did not have enough money for such extensive schooling, though, so Asa dropped out and spent the 1920s playing vaudeville and silent-movie houses. When another Asa, stage-named Al Jolson, sang on-screen in 1927's *The Jazz Singer*, Asa Martin's career playing theaters ended. That was also the year of the so-called Bristol sessions in which Ralph Peer brought to the world the Carter Family and Jimmie Rodgers. The latter inspired the square-jawed Asa, who began to sing in a Rodgers-like bright, nasally, robust voice and to play Rodgers's signature runs on the guitar. Asa first tried recording with fiddler Doc Roberts and Doc's brother James. Failing to make money selling records, he put all his efforts in radio, beginning with Louisville's WHAS, and forming a band called the Kentucky Hillbillies.[47]

By 1935 Asa was in Lexington on WLAP. The daily WLAP programs published in the *Lexington Herald* that year offer practically no mention of Asa or his band, so it seems likely that he worked as an announcer. His own band may have accompanied him and played in transition or with commercials. Asa may also have introduced and interacted with regularly appearing groups.[48] These groups included Uncle Henry and His Kentucky Mountaineers, Matt Adams and His Kentucky String Ticklers, Uncle Tommy and the Coon Hunters, and Bert Miller and His Kentucky Vagabonds. While these acts were often listed by name, there were also generic slots with names such as "Tonic Tunes" and "Noontimers," which may have allowed him to introduce new acts. In fact, Asa's greatest talent lay in his ability to spot other talent. It was when one of Asa's finds prepared to leave his band that David's opportunity came. "Lily May Ledford was playing with me, one of Coon Creek Girls," he said years later, "and, well, they were about to change over to Renfro Valley, and I needed a banjo player."[49]

While the exact date of Asa's contest in McKee is unknown, it likely took place sometime in the latter months of 1935.[50] That is because Ledford and her brother Kelly auditioned for WLS touring talent scouts in 1936, and she (but not her brother) was chosen to be signed on to *The Barn Dance*.[51] While at first glance this timing might seem to throw even the year of the contest in dispute, the 1935 date is one of the consistent details in David's story. Asa's ambiguous phrase that Ledford was "about to change over" may simply mean that he remembered that time roughly and maybe even that Ledford had stated her intention of leaving. Following such logic, it might be surmised, albeit inconclusively, that the contest was held in November or December.

Along with the mystery of the contest date is the puzzling mystery of why the contest should be held in McKee. Of all the tiny towns in all the counties in Kentucky—a state with banjo players throughout—why did Asa choose *that* one? It might be argued that Asa wanted to go into the hinterlands to find a banjo player. But the hinterlands were not that far from Lexington, and surely WLAP could have put out a call for banjo players and seen such hopefuls as poor Elmer Clark flocking to the city. Perhaps Asa had heard there was a higher concentration of banjo players in that area. Bob Baker claimed that the McKee courthouse was known to be a site for playing music:

> On Saturdays, we would take our guitars and a few people and got ahold of old cars and a few trucks and we'd catch us a ride with some of them and go to McKee. That was about ten mile from where we lived. And we'd play music on Saturdays. They'd hold court most every Saturday. They called it county court. And we'd play music for tips. People'd give us change, you know, and, oh, we thought that was great, that we was getting some money for our picking.[52]

This weekly gathering may have been what drew Asa to McKee, or perhaps he knew someone who knew someone there.[53] Whatever the reason, it would prove to be fortuitous for David.

The courthouse where the talent show was held no longer stands, replaced in 1950 by a new building with a surprisingly mod clock on the facade. But it is not difficult to imagine the scene. The event was most likely held in the courtroom upstairs.[54] We can envision a young David standing tall and thin among wooden benches lined in varnished ranks gleaming yellow in the glare of gaslight. Country folks, most of them knowing one another, would have had to jam into the building. Perhaps David smiled at the performers who just could not cut it—not a deprecating smile but one of sympathy—while keeping a wary eye on the strong acts, trying to gauge the competition. Finally, it was his turn to step up and play. What song(s) he played in the contest no one now knows, any more than what he thought and felt in that moment. Maybe memories of Luther filled his mind as he struck the strings. Maybe Alfred, Sallie, and Robert watched with their mother, and maybe their presence calmed his nerves as he played for such high stakes. Perhaps his father came, but he likely did not approve. David needed all the support he could get, especially if the winner was decided by the vigor and volume of applause.[55]

When the show ended, not only did David not win, he did not even place. But if he felt his dream crumbling in his stomach, it did not last long. Asa came up to him and said, "Well, say, boy, I wish you wasn't in that [CCC camp. . . .] I'd give you a job for a few weeks."[56] The invitation must have shocked David after not winning, and Asa would forever be cryptic, saying, "He didn't actually win first place . . . but I really wanted to hire him."[57] What exactly did Asa hear in David's playing that was not good enough to win a contest but made him someone to hire professionally? Given his penchant for spotting talent, perhaps Asa saw something in David beyond just his playing the banjo. It is difficult to define the difference between a technically outstanding instrumentalist and a person who possesses the elusive aura of stardom. There is no formula or training for attaining that aura. If Asa saw that in David as he did in others whom he helped in their careers, then that could explain how he could see a higher calling for David than for the contest winner (whose name, incidentally, has been lost to history).

STRINGBEAN AND HIS BANJO
1935-1942

A BEAN IS BORN: 1935

One wonders if David slept at all that night after the talent show. He may have gone back to the CCC camp to collect his belongings, but he more likely had brought his things with him and stayed the night at home. If he did, the atmosphere must have been strained because James's disapproval was palpable. "Pa told me when I left home that a lot of folks sittin' on their porches could play better'n me," David recalled. "I knowed that, 'cause I ain't never had that much talent. But I always had lots of determination."[1]

That determination — to succeed and perhaps also to prove his father wrong — put itself on display when David took the initiative the next morning. Asa would always claim that David hitchhiked to Lexington after getting out of the CCC camp, but Amon Jackson may have driven him.[2] There is a story that Amon drove David to Manchester, Kentucky, to appear on the radio, singing "Curly Headed Baby," which he dedicated to Amon's daughter Helen, who was born in 1933.[3] Since there was no radio station in Manchester until 1956, it may be that David played on some other station somewhere nearby Manchester.[4] It is more likely, however, that in handing the story down, Manchester became mixed up with Winchester, near Lexington, where David would soon be living, and that Amon drove him there.

The trip covered some seventy miles on winding local roads through the hills to Highway 25, which became Lexington's Main Street.[5] When David arrived that morning, he found himself in a city of around forty-five to fifty thousand inhabitants. A later article would colorfully assert that Lexington "looked like a big city to a bony boy coming from a town of fewer than 400." Although the third-largest city in the state, Lexington had a small, close, antique, residential feel. Since its hemp-rope manufacturing business had faded, it lacked the earmarks of a modern industrial city. The "absence of factory smoke and the presence of a lone skyscraper are noticeable," wrote Works Progress Administration writers at the time, explaining that the main products of the city were bourbon, tobacco, and thoroughbreds. That lone skyscraper was the fifteen-story Fayette National Bank Building, standing where Jordan's Row met Main Street. Riding west on Main Street toward that landmark, David would have seen the redbrick Phoenix Hotel on his right—the "mecca of thoroughbred horsemen"—while on the left a similarly shaped sign jutted from the front of the Ben Snyder Department Store.[6] Ahead on the right loomed the Hotel Lafayette, where civic organizations and people with interests in saddlebreds met. Among these tall structures, smaller buildings were jammed along Main Street with signs announcing their businesses: Dan Cohen Shoes, Meyers Art Goods, and Spengler Studio, which included the verbiage, "The New Home of the Old Reliable Spengler Studio, Leading Photographers Since 1900, Our Motto: 'Not How Near But How Good'."[7]

David made his way to the second-floor WLAP studio in the Walton Building on the northeast corner of Main Street and Esplanade.[8] WLAP had originally been located in Louisville, but *Lexington Herald* owners Lindsay Nunn and his son Gilmore bought the station and housed it in the Walton Building. There they affixed a 138-foot antenna on the roof that projected 250 watts by day and 100 watts by night, covering the central Kentucky radius of the paper. Broadcasting began March 17, 1934. Under Gilmore's leadership, it began to build a reputation. By 1938 the station would be moved to a new building (still referred to as the Nunn Building as well as the Lexington Herald Building) on the corner of Walnut and Short Streets and declared as one of the "South's Finest Studios" and "The Voice of the Bluegrass."[9]

The scene that greeted David in the studio that day must have been thrilling and otherworldly. If David was able to get a glance at the Direct Crystal Control transmitter's dials and knobs, he probably thought he had entered the laboratory of a mad scientist. The large studio room contained two or more microphones mounted on stands: the Western Electric 618 was a popular make at the time for broadcasting and may have been the kind WLAP used. The studio would have been bustling, with some performers on the air, others packing up to go, and still more preparing for their moment. The day's program was made up of five-, fifteen-, and thirty-minute slots all filled with live entertainment, news, devotional services, and even Roosevelt's fireside chats. Broadcasting began at 7:00 a.m. and ended at 10:00 p.m., Monday through Saturday, and 9:00 a.m. to 10:00 p.m. on Sunday.

David arrived in the studio in time for the noontime slot. If the talent show in McKee was held on a Friday night, then the next day's noon slot likely featured either Uncle Henry and His Kentucky Mountaineers or Matt Adams and His Kentucky String Ticklers. It may be that Asa inserted David into a "Noon Timers" performance (one ran at 12:45 on November 2), or perhaps David performed as part of an unlisted transition.[10] Whatever the case, Asa thrust Stringbean right into the action. As he told it years later:

> So the next day—he didn't tell me he was coming—and I went in on a program at twelve o'clock that I was having for the Pennzoil Oil Company on WLAP in Lexington, and String was in there with my players. I said, "Oh, here's the old boy from McKee. You want to play a number with them?" He said, "Hm-mhh." That's the way String talked back in those days. And I marched out a number, I said, "What are you going to play?" He said, "I'll play 'John Henry'." So, he did the number, and did it real well. And then I began to try to introduce him—well, no, he hadn't done the number, I began to try to introduce him—and I described him as a long, tall, curly-headed boy from back in the hills of old Kentucky, and I said, "Now listen, folks, I just can't think of his name, but for the present I'm going to call him 'String Beans'." Well, that surprised him. But, however, the name stuck, and we had many calls for String Beans.[11]

Thus it was that a slip of memory gave David the name by which he would come to be known. It might be noted that in his retelling of the story, Asa used the plural form, as in a mess of string beans. Citing another instance of Asa's telling the story, country music historian Charles Wolfe claimed that Stringbean did not officially change to the singular form of Stringbean until several years later.[12] But when David told the story—including in an interview on the night of his death—he remembered Asa using the singular form of the name, "Come here Stringbean, and play us a tune."[13] It is more believable that Asa said "Stringbean" to describe a single tall fellow who made Asa think of a bean than to apply the rather more esoteric plural. On the other hand, "Stringbeans" *was* used in publicity for David in these early years, and Asa really may have been thinking of beans in the plural.

Whether Asa said "Stringbeans" or "Stringbean," there is a reason that the latter stuck. It applied to David's physique and quiet personality in an evocative way that could both tickle and intrigue. It was a name that could not be improved upon, accidental but fated. It may even have been that Martin meant to say "bean pole," the nickname being then a slip of a slip. But "Stringbean" was better than "Beanpole," as is surely obvious seeing the two names so juxtaposed.[14] "Beanpole" is a thing; "Stringbean" is a living, organic entity. "Beanpole" is more abstract and also more common as a derogatory term for a thin person. Stringbean, on the other hand, appeals to the senses. The sight of long green beans hanging from the vining plants, the feel of them firm in the hand when stringing them on a hot afternoon, the smell of them cooking with country ham, the taste of them when they are ready and steaming, and the deliciously evocative sound of the name are all appealing—all combine for a complete sensory engagement.

Although David did not like the name at first, it would prove to be perfect and powerful for him. It gave him a sense of belonging and an identity. It set him apart in both aural and visual ways. What is more, "Stringbean" gave name to that entity growing inside him, making the name even more than a nickname or marketing opportunity to exploit in the moment. The invention of the name coincided with the birth of a kind of being who was and was not David Akeman—"Stringbean," who was David Akeman plus more. "Stringbean" described the particular kind of musical and entertainment genius David was gifted with and that he would develop. "Stringbean" would develop his own personality, his own style, his own legacy that would distill the best qualities of David Akeman. Those qualities would come to embody a set of ideals and values of hard work (in a field he cared about), honesty, integrity, humility, and, above all, not getting above his raising.

That latter idea—that David did not put on airs or pretend to be fancier or more important than his home and family had been—was crucial to David's/Stringbean's personality. Already he fitted in as someone whose easygoing personality combined with dedication to doing well and quietly going about his work made him someone other band members enjoyed being around. A name like "Stringbean" kept him at a comfortable level, effectively blending absurdity and seriousness in a mix that resonated with audiences and industry insiders alike. A human being has flaws, foibles, and inconsistencies, but a persona can exist without those. David the man appeared not to have many of those anyway, but Stringbean was born with the capability of channeling the best of David.

If David did not take a moment to savor his achievement, he should have. To play on the radio was a major deal for a musician. Radio was the centerpiece of public communication. Listeners tuned in to various stations to hear the latest antics of Lum and Abner and other radio characters. Far away up north, Frank Sinatra was making his debut on the radio at the same time. From the magic of that wooden box, lit in warm yellow in the darkness, a world of life and excitement could waltz right into a house in the remotest parts of the country. And now David Akeman found an open door to those homes too.

A PROFESSIONAL ENTERTAINER'S LIFE BEGINS: 1935–1939

David began the work regime of hillbilly performers at that time.[15] Money was a problem. Unless a slot had a sponsor, radio paid little, if anything. Likewise, recording also brought little income, since performers then were typically paid only flat fees and no royalties for making records. The most substantial income came from live performances, and the chief purpose for both radio and records was to provide exposure that led to bookings. Aside from traveling medicine shows and the relatively few movie theaters in Appalachia at that time, the most typical venues for performers such as David were rural schools, courthouses, and churches. It was a common practice across the industry for performers to play a radio slot in the morning or midday, then travel to a location near or quite far to play one or more shows, and then drive back in the middle of the night, in some cases arriving just in time to play the radio slot on the next day.

At first, David played the banjo only, but he soon began to expand his entertainment repertoire. Watching comedians onstage, David imitated them and developed a knack for entertaining other band members in their spare time.[16] His ability to make people laugh registered with Asa, and soon an occasion arose to call upon this newly discovered talent. Doc Roberts related the following story:

> One night this comedian got sick down in Hazard, when [Asa Martin's band] had a big show lined up that night in Hindman [Kentucky]. Acey insisted that Stringbean go on as the comedian—in fact, he said he'd fire him if he didn't. String had never sung in public, and he didn't think he could make people laugh, but he went backstage and got himself fixed up. When he came on stage, the crowd gave him the awfullest hand you'd ever want to see. He straightened up right then and made the best comedian Acey had ever seen. When they got into the car that night, Stringbean said, "Well, you can fire me if you want to, but I'll never play nothing but comedian again."[17]

So began another of the pillars of the developing entity that was Stringbean. The particular brand of comedy he plied was of the backwoods-rube variety practiced by countless performers. Stringbean was not necessarily unique at this point. He was becoming what he had been feeding on—a heavy diet from listening to the Opry, which included performers "telling wild stories about country characters" in good fun, which "was a scarce commodity in the hot, dusty days and nights of the Great Depression."[18] Paying attention to not only the artistry of entertainment but also the business side, David found that diversifying his skill set could make him more marketable to audiences as well as to other bands.

27

Into David's new life now came a vast and growing family of fellow entertainers. Doc and James Roberts became his friends, and he probably got to know Lily May and her brother. He befriended Cliff and Bill Carlisle as well as Henry Warren (Uncle Henry) and his wife, Sally, and brother Grady. Although he was currently working in Boston, Bradley Kincaid (who would play an important role in Grandpa Jones's career) was known to appear at WLAP and probably met David. To these names could be added many more, and countless others have been lost to history. They would hang together, forming close relationships that could equal and at times even supersede those of blood relations. These interconnections translated into a kind of fluidity when it came to onstage appearances. On any given night or day on the air or on a stage, a given band's makeup may vary, including picking up a performer who might not regularly perform with that band.

In fact, as the months rolled on through the end of 1935, through 1936, and into 1937, David worked to refine his image as the individual comic–banjo player Stringbean(s) while playing with multiple groups. One of these groups was Silas Rogers's Lonesome Pine Fiddlers, who were based in Winchester and often played on WLAP. The two fiddlers in the group were Silas himself and Thornton McCord, whose nickname, "Lightnin'," might have come from his being an electrician.[19] On guitar was Charlie Rogers, perhaps a brother to Silas. The bass player was Marty "Tex" Roberts, who would later perform with the Tennessee Ramblers.[20] In a column published not long after David's murder, Roberts told of his experiences with the band, explaining that while playing in Cincinnati one night Si Rogers offered him a job. "I loaded my bass fiddle and other effects in Si's 1935 Buick and we headed for Winchester . . . and the next morning I met the one and only Stringbean."[21]

Roberts discussed the monetary motivation of playing with multiple groups. "Room and board went for five bucks a week," he related, "and sometimes Stringbean and yours truly had a rough time making that." Roberts's comments offer insight into David's daily experience doing what he loved but struggling to make ends meet. A later article asserted that "nobody was willing to pay Stringbean and three other fellows more than $15—for the whole band per Saturday night."[22] Members of Asa Martin's Kentucky Hillbillies or Si Rogers's Lonesome Pine Fiddlers may have made as little as five dollars a week, possibly even less in what Roberts remembered as "some tough times."

Roberts also confirmed David's living in a rooming house, the implication being that he roomed with Roberts himself part of the time. Roberts commented, "You'd be surprised how many ways beans can be fixed and we ate 'em for every meal." David too recalled, "I could eat breakfast for 9 cents—bacon, egg, toast, jelly and coffee. It was the Depression years, though, and even 9 cents was a lot of money."[23] This pain of the ongoing Depression further deepened David's commitment to making money and keeping it away from banks. Roberts's mentioning that he rode in Si's Buick implies that he had no car of his own, and David even now likely could not afford a vehicle either, if he even wanted one. He was famous for not driving later in life, and he may have had little use for automobiles in his youth, as well.

A 1937 photograph features the young David with the band, and his separateness as comic banjo player is evident. Where the others stand, wearing western-style outfits, Stringbean sits in backwoods attire. He wears a round-crowned hat with a medium-size upturned brim, somewhat different from the small-brimmed porkpie he would later be known for. The hat sits back on his head, revealing a flowering of puffy curly hair. His long-sleeve shirt is a light plaid, and suspenders hold up his pants. He is barefoot, his long feet so conspicuous as to suggest they played a role in the humorous aspect of his look, accentuated by what appears to be a bandage tied to the big toe of the left foot. His expression blends a vacant stare with a slack-jawed snarl, his listing mouth with some of the teeth blacked out. That expression suggests that the comic role he then played was a kind of dumb hillbilly hick, perhaps a cognitively or socially disabled ancestor of Billy Bob Thornton's Karl Childers character.

The other arresting thing about this photo is the banjo he holds, a Gibson RB-11. This may have been the banjo David bought with rabbit skins. The RB-11 was first manufactured in 1935, its four-string predecessor TB-11 having been introduced as early as 1931.[24] This banjo looked the part of a fancy instrument and was described in the 1935 Gibson catalog as the "flashiest five-string banjo made." Its fretboard was made of brilliantly shimmering golden pearloid, which also covered the resonator, and both were decorated with black and red designs, with a rosette centered on the resonator and a four-pointed star or flower design in the center of the peghead. The rim and neck were often painted dark blue, which caused these banjos sometimes to be referred to as "blue banjos."[25] The beauty was only skin-deep, however, for the pearloid and paint actually hid "cosmetically flawed wood which might not have been suitable for more expensive models."[26] Moreover, the decorations were printed with silkscreen, far cheaper than genuine mother-of-pearl inlays to be found in the high-quality Mastertone models. As for the banjo's guts, it featured a traditional lightweight rolled-brass tone ring as opposed to the heavy cast rings of Mastertones. The tone ring had by now developed into a key element of a banjo's volume and particular sound, and this one lagged behind the technology. The price of the RB-11 matched the inexpensive make too, for whereas a Mastertone Granada could sell for more than $200 new, the RB-11 sold for around $50.[27] In a time when per capita income may have been as low as $474, such an investment could have represented a large percentage of David's income.[28]

David's pocketbook must have thanked him for joining a third band called the Bar-X-Boys. Their name was likely been taken from the X Bar X Boys series of novels "primarily for boys but which will be read by all who love mystery, rapid action, and adventures in the great open spaces," written by different hands under the pseudonym James Cody Ferris and published by Grosset and Dunlap.[29] Based in Columbia, Kentucky, the band, which was also sometimes called "Willie Clyde and the BarX Cowboys," played on WLAP and was made up of Gordon Kelsay, Casey Jones (a national fiddling champion), Clyde Royse, and a future mayor of Columbia, Hollis Keltner.[30] As for how David came to the group, Royse (whom David for some reason called "Richard") told the story that the group needed a banjo player and heard about David and drove from Columbia to Jackson County with their instruments to see him. Royse's grandson Mark Kelsay Royse tells that, according to Clyde, David responded to their invitation to play with them on the radio and live performances by saying, "I don't play anymore. I gave it up."[31] If David had given up at that point, his comments may be an insight into a moment when the struggles of the Depression and the obstacles to success had overcome him. Nevertheless, David said that since the fellows were there, they might as well pick a little, and thereafter he joined them for about nine months in 1938–39. A photo of David with this band exists also. In it, Stringbean again differs from the other band members' western clothing. David wears an even wider-brimmed hat, back on his head again, although with a less puffy flowering of hair visible. His dark coat obscures his shirt, but again he is barefoot. The vacant stare seems more indicative of what at the time would have been referred to as "idiocy" than of menace.

By 1939 David was definitely making a name for himself. Asa had begun his *Morning Roundup* show on WLAP, bringing in as many as twenty performers at a time. One notice of his band's performance that year in Stanford, Kentucky, stated that the *Morning Roundup* "program is broadcast daily on WLAP and consists of all kinds of string musical instruments."[32] David received his own billing, with publicity highlighting "String Beans and his Old Banjo."[33] Meanwhile, David continued to gain valuable experience and was starting to sing. His repertoire included "Suicide Blues," "Mountain Dew," and "Get along Home, Cindy."[34] As challenging as his schedule was, David was young and surely having the time of his life, doing what his hero, Uncle Dave, did. One also hears hints of David's having a wild streak at this time of life, as both Mark Royse and Marilyn Jones (Casey Jones's daughter) have distinct impressions of David joining other hillbilly performers at the time in drinking and carousing. Rumors also persist in Jackson County of David's kicking up his heels with Dood and others.

David was also emulating his baseball heroes and may have been making some additional money doing so. He later claimed he played in the Class D Mountain State League.[35] "Caught some, pitched some. Played outfield. Flew 'round them bases like a crow!" he reminisced. Although he had talent and wanted a shot at a career, he never found himself in the right place at the right time to get to the big leagues. "Not many scouts, then," he said. "Cut my career short. Nobody discovered me." He did allow that he could not develop his skills fully because there were no Little Leagues to play in then. "Little Leagues sorta knock the rough edges off you before you get up high," he said.[36]

Searches of baseball rosters do not produce any listing of David's playing on minor-league teams, but that does not prove conclusively that he never played any games.[37] A James Aikens is listed as having pitched for three teams in the Mountain State League in 1940, but no name resembles David's.[38] If David did play, there arises also the question of how he pulled it off and for what team. The Mountain State League played its first season in 1937, all of its teams being based in West Virginia, as per the league's name. In 1939 the Ashland Colonels became the only Kentucky-based team in the league and remained in it until the league transitioned from D to C and then dissolved the following year. It is entirely possible that no record was kept of David playing. That said, it is also difficult to imagine a carless David finding time to play baseball in a league in which the nearest team was a hundred miles away from Lexington, much less for him to play on one of the West Virginia teams.

Whether he actually played in that league or not, David almost certainly played as part of the general town-affiliated baseball competition in Kentucky. Throughout the 1930s, young men from neighboring towns in the United States would gather to enjoy a few hours' respite from the gnawing miseries of the Depression. David may have had a spot on a team in Jackson County by his midteens, and CCC camp teams were known to play town teams as well.[39] If he actually made money playing, it speaks to his resourceful drive to squeeze whatever earning power he could out of his talents in a time when every effort to make money was necessary. It also speaks to his athleticism and the need to exercise it while also revealing one of the ways he chose to spend what leisure time he had.

MARRIAGE TO BLANCHE: 193?

David was probably taking flak from his family for all this unusual and not very profitable activity, especially since his father sold the family farm back in Jackson County about this time to a man named Alfred Moore.[40] James may have been *forced* to sell his home and thus have felt betrayed, compounding any jealousy he may have felt. Perhaps from the combined squeeze of his father's disapproval and a real financial need, David took a job as a proprietor of a filling station near Winchester.

David's connection to Winchester involved not only a job but a woman. Her name was Blanche McQueen. Born April 10, 1910, five years older than David, she spent the first decade of her life on a farm in Jackson County. Sometime after 1920, her father, Dan, decided to try his luck as a driller in the oil fields in the western Kentucky town of Owensboro. While living there in Daviess County, she met and married Luther McIntosh in 1925, but by 1930 the two had apparently separated. Listed in the census as living in her father's household, in the "Marital Status" column, illegible letters are crossed out and above them the letter *M* written, suggesting uncertainty about her situation. Whatever was going on, she had gone back to live with her family and had taken her two children, Gene and Jack, with her. It is likely that she moved to Clark County in the Lexington area with the family when Dan moved there, now flush with cash and continuing to work in oil.[41] She was evidently divorced by this time.

How she and David entered into a courtship remains a mystery. They likely knew each other during childhood, living in the same sparsely inhabited county. She may have been working at WLAP (possibly in connection with the Pennzoil sponsorship), or she may have seen him at a show date. It is also possible that her father may have owned the filling station or been connected with it in some way and that David met her via that connection or got the job as proprietor from her father and then began dating her. The family remembers Blanche as being pretty, and a photograph of her taken when her two sons, Gene and Jack, were grown reveals her to have been a stout woman with dark hair and strong features.

What *is* known is that by 1940, David and Blanche were married, for he is listed as so in the household of Dan McQueen in that year's census. Census records are hardly a place to discern affairs of the heart, but Blanche's entries reveal a puzzling tentativeness, for after her strange marital-status listing in the 1930 census, in the 1940 census David's home is listed as being Tyner, back in Jackson County, even though his entry places him in the McQueen household. Blanche's niece Bernice Gibson provides a possible explanation, as she explains that Blanche's mother, Nellie, was often ill and wanted Blanche close by to care for her. Gibson also remembers her cousin visiting back in Jackson County at the Gibson household near Irvin, where especially good fishing was to be found. David enjoyed the home cooking there and the many children, for Mr. Gibson had more than twenty offspring by two different wives.[42] The relationship between David and Blanche seemed good, and the family remembers David as nice. But his constantly going on the road to perform would become a problem.

And their relationship was about to be tested by greater distance and time away than ever. Even as the ink was drying on the census page, David was leaving Kentucky altogether, chasing his dream of entertainment to a whole new level.

A KENTUCKY PARTNER: 1940–1941

Having attained visibility in the Lexington region in both radio and live performance, David was ready to take the next step in his career. In early 1940, as winter gripped the brown Kentucky hills, he got an opportunity to work for a major star in hillbilly music, Charlie Monroe.

Charlie and his brother Bill had achieved fame as the Monroe Brothers.[43] The two had come from the so-called Western Coal Fields region of Kentucky near the town of Rosine, growing up on a large farm there perched atop Jerusalem Ridge. As young men, the brothers migrated to Chicago, Charlie finding them work at Sinclair Oil and playing for the company's baseball team (both he and Bill loved playing the game just as David did). There, in the big city, they got on the WLS *National Barn Dance* and soon obtained the sponsorship of the laxative company Texas Crystals. Successes followed quickly, and under the new sponsorship of rival Crazy Water Crystals, the brothers settled into an intense pace of playing in the Carolinas. By 1937 it seemed they were headed only upward. But the two could not get along, and the next year they split up. Unfortunately, companies refused to sponsor either Charlie or Bill as solo acts, so each had to start over.

Charlie at first outstripped Bill, forming a band called the Kentucky Partners (sometimes spelled "Pardners"), which in 1939 went to Wheeling, West Virginia, for a tenure at the Wheeling Jamboree. By the autumn of that year, Charlie announced that he had set up an audition for the Grand Ole Opry in November. But on October 28, while the Kentucky Partners were playing the Jamboree, Bill and his own new band, the Blue Grass Boys, beat his brother to the punch.[44] After finishing their first two segments, Charlie and his band happened to tune in to WSM, which by now was booming at 50,000 watts, only to hear Judge Hay announce Bill and the band to play "Foggy Mountain Top" and his rendition of "Muleskinner Blues." Frantic to keep up with his brother, Charlie gave up the plumb position in Wheeling and headed to WHAS in Louisville, despite not having a sponsorship, for the sole reason that it also was also a 50,000-watt station.

It was sometime after the new year that David entered the picture. As Charlie remembered it years later, "The first time I ever heard [David] was at a service station where he was working near his home in Kentucky and he had a banjo there and I asked him to play a number and he whipped off 'Cripple Creek' about as fast as I'd ever heard it. I hired him on and brought him straight to Greensboro."[45] Charlie's account raises as many questions as it does answers. It suggests that perhaps he and his band may have stopped at the station en route to a performance, pulling his new Lincoln Zephyr to the pump only to find himself confronting Stringbean. Was this a moment in destiny, Charlie and his band just happening to stop in at *that* service station?

Charlie's story might be read as implying pure coincidence—that he happened to see David's RB-11 sitting in the corner and asked the young man if he could play it. But it could be that he had intentionally gone to that station at the recommendation of someone in the music family. It is also possible, but unlikely, that he could have learned about David through mutual acquaintances with Blanche or her ex-husband, Luther, since they had lived in Daviess County, which bordered Ohio County, where the Monroe family lived and where they had grown up. Charlie is known to have taken his band to Rosine at least once after they had settled in Louisville.[46]

There is another version of how David joined the band told by Tommy Scott, one of the Kentucky Partners at the time, who would form a lifelong friendship with David. Two years younger than David, Scott was born in Toccoa, Georgia, on June 24, 1917. As a child, he played the guitar and sang with his sister Cleo on Toccoa's WTFI, one of the first radio stations established in the country. At age seventeen, he ran away from home to join "Doc" M. F. Chamberlain's Medicine Show, where he learned to sing, play guitar, perform as a ventriloquist, and brew patent medicines, including Doc Chamberlain's special laxative, Herb-O-Lac. When Doc Chamberlain finally retired, he helped Tommy find a job, landing him a position in 1938 with John and Minerva Ray on WPTF in Raleigh just as the Monroe Brothers were unraveling. It so happened that the first person Tommy met in town was Charlie, and the Monroe brother planted a bug in his ear that he would be looking to build a new band soon and would want Tommy in it.[47] Tommy joined when the band headed to Wheeling and went with them to Louisville.

According to Tommy, it was David who came to Charlie "on a cold morning in January." David sought work as a comedian, Tommy claimed. "Well, Charlie's not hiring right now," Tommy said, knowing that Charlie had grown tight with money, "but we sure could use another black face comedian. Why don't you show us what you can do?" David evidently impressed Tommy, who explained that he could not do the hiring himself. Tommy claimed Charlie did not even listen to David's pitch, simply declaring, "We aren't hiring." At that point, Tommy took David aside and said, "I'm going to talk to the others in the band. If they can donate a few dollars a week from their check, and I'll do my share, we'll pay you. We'll just let on to Charlie that you're doing it for free until you find a job." Charlie agreed to take David on if he did not have to pay him. Eventually, Charlie figured out the arrangement, telling Tommy, "I suspect you men in the band are paying Dave's wages. Well, that has to stop. I'll pay him from now on."[48]

It is difficult to reconcile Charlie's and Tommy's stories. Perhaps David originally signed on in Louisville doing comedy only. Then perhaps at a later point when the band was passing through the Winchester area, they stopped at the filling station, where David played the banjo for the first time in Charlie's hearing. It may be that David had gone back to Winchester and Charlie and the band stopped by on the way to Greensboro, North Carolina, to say hello or pick him up. Bill was known to park his trailer for the night next to filling stations, so it may be that Charlie did the same, although the fact that Charlie and his band were staying in hotels and boarding rooms in Wheeling suggests that he had dispensed with the trailer at that point. It is also possible, of course, that one of the stories is a complete misremembering or deliberate fiction. Each story is striking for making its teller the hero who brought David into the band.

What both stories agree on is David's talent and character. Tommy observed, simply, that Charlie "got more than his money's worth, for Dave was good."[49] David was a "mighty good and an honest and hard worker too," Charlie said. "I've had a lot of people play with me but I don't believe I've ever had a man who took his work more serious than Stringbean did."[50] These qualities of goodness, honesty, work ethic, and seriousness formed a key part of David's reputation. They were values the young man dedicated himself to and that people in the growing music industry appreciated greatly. David, they knew, would go about his work quietly and, consequently, become an addition to the band who fitted in and whom people liked.

However David came to be a part of the Kentucky Partners, he went with them to Greensboro in March 1940 where Charlie was trying to get back on WFBC on which he and Bill had once been regulars. Greensboro's population was a little larger than Lexington's at nearly sixty thousand, and the city's humming textile industry gave it a more industrial feel than the more staid Kentucky city.[51] The Spanish-flu pandemic had created tremendous demand for VapoRub and NyQuil, both manufactured by the city's Vicks Chemical Company, and Greensboro also boasted its own steel industry. Prosperity showed in robust building, from the Guilford County Courthouse to the eighteen-story Jefferson Standard Building.

Although the plan was to appear on WFBC, the radio station still had no interest in sponsoring Charlie without Bill. For sponsorship, Charlie took action on a plan he had hatched back in Louisville. Knowing Tommy had the recipe for Herb-O-Lac, Charlie convinced him to rename the product Man-O-Ree, with Charlie owning the patent over Tommy's protests.[52] Charlie's promising a fifty-fifty split of the proceeds, and buying Tommy a brand-new Ford, neutralized Tommy's objections. Tommy wrote a jingle for the medicine, which soon began to sell at a rate of ten thousand bottles a week.[53] Successfully creating their own sponsorship, the Kentucky Partners now began to broadcast weekdays 12:00–12:30 and Saturdays 6:00–7:00 on Greensboro's WBIG. Before long, they started broadcasting over telephone lines to as many as fifteen stations simultaneously. In these high times, David may have been making as much as fifteen dollars a week, which was Tommy's salary, although Tommy later found out that Curly Seckler, who had departed while the band was still in Louisville, was making twenty dollars to be Bill Monroe's clone.[54]

Tommy described the typical radio set the band would do. It would open with the Man-O-Ree theme song, followed by an announcer saying, "Now it's time for the noontime program you've all been waiting for, and here they are; live and in person: Charlie Monroe and his Kentucky Partners, brought to you by Manoree, the makers of the tonic laxative that keeps everybody hale, hearty, and healthy!"[55] There would follow a duet sung by Charlie and Bill Coy (Seckler's replacement, who happened to come from Rosine and sounded like Charlie's brother Bill) while David, Tommy, Tommy Edwards, and Paul Prince played.[56] After another Man-O-Ree advertisement, Tommy Scott would do a solo, and then one of the band members would step to the microphone to announce where the band would be playing that evening. The band played a fast song after that and then finished the set with a hymn for the shut-ins, signing off with a final Man-O-Ree advertisement. Whether David was allowed a solo or even mentioned by his own name or by Stringbean is not known.

Once the broadcast ended, the band would pile into Charlie's Zephyr with a trailer in tow for their evening engagement. A photograph pictures the band surrounding the trailer that bears the words CHARLIE MONROE AND HIS MORNING JAMBOREE. David kneels in the front row, dressed in a smart light-colored suit and holding a homburg that matches the other band members.' Charlie insisted on dressing well just as his brother did with the Blue Grass Boys. David smiles at the camera, his head tilted forward with his torso. The shadows stretch to everyone's left, suggesting midmorning or midafternoon as the time the photograph was taken, perhaps just after one of the daily four-hour rehearsal sessions Charlie insisted on, or perhaps along the way from the radio station to their venue.[57]

When the band reached the schoolhouse or other site for the show, David's appearance changed, and he transformed into Stringbean. True to Tommy's hunch, Tommy and David not only played blackface together, but also played a couple in which David, under the name "Stringbean," played his wife. As Tommy tells it:

> In the skit, I would invariably come home late and "she" (Stringbean) would be mad as a wet hen, sporting a cast iron skillet in long thin hands, accusing me of being out with a "woman" and "drinking and carousing around." We would ad-lib a lot in the way which was later made famous by Bob Hope and Red Skelton, as well as many others of the era, minus the black face of course. The audience loved it, and Stringbean loved the audience.[58]

While David's minstrelsy participated in stereotyping in his time and place, there is also a possibility that he was directly channeling authentic Black cultural forms and performances he had witnessed himself. Although Appalachia has often been characterized as a racial monolith, it has never been purely white. The region around Kentucky's Cumberland Gap especially harbored an extensive population of Melungeons, whose roots as free people of color intermixed with European and Native ancestry likely reach back into the 1600s and who preserved such cultural items as the banjo. David's hero, Uncle Dave, despite conforming to prevailing racist attitudes of his moment, nevertheless received part of his musical education from an African American man named Tom Davis, who taught him his signature song, "Keep My Skillet Good and Greasy."[59] David Akeman, via Uncle Dave and whatever Black musicians David himself may have encountered, had a sensibility shaped by Black culture that indirectly resonated with that culture. David's blackface performing meant engaging with that culture, problematic as such performance was. In simultaneously tantalizing parallel and aching distance, while David was performing in blackface, his birth-year sister Billie Holiday had encountered virulent racism while performing in Louisville and, in 1939, debuted her painful lynching song, "Strange Fruit."[60]

It may have been during this time that David began to spell his surname with an *a* in the second syllable instead of the more typical *o*. The 1940s census spells his name as "Akeman," and when he filled out a draft card on October 16, 1940, he wrote "AKEMAN."[61] Filling out the card in accordance with President Roosevelt's establishing the draft as he eyed the war in Europe, David wrote his address as 247 Summit Avenue in Greensboro. He lists "Mrs. BLANCHE AKEMAN," his wife living on Route 1 in Winchester, Clark County, Kentucky, as being the person "who will always know your address." His height was listed as six-foot-one, and for weight he first wrote 148 but changed the 4 to a 3. For race, he put an *X* by "White," eye color brown, hair color brown, complexion "Ruddy." Under employer, David wrote "CHARLEY MONROE" and place of employment as WBIG in Greensboro.

Why David changed the spelling of his last name is not clear. It may have meant nothing, just a variation on the typical spelling. But he may have made the change intentionally as a way to distance himself from his family, particularly his disapproving father. Less combatively, he may have been seeking simply to separate his public entertainer self from his private self. If the latter was true, then this draft card may be evidence of the growing public-private divide in David.

Despite success, trouble was brewing beneath the surface with the Kentucky Partners as 1940 drew to a close. Charlie was not keeping up his end of the Man-O-Ree bargain with Tommy Scott. Tommy claimed he received not one penny from the proceeds. Disgusted, Tommy left the band.[62] David exited the band around the same time, around the end of 1940 or the beginning of 1941. Maybe the rift with Tommy had caused the climate of the band to deteriorate, or perhaps David left out of loyalty to Tommy. It may be that David simply missed Kentucky and Blanche. Or maybe he hoped to take another career step.

KENTUCKY WONDER: 1941–1942

Back at home, David mulled his next moves. One thing he wanted to do was try out a new name. He started billing himself as the "Kentucky Wonder." This name conveyed a loftier persona than Stringbean while still maintaining a connection with string beans via the "Kentucky Wonder" variety. David's rural audience would have recognized the strain of bean: former Davidson County, Tennessee, court of appeals judge Ben Cantrell remembers laughing when as a child he would hear announced on WSM, "Stringbean, the Kentucky Wonder!"[63] There were other dimensions to the name, too. David may have been trying to capture the allure of a locomotive such as the Festiniog Railway Little Wonder, perhaps drawing on the railroad appeal Jimmie Rodgers had so effectively wielded. Furthermore, the word "Wonder" suggested immense and surprising talent, as though the entertainer were a wonder of the world. The "Kentucky" part also brought into play the connection with the state and with Charlie's Kentucky Partners. It was a name David would always like and use and, to some degree, prefer. But it never managed to stick as thoroughly and intimately as "Stringbean," and it failed to match the evocative power of the name he would be best known and remembered by.

David went back to work playing music, likely playing on WLAP again. He may at some point have assembled his own group called "Stringbean and His Kentucky Wonders." It is possible that David made appearances on the *Renfro Valley Barn Dance* show, which John Lair had established in 1939 near his hometown of Mount Vernon, Kentucky (in Rockcastle County, which adjoined Jackson County). Lair brought musicians with him, including Lily May Ledford and Red Foley. A native of Blue Lick, Kentucky, Clyde Julian "Red" Foley was almost exactly five years older than David, born June 17, 1910. He grew up in Berea, near David's home, and, like David, participated in a talent contest (although, unlike David, he won first prize). Nicknamed for his red hair, he joined with John Lair in Chicago and went with him back to Kentucky to help start *Renfro Valley*. David and Red became friends, and their connection may have begun during this time.

The most influential *Renfro Valley* regular for the development of the Stringbean persona was fiddler-comedian Homer Miller, who went by the stage name Slim Miller. David took particular notice of this man with whom he shared a similar tall, lean physique. Always wearing a woe-is-me expression on his long face, Miller typically dressed in a checkered shirt, suspenders, and small hat. This look designated him as a rube, an image that Lair had no problem promoting, even if it raised the hackles of some performers uncomfortable with playing up hillbilly stereotypes. In one of the few extant photographs of him, Miller stands with his shoulders slumped, fiddle in left hand, bow in right, his eyes cast upward, mouth slack-jawed, and head tilted, conveying a look of dour resignation that life will never be right.

It was a look and style that resonated with David as a different take on the hillbilly comic role—a kind of Pierrot. Neither Miller nor David may have realized they were channeling the sad clown from Europe's stock characters of commedia dell'arte, but their doing so tapped into an imagery that reached back into the seventeenth century and that had inspired fellow southerner and high-modernist writer William Faulkner. The character also inspired Charlie Chaplin's little-tramp character, and Stringbean would later exhibit evidence that David had been studying that ultimate comedian as well as Buster Keaton, whose stone face Stringbean imitated. In the image and style of the sad clown,

David, like Emmett Kelly, may have seen a way to express a decade's worth of national pain as well as whatever personal pain he felt at losing his brother and his homeplace. David's mother, father, and youngest brother, Robert, all now lived in Jefferson County, Indiana, on the western Kentucky border, where his father was farming again. David's younger sister, Sallie, was also living in Jefferson County, now married to a farmer named Owen Russell and with a one-year old son they had named after James. Meanwhile, David's brother Alfred had filled out his draft card only a month after David had, listing his occupation as the Morgan Packing Company in Scott County, Indiana, and the 1940 census lists him as a soldier at Fort Thomas, Kentucky.[64]

Alfred's military post coincided with the war intensifying in Europe and in the Pacific in ways that were increasingly affecting a resistant United States. Not long after David had arrived in Greensboro, Germany had launched its attack on France and Paris fell only a few days before David's twenty-fifth birthday. The Battle of Britain began the next month, and in September the United States established the Selective Service, following which David filled out his draft card. As the war inched closer to affecting the United States, the cloudier the future looked, and with more men entering the military, it may have been a difficult time to put together a band. Newsreels showing the Nazi bombings of London, England, must have been terrifying to folks in London, Kentucky. It was a relief when the Luftwaffe left off attacking in September, and the British celebrated. But it was folly to think that dangers no longer threatened.

Those dangers became reality with the Japanese attack on Pearl Harbor on December 7, 1941. The attack and the nation's entry into the war represented a second cataclysmic change in David's conscious life—first the Depression and now a war—a piling up of horrific circumstances that defined his generation and made already hard lives even harder. Yet again the voice of Roosevelt sounded to deal with crisis. Beginning in January 1942, rationing began, first with tires and then with gasoline (constricting musicians' touring), while national propaganda encouraged people to save money. Still, many in the country wanted distraction and continued to turn to the forms of entertainment that had gotten them through the Depression. David would help provide that entertainment and escape, as his career clicked into high and historical gear.

GOIN' TO THE GRAND OLE OPRY TO MAKE MYSELF A NAME

1942–1945

BECOMING A BLUEGRASS BOY: 1942

Decades after the grim days of 1942, Bill Monroe reminisced about his career in an interview with country music historian and archivist John W. Rumble. As he spoke in his quiet, dignified way about the development of his band and style of music, Bill answered Rumble's question about how he first added a banjo player to his group:

> Well, I guess he come to where I was and wanted an audition, and I tried him out, and he played the banjo. He was the first banjo player I ever had, and he was a good singer, and he could also do some comedy too. I just wanted to get a fellow who could sing and not play too much banjo, just to fill in with it; let them hear the sound of the banjo.[1]

It is quite a statement from the man whose band would give its name to the genre of bluegrass music. Bill's words succinctly outline David Akeman's place in a pivotal stage of that genre's development.

It is not clear exactly when Bill decided the banjo would make a good addition to the band. In another interview, Bill explained, "What I wanted was the sound of the banjo, because I'd heard it back in Kentucky, and I wanted it in with the fiddle and the rest of the instruments."[2] His beloved uncle Pen was known to jam with a couple of banjo-playing buddies, Cletis Smith and Clarence Wilson.[3] Bill remembered hearing them, but as someone inspired by and thoroughly familiar with Jimmie Rodgers's discography, he likely also remembered the plectrum and four-string banjo playing featured in such recordings as "Mississippi Delta Blues." Channeling Rodgers's musical catholicity, Bill sought to embrace and even combine Appalachian-based clawhammer style with a bluesy, jazzier style.

Now, in his adulthood, Bill found himself again in close proximity to banjo players. In the spring of 1940, after securing a spot on the Opry and while David was learning blackface with Charlie's Kentucky Partners, Bill and his Blue Grass Boys were touring with Silas Green's tent show. Accompanying them was Uncle Dave Macon, whose banjo playing may have recalled the particular power of that instrument for Bill. There was another curious little twist of history with the banjo in relation to Bill and his future succession of banjo players. By the fall of 1941, despite being married, Bill had a "road girlfriend" named Bessie Lee Mauldin, of Norwood, North Carolina. She would go on to be an official member of the band, playing bass and singing. Her father, Samuel, picked the five-string banjo, and he worked at Norwood Manufacturing, which would later be renamed Collins and Akeman Company.[4] Uncle Dave, North Carolina picking, David's last name—striking intersections that foreshadowed the formative banjo players who would soon come into the band in succession.

It was in July 1942, while touring with the Grand Ole Opry tent show along with blackface comedians Bunny "Jam-Up" Biggs and David Lee "Honey" Wilds, that Bill found his banjo player in David. Bill may have tried first, unsuccessfully, to hire the three-finger picker DeWitt "Snuffy" Jenkins around this time. But whether David was Bill's first choice or not, to him would go the history-making position of being the Blue Grass Boys' first banjo player.

The precise circumstances of David's joining the group are unclear. Common wisdom holds that baseball brought David to the band, Bill hiring him to play on his team without even knowing David played the banjo. Such was the claim David's brother Robert made.[5] But the fact is that Bill did not form his baseball team until sometime in 1944, well after David joined.[6] While that myth may be debunked out of hand, no other story quite has a definitive feel to it either. Bill's mentioning an audition came with an "I guess," and elsewhere he claimed Stringbean wrote him asking for a job. Bill "Cousin Wilbur" Wesbrooks, the Blue Grass Boys' comedian and bassist at the time, remembered it that David had come to Nashville trying to get on the Opry and that he, Cousin Wilbur, urged Bill to hire him.[7] Meanwhile, there might have been some truth in Robert's claiming that David joined with Bill in Winchester, for Bill surely knew of David already from his playing in Charlie's band. However peeved Bill may have been at his brother, he kept tabs on performers, listening for those who might be a good fit for the Blue Grass Boys and the sound he was trying to develop.[8]

Whatever the details, David joined the band in late July 1942.[9] Bill put him right to work with Cousin Wilbur, seeking to capture the comedic duo power of Jam-Up and Honey.[10] In fact, Stringbean and Cousin Wilbur established a kind of independent act within an act, the August 1942 *Billboard* announcing that the two "are striking out on their own to form a new act called String Beans and Cousin Wilbur. They'll be used with the Monroe crew on the Grand Ole Opry program." The two did their bit in the show, Stringbean playing a deadpan role and Cousin Wilbur a smartmouth.[11] Cousin Wilbur remembered one night:

> String could never remember the name of the town we were in. Right in the middle of the act he'd get the audience laughing and then he'd ask me out of the corner of his mouth, "What's the name of this town?" and I'd tell him. One night in Arkansas I really fixed Stringbean up. The name of the town was Rector, Arkansas. And Stringbean asks out of the corner of his mouth, "What's the name of this town," so I told him it was Rectum, Arkansas. That's what Stringbean up and said, "Right here, folks, right here in Rectum, Arkansas." And he liked to wreck the audience. They must have laughed for fifteen minutes. And I got so tickled that Stringbean got broke up. . . . I looked backstage, and there was Bill Monroe and Honey Wilds—Honey was a big fat guy—and they were backstage of the tent lying down on the ground just holding their stomachs.[12]

The moment David became a Blue Grass Boy, he knew that meant realizing his greatest dream. Now he, David Akeman, would be on the Grand Ole Opry. His first appearances put him on the stage of the War Memorial Auditorium, a neoclassical structure built in 1925 to memorialize the Tennesseans who died in the Great War. While the acoustics were excellent, the Grecian columns clashed with the Opry's homespun style.

Or it might be better said that the Opry's homespun style clashed with Nashville's Grecian aesthetics, for the city had long possessed a tony character. Officially founded in 1779 as Fort Nashborough, named for Revolutionary War hero Francis Nash, the city grew to become the central urban space of the state and was made the capital in 1843. It was the first Confederate city to fall to the Union army in 1862, but, by the end of the nineteenth century, it had recovered through both its agricultural and its industrial production. The city maintained a genteel character, its tradition steeped in Old South lore, its aristocratic citizens' accents and lifestyles distinctive. Nashvillians loved fox hunting and fox-trots and were proud of their neoclassical architecture and institutions of higher education. Since the mid-1880s, the city had thought of itself as the "Athens of the South" and thus quite naturally built a full-scale replica of the Parthenon for the 1897 Tennessee Centennial Exposition. The War Memorial Auditorium replicated the Parthenon's precedent and the city's general Athenian echoes. That classical self-conceptualization involved a rigid hierarchy and strong racial segregation, with the African American community focused around Jefferson Street by the 1940s. While a jazz scene existed in that contained section of town, the hillbilly music at the Ryman pervaded the city and bothered the aristocracy greatly. The upper class was horrified to see predominantly poor white music starting to define their city's image.

In 1942, when David arrived, Nashville's skyline was still low, the capitol building perched on the hill that marked the highest point of downtown. Blocky buildings of the style of the previous decade filled the city center, but Nashville was moving forward, including the opening of a modern department store, Harvey's, on the corner of Sixth Avenue North and Church Street. Harvey's boasted Nashville's first escalators. The main thing on the city's collective mind, however, was the war, and in town could be seen the green woolen uniforms of soldiers on furlough, while those not in the military contributed to the war effort either through personal contribution or by working in such facilities as the Vultee Aircraft Company. The strains of big-band music filled the airwaves along with the classical music wealthy Nashvillians loved. The only thing that brought grudging aristocrats to accept hillbilly music was the money it brought.

It must have been an overwhelming moment for David to play the Opry for the very first time. So many nights he had listened in the dark on that radio at the Welchburg store. No longer just one of many radio barn dances, the Opry had now grown even more prestigious and held audiences spellbound all over the South and as far north as the Great Lakes with WSM's increased range. David was experienced enough as a performer to take any venue in stride, but this was not just any venue. It is not hard to imagine him shaking with excitement and nervousness as the Blue Grass Boys broke into whatever number they played on his first night. Looking out over that audience, did his mind wander back over the journey to this point? He never seems to have spoken about that night, but he expressed his adoration of the Opry in two different songs, "Opry Time in Tennessee" and "Going to the Opry (to Make Myself a Name)." The second one is the first of his biographical songs:

> I come out of old Kentucky, it was early in the spring.
> I was heading to the Grand Ole Opry, boys, to make myself a name.
> Oh, there's never been a show on earth of Grand Ole Opry fame.
> I'm going to join up with them folks, make myself a name.[13]

Now David entered the Grand Ole Opry family. Some members of it he knew already: for example, Casey Jones, the fiddler David had worked with as part of the Bar-X-Boys, was now making appearances on the Opry. Other cast members he was probably meeting for the first time. David became friends with fellow comic "Cousin" Minnie Pearl, who was already on the rise as a fan favorite. A couple of East Tennesseans would become particular friends to David. One was comedian "Bashful Brother" Oswald. Born Beecher Ray Kirby in 1911, later changing his first name to Pete, Brother Oswald was a strapping man with a big voice and braying laugh. He played resonator guitar and sang with the Smoky Mountain Boys. The other friend was the leader of that band, Roy Acuff. Roy shared David's love of baseball, having once played for the Knoxville Smokies minor-league team. Unsurprisingly, David and Roy formed a lifelong friendship.

Of course, the most important Opry member for David was his musical and spiritual uncle, Dave Macon. David could not hide his admiration as he went to work taking notes from the great entertainer. Kirk McGee, another Opry member, told a story of the young David watching his idol:

> He would stand in the wings watching him, watching him real close, trying to get down every little move he made. We used to kid Uncle Dave about it, saying, "Uncle Dave, he's gonna steal your stuff, you better watch out," and he didn't think much about it, but one night while he was on stage, he turned around and looked back over to us, and String was right in the middle of imitating him and String just stopped dead in his tracks, and Uncle Dave turned back and snorted, "Oh hell."[14]

Even with imitation being the highest form of flattery, Uncle Dave might not have handled a less likeable young man mimicking his every action so well. Already he was facing Roy Acuff's challenging his status as the Opry's premier star, and now here was a young man transforming himself into the next Uncle Dave—a young man who shared his own name, no less. But this young "Stringbean" fellow was especially likable, and he clearly appreciated Uncle Dave. Seeing a protégé, Uncle Dave took the younger man under his wing.

COSTUME: 1942–1943

It was soon after joining the Blue Grass Boys and the Opry that David fashioned his famous costume. The single greatest stroke of genius in developing "Stringbean," after the name itself, was creating the look that set him apart from other banjoist/bassist comics. Remembering Slim Miller's Pierrot-like look, David began painting on eyebrows that hoisted upward, giving him a woeful expression. David also donned a striped shirt, suspenders, and a small-brimmed hat like Miller's. Kirk McGee claimed, "String once told me that he borrowed that idea from an old comedian somewhere up north, I don't remember his name, who had worn a costume like that and String had seen him. When he retired and didn't use it any more, that's when String started working with it."[15] Whether it is exactly true that David waited for Miller to retire or not, David clearly patterned his look on Slim's.

But David took the concept a step further that would make all the difference. He replaced the regular shirt Miller wore with a long nightshirt and jeans buckled just above his knees. In that one move, David effected the embodiment of a human string bean. He might have achieved this living legume look in other ways by putting on green makeup and wearing a green outfit or by wearing a hat with the tip of a vine sticking out of the crown. But the way he chose was brilliant and audacious. It was so ridiculous it should not have worked. Yet it did because that long shirt and short pants captured "Stringbean" more effectively than any other could have.

The outfit is completely David/Stringbean, as full an expression of the man/persona as his banjo playing. It conveyed "stringiness," creating a subtle kind of intimacy and familiarity in the way it combined everyday materials with exotic freakishness. It managed to be both understated and loud at the same time. The weirdness of the costume contrasted comically with his mournful expression and dry demeanor. From henceforth (if it had not already), the Stringbean persona balanced on a razor-thin edge of dark and light, sad and happy, somber and ridiculous. This character was a pathetic victim of the world. "Lord, I feel so unnecessary," he started saying between verses of songs. It was a look and style that channeled pain into humor, and one wonders if the pain of a dead brother, an estranged father, and a shaky marriage underlay David's comedy. David and Stringbean were fully simpatico, but Stringbean increasingly subsumed David, himself, perhaps by design. Both strange and funny, Stringbean invited friendly warmth while also keeping aloof and secretive.

That long-torso look also marked a nexus of racial performativity. It has been observed that the "exaggerated hayseed imagery that became such a lasting part of country music was a show business affectation, a transformation of the blackface mask into a new clown face. . . . The banjo player was especially susceptible to 'whiteface' minstrelsy. Ridiculous costumes, oversized shoes, and comedy gags were part of being a banjo player."[16] Given this transformation of elements of minstrel performance into country-bumpkin performance—which mirrored the five-string banjo's own history of "whitening"—David's performing in blackface marked a step toward his development of the Stringbean persona as one that resonated on racially inflected levels. It is not entirely a cultural accident or coincidence that this torso-lengthening look crosses racial lines because it is part of a larger intersection of poor white and Black performance to be found at work in nineteenth-century dialect fiction of local colorists and southwest humorists. "Once blackface fell out of style, a lot of the stock characters kept a lot of the jokes, the sketches, and the sort of banter that were a part of the blackface minstrel show and repurposed them so that they fit with the normal show," says Dom Flemons, singer-songwriter-interpreter, who has deeply researched African American forces in roots music.[17]

At the same time, the long-torso illusion bore relation to an African American sartorial style of the moment, the zoot suit. That urban hepcat costume of a long, angular coat was famously modeled by Cab Calloway. Stringbean represented a countrified white version that arguably keyed into late-modernist style not unlike the kinds of southern literary modernism that used contemporary experimental techniques to present old-fashioned, rural, peripheral places and characters. Considering the ways Stringbean's costume raised the rube outfits of other hillbilly comics of his time and earlier to a higher level, Flemons observes, "That costume is the pinnacle of that style of costuming. [Stringbean] brings on the modern equivalency of what those early pioneers were doing."[18] There was something almost cubist about the Stringbean look, and the contrast of that edgy modernist appearance created both the tension and the humor that persona projected.

Stringbean's appearance not only drew upon the past and interfaced with the present, but also uncannily anticipated future race-based performative style. Funny as it may sound to say, in appearance and perhaps in some ways in affect, Stringbean anticipated the gangsta image. Matt Powell has well said, "His iconic costume is a cultural anomaly—simultaneously old-fashioned and ahead of its time." It was the kind of outfit Snoop Dogg would wear decades later. It is not that Stringbean made a direct impact on these later clothing styles. Rather, his costume frames gangsta clothing as coming full circle in a progression of race-inflected performance, the minstrel morphed into a hillbilly morphed into twenty-first-century African American performance and style.

VEGA NO. 9: 1943

Sometime in the first half of 1943, as he settled into his new look, Stringbean acquired the banjo he would play the rest of his life, the Vega No. 9 Tubaphone, serial number 81268.[19] Exactly when and where he bought it is unknown, Stringbean revealing only that he bought it secondhand and that he understood it to have been manufactured in 1930.[20] How much he paid is also not known, although it should be noted that his purchasing power had probably grown to a greater level than ever, for Bill paid ten dollars a day for six days a week plus another ten dollars if a band member worked on Sunday. Stringbean may have traded the Gibson RB-11 for it. Certainly, the Vega No. 9 was superior to the RB-11, and it differed significantly from the direction in design Gibson had taken. Stringbean's banjo was an instrument perfectly suited to his style of both playing and performing.

In appearance, the Vega No. 9 had an elegant beauty. The neck was fashioned of laminated figured maple, its flaming zebra-like stripes curling around its delicate circumference. The heel was carved in oak-leaf bass relief, and the heel plate featured an artichoke-shaped mother-of-pearl inlay. At the other end of the neck, the back of the peghead bore a six-pointed flower-shaped mother-of-pearl inlay. The front of the peghead sported gold-tinted pearl inlays in a late 1800s Victorian design brought in from the A. C. Fairbanks Company Vega had acquired. The Fairbanks inlay designs continued down the ebony fretboard, the mother of pearl shaped and engraved in flower designs.

The Vega No. 9's pot design was also distinct. The head was 10 15/16 inches, held tight by twenty-eight hooks. These hooks screwed into shoes with individual flanges as opposed to the single flange commonly used in Gibsons and in most banjos now. The resonator was an especially elegant work of art, composed of eight pie-shaped pieces of figured maple with thin rosewood inlays along the joints. It attached not via four thumbscrews in receptacles in the resonator wall but by a single bolt that screwed into a clamp on the wooden dowel that ran through the head. The resonator was relatively shallow, giving the banjo a thin profile, and that wooden dowel made the banjo lighter than the one or two metal-rod construction of most Gibsons.

Unlike the bell-shaped profile of the cast tone ring in Gibson Mastertones or the scalloped ring used in Vega Whyte Ladies, the Vega No. 9 tone ring was composed of a spun outer shell, a hoop, and square inner tube with holes. Developed in 1906 by Vega, it was that tubular inner ring that made it a "Tubaphone." Its distinct tone has been described as a "warm, round sound with a sweet, golden metallic ping in the tone. It doesn't have the sharpness of a heavy cast tone-ring and for that reason, it is popular with folksingers and old-time clawhammer players who like a fuller sound. For the player who wants a sweeter, gentler sounding banjo, that is crisp and full, with a little less 'bite' than a cast bronze tone-ring, this is a classic and a beautiful choice."[21] While great for clawhammer style, it also served well for David's two-finger picking, as this loud tone ring has been referred to as "the SUV of tone rings, in that it is an all-purpose tone ring."[22] This crucial part of the banjo, with its tremendous range, worked in wonderful conjunction with Stringbean, forming his particular sound.

In fact, the Vega No. 9 projected a personality inextricably tied to Stringbean. A photograph taken at the time features David dressed in a sharp suit and a wide-wing collar with no tie as he holds his new banjo. His grin shows his pure joy, and the banjo itself seems to beam in his grasp. The fancy clothes and the ultra-fancy banjo present a young man who had come a long way from the hills of Kentucky. The Vega's beauty would have clashed with another performer's rube look, but with Stringbean it simply melded with his peculiar style, strange and illogically logical. At the same time, both clothes and banjo suited the fancy style of clothing Bill Monroe, like his brother, preferred his band members wearing. In short, this banjo had all the makings of an icon.

And David carried it with him in Bill's new tent show that spring. Leasing canvas from Billy Wehle out of Louisville, the Blue Grass Boys hit the road in May. Their path took them from Georgia into Tennessee, over to North Carolina, up to Virginia, then back down through South Carolina and into Georgia again.[23] Frank Buchanan, who became a Blue Grass Boy years later, remembered walking seven miles to see one of these performances in Spruce Pine, North Carolina, when he was nine years old. "Now I remember very well who was with [Bill]," he reminisced. It "was Clyde Moody, Stringbean, Cousin Wilbur, Chubby Wise. . . . And I remember just about all the songs they did. I can remember Clyde done 'Six White Horses.' And Bill done 'Mule Skinner Blues.'"[24]

THE RYMAN: 1943

The Stringbean character's jelling coincided with an iconic conjoining in Opry history—the program's move to the Ryman Auditorium. The War Memorial Auditorium was, in truth, never a completely logical place for the Opry. Although larger than previous Opry sites, at two thousand seats, it still could not accommodate the thronging crowds of hillbillies who differed profoundly from the neoclassically turned aristocratic audience the building best suited. Even charging a whopping twenty-five cents per ticket did not discourage fans from seeing their heroes. Citing damage to the seats' leather upholstery—people were carving their initials in them—the War Memorial Auditorium's administrators tendered a "polite but firm request" for the Opry to leave.[25] The Opry managers began to cast about to find a new venue.

They found it in the Ryman Auditorium. This splendid edifice was built as a church in 1892 by Captain Thomas Ryman. An old riverboat captain who owned gambling saloons and riverboats and was a great lover of vice, Captain Ryman had been converted by the preaching of the famous minister Sam Jones. Ryman had gone to Jones's Nashville tent meeting to heckle the preacher. But Jones, who had himself been a notorious drunk as a young man, had a way of speaking that got down to the bone, eloquent in its directness: "I believe the Bible from lid to lid," he would say.[26] His biggest phrase he projected straight into the faces of sinners, simply, "Quit your meanness." His words hit the captain hard. He went straightway and changed, so profoundly converted he spent $100,000 (nearly $3 million today) of his own money to build the beautiful church building he called the Union Gospel Tabernacle in 1892.

The tabernacle was grand and elegant, with just the faintest touch of the riverboat aesthetic to give it something extra without detracting from its spiritual purpose. The basic structure of the building was simple enough, a kind of glorified brick barn. The facade varied the front with tasteful decoration, including a bank of Gothic stained-glass windows that broke the sunlight into a million colors. Inside, ranks of warm wooden pews curved in a semicircle around a pulpit, and five years after the building was complete, a second level was built called the Confederate Gallery, increasing the seating capacity to six thousand souls. True to his new selfless piety, Ryman refused to name the tabernacle for himself. Not until he died in 1904 did Sam Jones himself urge that it be renamed the Ryman Auditorium.

By 1943, a curious blend of the spiritual and artistic had distilled in those wooden pews, stained glass, and redbrick walls. Many an eloquent orator had delivered lectures and sermons there along with opera and orchestral productions. Since 1920 the Ryman had been managed by the visionary Lula C. Naff, who had brought no less famous and varied performers than Charlie Chaplin, Harry Houdini, and W. C. Fields to the stage. This eclectic blend brought a special kind of pulse to the auditorium. Although the Opry may not have seemed an obvious match at first glance, nevertheless here hillbilly music could be itself, not an out-of-place stranger misunderstood by those who would look down on it. In this temple of sincerity to religion, music, and life, generally, the music of country people would have plenty of room to grow and deepen. The corny side could and would stay, but now this kind of music and performance could allow itself to manifest its other dimensions. Naff may not have favored the hillbilly scene herself at that point, and she probably did not foresee how ultimately appropriate and legendary the wedding of the Ryman to the Opry would be.[27] But her business sense overpowered her taste, and a contract was drawn up for the Grand Ole Opry to debut on the Ryman's stage on June 5, 1943. David was part of the Opry regular cast that made this momentous transition.

MILITARY: 1943

Just as David was establishing his iconic costume, he received a call to don the green uniform of the U.S. Army. His enlistment form puts him in the army as a private on June 30, 1943, serial number 34738550 at Fort Oglethorpe, Georgia. His civil occupation was listed under "Actors and actresses." A photograph of David has floated up onto Ancestry.com, apparently sent to and kept by Blanche. It features him in uniform, smiling, against a painted background featuring a palm tree.

He may have been smiling, but the timing could not have been worse for David. The career momentum halted. In such frightening and uncertain times, David may have fretted about whether he could keep his position in the band. Any anxieties he may have felt could have been alleviated by the fact that Howdy Forrester had been in the military now for months and Bill had kept his wife, Wilene "Sally Anne," on and in the band. But while David was away, Bill encountered sixteen-year-old banjo player Don Reno in September in Spartanburg, South Carolina, and told Clyde Moody, "This is the sound right here that I want."[28] Reno's sound was a three-finger picking style derived from Dewitt "Snuffy" Jenkins that differed from David's clawhammering and two-finger picking. If word of Bill's comment got back to David, he might have worried.

By November David was in Camp Fannin, Texas. Sometime during that month, he was admitted into a hospital with an undisclosed condition that "existed prior to entry into the service."[29] On December 21, he was honorably discharged, with the cause-of-separation code CDD Sec II AR615-360. The notice to the Veterans Administration section in the paperwork provides more information on the diagnosis: "disability." The following conditions were listed: "psychoneurosis, hysterical type, severe." To these were added, "Pain in the back, bed wetting and numerous other somatic complaints not on an organic basis."

David would not have been alone in experiencing extreme anxiety at the prospect of being in combat. On the other hand, he may not have feared war so much as he struggled with it morally, ethically, or politically. He had no qualms about hunting squirrels, but shooting at other humans may have been a very different matter. David was already playing a song titled "Crazy War," which was originally "an old Spanish-American war protest song."[30] No record exists of David conscientiously objecting to military service, but then he might have felt societal pressure to fill out his draft card and enter the military. Once in the service, his conscience may have overcome him.

The indication that David's psychosomatic ailments preceded his entry into the service raises questions about his health generally. Should we read in this military record a troubled and ill person hidden behind the comedian's mask? The high-profile suicide of Robin Williams points to the many funny people who wrestle with depression, and David may have been one of them. His struggles may have been greater during his time in the army and ended once he was out. But they may also have continued, and that possibility is worth remembering in seeing the full depths of this man who made so many laugh but may have wrestled with demons of his own. The lines between the person and the persona are not always easy to delineate; David channeled his own energies into his persona in complex ways.

Unsurprisingly, David kept the full extent of his cause for discharge secret. Just before his death, he did tell an interviewer a back injury caused his discharge. But he said little else, at least publicly, about his time in the service. Aside from obvious reasons of privacy not to provide details, there were potent professional motivations not to play up a discharge. A month before David's hospital visit, a furor had erupted over Frank Sinatra's not being enlisted due to physical unfitness, although the examining doctor specifically wrote, "The diagnosis of 'psyochoneurosis, severe' was not added to the list." David surely did not want to draw such controversy to himself. The country music industry too took care not to call attention to David's army experience. A column in Minnie Pearl's *Grinder's Switch Gazette* mentions that the "Gazette is anxious to give credit due the boys on the Opry who have gone to war—those who are still in service and those who have received honorable discharges. . . . 'Stringbean,' comic and banjo player with Bill Monroe, spent six months in the service, too."[31] But that notice appeared in the December 1944 issue, a year after David's discharge. If people in the industry knew about the diagnosis and that David struggled with psychosocial illness, they shielded these details from public view.

PRINCE ALBERT OPRY, BASEBALL, AND TOURING WITH UNCLE DAVE: 1944

As if not enough had happened to David and the Opry in 1943, one more major development occurred while David was away scaling obstacles and crawling in the mud as a basic trainee. Since 1939 the R. J. Reynolds Tobacco Company had sponsored an Opry segment called the "Prince Albert Opry." On October 9, 1943, that thirty-minute segment went from appearing on a handful of NBC affiliates in the South to broadcasting on as many as 129 stations across the nation. With this widened exposure, the Opry and the Ryman together achieved national fame, and hillbilly music became hotter than ever, bringing the "beginning of the explosion of country music," as Minnie Pearl put it.[32] In wartime, when death constantly loomed, this music that veered from down-home comical to unabashedly sentimental touched and inspired soldiers and the families who missed them.

In the midst of such trying times, the Opry proceeded in madcap informality. Performers crowded the stage, even when not performing. The audience eagerly awaited Cousin Minnie stepping forward to one of the box-shaped, silver-glinted RCA 44 microphones on stands decorated with WSM plaques and hollering, "How-deeee! I'm just so proud to be here." The audience laughed and felt the comfort of the transpiring of the expected. The same went for when Roy Acuff sang "Wabash Cannonball" or "The Great Speckled Bird" in his full-throated, unself-reflexive sincerity. And when Bill Monroe and the Blue Grass Boys brought their driving rhythm and high-pitched harmonizing, all could seem right in the world for a couple of hours.

Later advertising implies that David performed on the Prince Albert segment beginning in 1944, and that *Grinder's Switch Gazette* notice of his military service affirms that he had gained some visibility as Stringbean as well as a Blue Grass Boy.[33] Backstage, his friendships with his fellow performers deepened, his quiet, affable personality and wittiness endearing him in the collective dressing room. During this year, Tommy Scott joined the cast. But he left after only a year, mainly because the Opry did not pay at the time and demanded a percentage from road-show dates.[34] Grand Ole Opry members, including Stringbean, in fact, found themselves in a dilemma: despite the publicity the Opry brought, the car rides to show dates were grueling and the split of the money was small.

In the summer of 1944, Bill created his baseball team as part of his touring tent show. Loving the sport as much as David did, Bill started his own team to play teams in the towns where shows were held as a promotional stunt. He reasoned, "It seems like the people that loves baseball are the people that loves bluegrass music."[35] Bill's team was made up of band members as well as hired ringers. By all accounts, David was the best musician player and one of the best on the field, able to play any position and a strong hitter. "He was a hard man to strike out, boy," Bill said. "He went one year, and I think maybe they only struck him out a couple of times."[36]

A photograph pictures Stringbean standing in the middle of a lineup of Blue Grass Boys players in uniform for the diamond. He is flanked by Chubby Wise and Clyde Moody. On the end to his right stands Howard Watts, a bassist who had replaced Cousin Wilbur and "Cedric Watts." To the left, Bill, a little apart, stands with his hands on his hips. David smiles, holding his bat. In the background, the tent looms in glorious promise.

We might imagine a summer day in a small town somewhere in Kentucky in 1944. Posters and window cards have bloomed in town for the past few weeks, the work of an advance agent.[37] Now the day has arrived, and we watch as a procession of trucks snakes into town, led by a 1941 Chevrolet airport limousine with BILL MONROE AND HIS BLUE GRASS BOYS WSM "GRAND OLE OPRY" painted on the side.[38] It is midmorning, and clouds list across the bright sun as the procession comes to a halt on an empty field. The tall, solidly built Bill Monroe gets out of the limousine first, and the other men unfold out of the other doors, each man well dressed in shirts, ties, coats, and possibly even the jodhpurs they will wear later onstage. With them may be a blonde woman, Bill's girlfriend, Bessie, and along with her dark-haired Sally Ann Forrester.

Bill asks if this town has a baseball team, and when he learns it does he sets up a game for the afternoon. After lunch some of the tent crew don baseball uniforms and join the band members to play. The tall Blue Grass Boy with the funny name, "Stringbean," shines. Standing at the plate, his long face peers intently at the pitcher, and when he swings his bat connects with a telltale report. His long legs, wheeling, propel him around the bases just as his long right arm hurls the ball straight, true, and strong from anywhere on the field.

As the sun lowers on the hot day, people line up at the ticket stand, adults' tickets selling at sixty cents, children's at thirty. They buy Coke and popcorn, and some also buy song and picture books from the Grand Ole Opry. Inside, the people begin to fill the tent, the bleachers capable of seating a thousand. While they eat the popcorn and sip the Coke, they look at the bass fiddle on the stage under the lights, their excitement building. Then the band comes running out, most in their fine clothes, but Stringbean appears with his Vega No. 9 and dressed in his countrified style.[39] Cedric Rainwater stomps on the bass's stand pin, and the instrument leaps up into his hands. Then the band breaks into whirling sound.

After twenty minutes of music, the Blue Grass Boys pause for fifteen minutes of comedy. Stringbean and Cedric go to work, telling their homespun jokes. When the comedy interlude ends, the band comes back out. They play gospel songs and then more of their hard-driving secular numbers. The show ends then, and we stream out and break into clumps to walk home in the dark. After a day and evening of joy and entertainment, troubles may return, anything from a broken heart to money worries to fears about loved ones far away at war. But while the show has ended, the memories are only just beginning their long lives. Those memories recall a moment of stepping into another world full of soft lights and bright sounds. We will remember Bill's careening mandolin, Chubby's fiddle, and Stringbean's banjo. We may not remember the punch lines of every Cedric and Stringbean joke, but we will always remember laughing at the bizarre-looking man with the sad face.

While barnstorming around the country playing the banjo and baseball and making people laugh, David reveled in the time he was getting to spend with his idol. Years later—in 1970, the hundredth anniversary of Uncle Dave's birth—Stringbean remembered these days: "I traveled with Uncle Dave. I roomed with Uncle Dave for two or three years, I guess." Stringbean roomed at Ma Upchurch's so-called Hillbilly Heaven at 620 Boscobel Street in the Edgefield neighborhood in East Nashville. The gabled and dormered stone house was home to many performers, as Delia "Ma" Upchurch offered the rooming house to entertainers for five dollars a week, with breakfast for seventy-five cents and dinner for eighty-five cents, although she was known to feed a down-on-his-luck entertainer for free.[40] A photograph of David and Uncle Dave pictures them in suits and hats and shaking hands in a comical pose.[41] David looks at the camera smiling, while Uncle Dave looks at David, cigar in mouth, leaning back, his left leg bent, the right one forward with the toe of his shoe pointing upward.

David was learning professionalism as an entertainer from his mentor. "He was one of the greatest entertainers I ever knowed, and I've knowed a lot of them," David said of Uncle Dave. "I've seed him work forty-five minutes and have to come back and take seven or eight encores, and it takes a hoss to do that, I think." Along with learning to emulate the older entertainer's stamina, David picked up Uncle Dave's ability to introduce witty comments at unexpected moments in order to get a laugh, as when Uncle Dave would take off his coat onstage and say, "Now, ladies, don't get alarmed. When I get through undressing, I'll have on more clothes than you have."

David acquired some banjo technique from Uncle Dave. He studied how to sweep his hand up the neck toward the peghead and down on the head below the bridge, quirks and peculiarities that could keep an audience's attention. He did *not* adopt Uncle Dave's banjo twirling as has present-day protégé Leroy Troy, perhaps because the resonator on his Vega No. 9 made that less practical. Gibson manufactured some special RB-1s for Uncle Dave that were designed for his antics. Open-backed and light, they used old-fashioned wooden dowels in the head instead of Gibson's metal rods.[42] At least one of these RB-1s sported less metal hardware, using sixteen instead of twenty-four hooks to keep the head tight, which would have made the banjo twirling even easier. Typically, Uncle Dave carried three banjos with him, each tuned to a different key (marked with different colored ribbons for ease of identification). But, David explained, "When I went on the road with him I let him use mine, you know, and that cut down on him carrying. . . . I let him use mine, an A banjo, you know. And I was honored for him to play my banjo."[43]

All was not well during this time, though. Bessie abandoned Bill to marry a petty officer in the navy living on the West Coast.[44] This heartbreak inspired Bill to write "Blue Moon of Kentucky," the song that would become his greatest hit. David's marriage was also suffering. Although Blanche sometimes accompanied him to Nashville, she was torn between David and her ailing mother. It got to the point to where Blanche would ask David if he really had to go to the Opry every weekend. "Blanche, honey, I wouldn't quit the Grand Ole Opry to go to heaven," he told her.[45] An impasse was swiftly approaching.

Meanwhile, over everything hung the reality of war, which now mixed victory with gnawing grief. June brought D-day. The results of the offensive hung in the balance and even looked doubtful at first. But as the weeks and then months passed, the Allies began piling up victories. By year's end, large numbers of Americans were in the fight of their lives in the forests of the Ardennes. This Battle of the Bulge, as it came to be called, continued into the new year, with the fate of civilization still an immense question mark.

ON RECORD: 1945

A month and a half into 1945, on February 13, David found himself on North Michigan Avenue in Chicago at the door to the Wrigley Building while an icy, whipping wind squeezed a few flurries out of heavy gray clouds.[46] He may have been overwhelmed not only by that building's tower but by a city this massive, far larger and more urbane than Nashville, Lexington, or Greensboro.

He went into the building with his bandmates, and they made their way up to the second floor, where they entered the CBS-affiliated Studio 12 in the WBBM radio station.[47] As David opened his case and checked the head of his Vega for tightness after being in the cold, Chubby Wise started tuning his fiddle. Sally Ann readied her voice and her accordion. On guitar was Tex Willis, who had joined a month earlier. Cedric Rainwater tuned his bass. Bill Monroe grasped his new acquisition from a Miami barbershop, a 1923 Gibson F-5 Master model mandolin, tested and approved by legendary engineer Lloyd Loar. It was to become one of the most revered instruments in country music history, and Bill was playing it on record for the first time today, while David played his Vega No. 9.[48]

The group was here to record on the Columbia label with producer Art Satherly. A Brit who, like his fellow Bristol native Cary Grant, had come to the United States to find success, he had begun his career as a secretary for Thomas Edison. As he worked his way up through the ranks, he famously recorded the blues singer Lead Belly and in 1938 became head of Columbia's country and blues departments. A handsome, impeccably groomed man, Satherly talked quietly with Bill, their English and Kentucky accents blending in lovely counterpoint. Bill referred to Art as "Mr. Satherly" in his formal way. Once they were finally set up, they started recording.

The recordings that day marked the first known ones of David's banjo playing. The Vega No. 9 snaps along just audible enough in "Rocky Road Blues," a number David himself supplied.[49] The same went for "Footprints in the Snow," one writer noting that by "listening carefully one can hear delicate finger picking by" David.[50] In "True Life Blues," David got his first ever on-record solo. He also took a solo in "Blue Grass Special," while his playing in the Jimmie Rodgers–like "Goodbye Old Pal" resembles the banjo strumming in certain numbers Rodgers recorded. These recordings made history by foregrounding the banjo in Bill's music.[51] Inching Bill's sound closer to its destined bluegrass style, David's two-finger picking rings distinctly. David's solos manage the rhythm even as they delineate the melody, the result being a rousing plunk swing. He builds repeated climbing phrases that might be represented as:

one- - -two-three-four-five- - - - - - -six-seven
one- - -two-three-four-five- - - - - - -six-seven

The picking hops along like a fawn learning to walk, taking a few steps, then faltering, then taking a few more before faltering again. But that hesitance does not betray inexperience or inability. It rings exotic in the way David/Stringbean himself was. More important, it draws on the equally powerful comic-tragic ambiguity of blues music itself.

The recording session marked a pinnacle for David. He may have felt he was on top of the world that day in the big city. The next day was Valentine's Day, and perhaps he took the first train back to Kentucky and Blanche to celebrate his success and their love. But life was taking him on a different track far away from his wife and to new horizons.

BIG BALL IN NASHVILLE
1945-1952

LEAVING BILL AND A DUO WITH LEW: 1945

A month after the Chicago recording session, in March 1945, the Blue Grass Boys' sound began a dramatic shift toward what is now thought of as its defining style. Howard Watts, Chubby Wise, and Tex Willis all left the band only a few weeks after that Chicago session. Andy Boyette stepped in for Watts to play bass and perform comedy with David. Jim Shumate replaced Chubby. For a new guitarist, Bill turned to another musician who had previously played with his brother. His name was Lester Flatt.

Lester was born on June 19, 1914, almost exactly a year before David, in Overton County, Tennessee. While working in sawmills and textile mills, he made his radio debut in 1939 on Roanoke, Virginia's WDBJ with Charlie Scott's Harmonizers.[1] Lester and his wife, Gladys, became Kentucky Partners in 1943, but Lester quickly tired of Charlie. "I didn't particularly like working for him," Lester said later, "because I was singing tenor with him, and he sang everything so high; almost out of this world. He was the hardest man to work for I have ever known. Sometimes we worked as many as three shows a day."[2] After quitting Charlie, Lester went back home and started hauling timber. But he could not stay away from the guitar, so in March 1945 he joined a group to play a show on WBBB in Burlington, North Carolina, only to be surprised by a telegram from none other than Bill Monroe.[3]

When Lester joined the Blue Grass Boys, the tempo began to change. He has been described as "an extraordinary fluid rhythm guitarist, scrupulous about timing." He not only played guitar and sang, but also emceed and worked with Bill in writing songs, including "It's Mighty Dark for Me to Travel."[4] Outgoing and jovial, Lester complemented the quiet Bill in ways Charlie once did. His importance in the band grew quickly. As much as he got along with his bandmates, he held strong opinions about music and quickly grew frustrated with the most likable member in the group. "I felt that type of banjo playing did not fit in with what we were doing," he explained later, "and Stringbean had dragged us to death."[5]

David may already have been seeking to strike out on his own; if so, the new pace and rhythm may have urged him more. He found an opportunity for taking this step in a new friendship with an entertainer who joined the tent show, Lew Childre. Born in Opp, Alabama, in 1901, Childre had extensive experience in professional music.[6] He had joined a tent show in 1923 and formed a jazz band that included Lawrence Welk called the Alabama Cotton Pickers. Lew then got interested in country music and learned to play the guitar. He went back to work with tent shows, eventually landing a spot on XERA with the Carter Family on the Texas border in the late 1930s. In the early 1940s, he made his way up to the Wheeling Jamboree, either contemporary with Charlie's Kentucky Partners or shortly thereafter. He seems to have joined the Opry, perhaps in some capacity with the Blue Grass Boys, in 1945.

In that summer of 1945, David and Lew not only worked well together onstage but also became friends offstage. The two shared a love of fishing.[7] Perhaps it was during one of their days on the water that David and Lew hatched the idea of creating their own musical-comedy duo. By September, with atomic bombings in Japan bringing the war to a close, the men made up their minds. David informed Bill he would be leaving the Blue Grass Boys. Jim Shumate "hated to see ole String go. When he quit, it left a big hole."[8] But Lester was relieved, later commenting, "As much as I love drop-thumb style banjo playing, I was glad when Stringbean (David Akeman) left Monroe's group." In fact, Lester did not want any more banjo playing in the band.[9] But Bill still believed the banjo could make a difference. It was actually Shumate who recommended David's replacement, a young man from North Carolina named Earl Scruggs.

Scruggs's addition thrilled and overwhelmed the Opry audience and achieved the defining sound of bluegrass. It has become commonplace to speak of this turn the band took with an implied if not conscious disparagement of David's playing. Earl's three-fingered arpeggio-based style evoked a new science-y sensibility ushered in with the beginning of the atomic era. The precise, bloodless playing drew the ire of the old-time entertainer Uncle Dave. Lester Flatt remembered Uncle Dave saying, "That boy sounds pretty good in a band, but I bet he can't sing a lick."[10] Not only that, the jovial Uncle Dave also grumbled that Earl was not a bit funny.[11] Uncle Dave turned even more urgently to bestowing his blessings on Stringbean as the one who would carry on the entertainer–banjo player tradition on the Opry.

If David Akeman felt any resentment, however, it is not known and is actually highly unlikely. While history tends to present David and Earl as opposites, with the latter as greater, the record reveals much continuity between the two. Just as David played a Gibson RB-11 when he replaced Lily May Ledford in Asa Martin's band, so Earl played an RB-11 when he replaced David in the Blue Grass Boys. While Earl's playing clearly moved the Blue Grass Boys into their iconic style, it must be remembered that David's two-finger picking had already done its part to loosen the band's rhythms, even if it did not go quickly enough to please Lester. In fact, David had been an important contributor to the band in his own right. As Dom Flemons observes:

> Stringbean is an interesting transitional character. He is a part of Bill Monroe's band, but he is not the big innovator, like Earl Scruggs. Yet his role in Bill Monroe's band is unique as someone who is an innovator for a certain period of time. The idea of string-band music, ragtime, and jazz in certain regards are being incorporated freely into one type of music. And Stringbean is part of the melding of all those different styles. . . . He stays in an old-timey style, but he's featured in acts that were much more modern.[12]

David, meanwhile, began working up his material with Lew. Childre was, like David, an entertainer. Studio recordings he made feature the whooping, train-whistling, and generally rambunctious personality that entertained audiences. "Doctor Lew," as he was sometimes called, was "an old veteran minstrel man who was as fast-talking as String was laconic."[13] He had an energetic, ad-lib way of performing that complemented Stringbean's drier style. Their contrasting personalities would be the draw, and they prepared to get their performing well under way by the beginning of the new year. In the meantime, David entered into an entirely different kind of duo.

ESTELLE: 1945

Estelle Stanfill was born in 1914 in Fly, Tennessee, about forty-five miles south of Nashville in Maury County, close to the Williamson County line. The small community of Fly lay along the Natchez Trace, the famous thoroughfare from

Nashville to Natchez, Mississippi. The rich soil in the area supported the production of both cotton and tobacco. At some point, the Stanfill family seems to have moved closer to Theta, another small rural community east of Fly.[14]

Estelle's father, Rufus, went back and forth from farming to working as a sawmill laborer from the 1910s through the 1930s.[15] Her mother's name was Nellie Beard, whose family in Williamson County was very poor and known for basket weaving and even moonshining in order to survive, given that county's far fewer arable acres.[16] Estelle had two older sisters, Elsie (born in 1907) and Luddie (born in 1910). Elsie was sometimes referred to as Esther, and Luddie's name was variously spelled Ludy or Ludie. Estelle's name also bore a peculiarity, for the name "Burbon" would be attached to it, sometimes as her first name but usually as her middle name. In keeping with middle-Tennessee country dialect, people tended to stress the first syllable in her name: É-stelle. Her younger brother, Ennis, was born in 1911, and the boy would be drawn to sawdust like his father.

Little is known about Estelle's youth. She quit high school in or after her sophomore year and married a local man named Daniel Boone Whitaker in 1938. Later known to be a carpenter, he may have worked with Rufus at the sawmill. The marriage went sour quickly: Estelle divorced him in 1940 on the grounds of drunkenness.[17] By 1942 she was living with Luddie; Luddie's husband, S. Dalton Sparkman; and their two children, Nelda Jean and Harold Dan, in their home at 1305 Forrest Avenue in Nashville.[18] Ennis, whose nickname was "Big," had also moved to Nashville and was renting an apartment at 416 Main Street and working with Dalton for Central Construction Company.[19]

Exactly how, when, and where Estelle met David Akeman is difficult to pinpoint with certainty. A 1956 article asserts that "David found Estelle about fourteen years ago," which puts the two meeting when David first came to Nashville in 1942.[20] If that timing is correct, then David's connection with her may have played a role in ending his marriage with Blanche. When exactly David and Blanche parted ways is also not clear, as there appear to be no records of marriage or divorce in either Clark or Fayette County in Kentucky. There is a story that Estelle may have been working as a waitress in a restaurant David frequented. However, a man named Joe Denton wrote, years later, "I had the pleasure of watching 'Stringbean' Akeman and a pretty young teenager named Estelle Stanfill standing in the back of a crowded little school room in rural Williamson County (Boston community) flirt with each other as he was performing on stage with, I believe, the Bill Monroe band. They met after the show and were married soon after that."[21] Denton's memory would seem to place their flirting (if not their actual meeting) around September 1945. A year older than David,

Estelle was obviously not a teenager at that point, but she may have seemed so to Denton. As for the Williamson County location, perhaps she had moved back closer to home by that time or was simply staying with friends or family and went to see the Blue Grass Boys in the neighboring county. A recently discovered photo features David standing with her, and he is wearing the jodhpurs typically worn by Bill's band members at the time. The fact that they were married in Williamson County on December 14, 1945, lends further credence to Denton's memory and the likelihood of their having met the previous summer.

Another portrait presents the couple as newlyweds. David's wiry hair rolls up his head in a finger wave. It is a handsome face, although again the teeth weaken it. He wears a striped tie, white shirt, and suit. Estelle's blouse is gray with a flouncy white collar. She wears her brown hair in the pompadour style of the time. Her brown eyes are not unlike her husband's. The lips are thin, even with lipstick on. Her face is wholesome, pretty in a sensible way. They make a sensible couple, their quiet wedding taking place nine days before Christmas and away from the city. It was an understated and grounded wedding.

And they made an understated and grounded couple whose marriage differed greatly from David's first. Where no one in the industry spoke of Blanche and perhaps did not know about her, Estelle would become part of the very fabric of the Opry. Where Blanche mostly stayed home in Kentucky, Estelle would go practically everywhere David went. Estelle not only went with him to show dates, but also shared his love of fishing and hunting. She may have already enjoyed those pastimes or learned to once she met him, but she proved to be even better at both than he. David and Estelle also shared a passion for simple country living and dreamed of having their own farm. Both had been scarred by the Depression, along with so many in their generation, and they nursed a strong distrust of banks. That scarring would fuel an obsession with making and saving money that may already have begun to grow and that would lead to their violent deaths.

Life must have taken on a new freshness for David as he celebrated the holidays with a new wife and a new music partner. In 1946 the appearances with Lew began in earnest. The February 1946 issue of the *Grinder's Switch Gazette* featured a notice of Lew and String, including a photograph of the two along with two young guitarists identified as Rusty and Dusty. Except for a still relatively wide-brimmed hat, there is little Stringbean-y about David in this picture. Lew Childre receives first mention, for he was the more established star at the time. The same was true in the September 1947 issue of *Barn Dance Magazine*, which notes, "One of the most popular singing comedians of all time on the Opry is Lew Childre, the boy from Alabam'. For years he and his six foot four inch side kick, Stringbean, have been Opry regulars."[22] Capitalizing on Lew's Alabama connections, a surviving WSM advertisement presents Stringbean appearing with "the hometown" boy Lew in Birmingham, Alabama.[23] The duo's success on the Opry soon brought an invitation from Atlanta's WSB, but the two remained with WSM, and Stringbean (sometimes still referred to as "Stringbeans") and Lew became even more widely known as performers in their own right.[24]

GRANDPA: 1946–1948

It was in the midst of these heady times that David intersected with the man who would become his best friend. Louis Marshall Jones was born on October 20, 1913, in Niagra, Kentucky, only two counties west of Bill Monroe's hometown, Rosine. Initially a guitar player, he won a contest as a teenager in Akron, Ohio. That exposure led to his joining with Bradley Kincaid in Wheeling and then New England. It was on one of the morning broadcasts on WBZ in Boston after a late night that Kincaid told the cranky, groggy Marshall, "Get up to the microphone. You're just like an old grandpa." The idea resonated with fans, and the Grandpa character first emerged in 1935, the same year "Stringbean" was born. The newly minted Grandpa began to work solo at Fairmont, West Virginia's WMMN, then back at WWVA in Wheeling, and finally WLW in Cincinnati, where he stayed until 1944. In that year, his father died, his songwriting and recording were not going well, and relations with his first wife had grown strained, so he enlisted in the army and headed to Europe. Upon Jones's return to the United States, Kincaid arranged an audition for him with Pee Wee King's band. On March 16, Grandpa made his debut on the Grand Ole Opry. He met David shortly thereafter, and, as he put it, "we hit it off right away."[25]

What established the relationship between these two men were hunting and fishing. Despite their being from Kentucky and having worked in a profession with such a tight-knit family, the two had never met before Grandpa's arrival on the Opry. Grandpa's developing his banjo playing and comedy skills at that time may have played a role in their becoming close. But when remembering those early days, Grandpa's chief recollection was that they "talked hunting and fishing all the time and did a lot of it, too."[26] These memories bore a distinctly Jim-and-Huck nostalgia for Grandpa:

> String and I started floating the Stones and Harpeth Rivers, staying all day and cooking the fish on the bank. I had a box rigged up that had everything to cook fish with, everything to season them with, and everything to wash the dirty dishes with. We had some good times on those rivers. As we floated along we would

gather wood here and there to build the fire with later. I had a grill that stuck in the ground and you could build a fire under it. We had a coffeepot that you boiled the coffee in. String would say, "Make me some of that Agrifortus coffee." He meant very strong, and I did, and it was.[27]

The two had a routine for these fishing trips, and Grandpa's memories offer insights into David's personality. For one thing, these days started at a reasonable hour. "String never liked to get up at four in the morning to fish," Grandpa explained. "He said if he had to work at it, he'd just stay home." This was the kind of dry, practical philosophy that would come to be Stringbean's trademark. It reveals something of where he drew the line between work and leisure, and no matter how much effort or money he put into fishing, he always kept it squarely in the latter. This philosophy also points to a streak of contrarianism in David, for while most people get on the water before sunup, "he'd get out there about nine o'clock and fish all day and have as many fish as any of them." At the same time, the aesthetics and the feel of fishing appealed to David. "He went for the joy of fishing and being out in the open air on a beautiful stream or lake," Grandpa noted, explaining David's drive to wax poetic about his pastime.[28]

Their routine involved some maneuvering. Grandpa detailed the arrangement in which they drove two cars with boats mounted on top to a certain point along the river. There they unloaded both boats and then drove both cars to the end point, leaving one car parked there and driving back to the boats. Then they would each get in a boat and float slowly down the stream, one river bend being "so long we could float all day and be only about a quarter-mile from where we put in the river." There, away from the public, the two men exulted in their time together, their bond deepening. "String was a funny man," Grandpa said. "He kept me laughing on all the floats. Those floats were much, much fun. He always cleaned the fish, and I did the cooking and fire building." Grandpa's memory has David being funny even off duty, maybe even if he did not mean to be, and that wartime psychoneurosis diagnosis either seems unimaginable in such scenes or throws a shadow over the otherwise glowing past. There is reason to believe, though, that both men felt the warmth of their escape and the pleasure of knowing they would return home to women they truly loved.

By this time, Grandpa and his first wife had parted ways, and he was in love with another musician named Ramona Riggins. Grandpa had met her before the war when she was playing the fiddle with Sunshine Sue and Her Rock Creek Rangers. He reconnected with her when he returned from the war and right after his divorce was finalized. Ramona came to Nashville to join Kincaid's band and then the Bailes Brothers, whom Grandpa also joined soon after. He boarded at Ma Upchurch's, and Ramona stayed next door with the Estes family.[29] As the summer progressed, their relationship blossomed, and they married on October 14, 1946.

The Akemans and the Joneses quickly became close, and Grandpa's description of those halcyon days evokes quiet happiness for people who had survived hard times and hoped for new successes. Grandpa and Ramona soon began performing as their own duet just as String and Lew were, both acts playing a spot on the Opry, and the following May, in 1947, Grandpa's "Mountain Dew" sold twenty thousand in its first month.[30] The next summer brought more days of floating and fishing whenever the opportunities came. Grandpa and Ramona may already have been touring with yet another duo, a comedy team called Lonzo and Oscar. These two had begun their Opry tenure playing in Eddie Arnold's band. Lonzo, whose real name was Lloyd George, played bass, and Rollin "Oscar" Sullivan played the mandolin. In 1947 they struck out on their own with the Lonzo and Oscar act and became particular friends of Stringbean's

Meanwhile, David continued to learn from Uncle Dave, and it may have been in this year that he experienced what he later called "the biggest thrill of my life" because, in his words, "one time me and him done a couple of numbers on the Opry."[31] The Prince Albert segment of the Opry was now being directed by String's friend Red Foley. Also coming onto the Opry in 1946 were the Willis Brothers. Hailing from Oklahoma, James "Guy" and Charles "Skeeter" Willis had played with various other configurations of a group they called the Oklahoma Wranglers. By 1942 they were a trio with their brother, John "Vic." The war separated them, but they reunited and got onto the Opry, each of the brothers forming relationships with Stringbean.

January 1948 brought Stringbean renewed work with Bill Monroe. The year began with Lester Flatt, Earl Scruggs, and Howard Watts (who had rejoined Bill) leaving the Blue Grass Boys to form a rival group with Jim Shumate and Mac Wiseman called the Foggy Mountain Boys. Bill was incensed at them, but he carried on, bringing back the baseball playing after a hiatus. Stringbean played in these games; one attendee of a game against the Rosine Red Legs remembered Stringbean pitching. "He'd do a little jig, then he'd wind up and throw that ball hard," Darrel Dukes recollected.[32]

When summer came, the days of fishing and floating came to an end as Grandpa and Ramona headed north with their children to join broadcasting entrepreneur Connie B. Gay on WARL in Arlington, Virginia. If Gay invited Stringbean, he refused, although part of him may have rued his decision when he heard about the fishing and hunting, especially with Joe Wheeler, to be enjoyed in the Virginia countryside. Joe and Grandpa hunted "everything from groundhog to bear" together and shared a love of shooting .44 Magnum pistols without earplugs, which Grandpa would blame for losing his hearing later.[33]

Back in Nashville and on the Opry, even more changes were developing. The year brought two new faces to town and into Stringbean's life. One new member was the tall, lean, impeccably dressed George Morgan. The other was the diminutive, spunky Little Jimmy Dickens. David formed friendships with both and paid particular attention to their sartorial styles. Meanwhile, Stringbean and Lew's duo was fizzling out as 1948 passed into 1949. Even as he continued working with Bill Monroe, playing music, and coaching the baseball team, Stringbean was performing more and more as a solo figure.[34]

HONKY TONK: 1949–1952

On June 11, 1949, the sensational "Lovesick Blues Boy," Hank Williams, performed during the "Warren Paint"–sponsored segment of the Opry that ran from 9:30 to 10:00.[35] The segment kicked off with Lew heading solo. David stood in the wings, while the new Alabama boy—the tall twenty-five-year-old Williams—went out to play his smash hit, "Lovesick Blues." Stringbean played in that very same segment in the third slot after Hank, following the Crook Brothers and Earnest Tubb. The honky-tonk style of music had already invaded the Opry, but this young newcomer, named at birth after the Phoenician king Hiram I, planted the flag. This new sound's wailing electric tones expressed an atomic-era zeitgeist in which scientific innovation was invading even the hillbilly world's county-line joints. With it came a new edge to country music, giving it a harder, wised-up, noir feel that was as rural based as ever but pointed to a new kind of rhythm and instrumentation.

For now, though, Stringbean was riding high as an exemplar of old-time music. He and Estelle were living in apartment C, 407 Fatherland Street, still in the city but dreaming of a home in the country like the one Grandpa and Ramona were enjoying in Virginia.[36] When June of the next year, 1950, saw conflict heat up in Korea, Stringbean played in the Opry's Armed Forces Radio shows. In one program, he sang his own version of "Mountain Dew" after Hank Williams and Minnie Pearl joked around for a few minutes. On a November 11 installment, Stringbean again sang "Mountain Dew" immediately after Hank Williams sang "Nobody's Lonesome for Me" with Grant Turner introducing him with, "Here's a man that everybody's sort of giggling at. . . . [O]ld String's inviting us in for some of that good old mountain dew."[37] Offstage, David's self-deprecating personality endeared him to everyone as he treated women with deference and referred to men, young and old, as "Boss" or "Chief."

David capitalized on his popularity by publishing *String Bean "The Kentucky Wonder" Songs, Jokes and Picture Book*. This booklet featured a dozen songs, including his versions of "John Henry" and "Little Log Cabin in the Lane." His quasi protest song "Crazy War" appeared along with one of the oldest songs in his repertoire, "Suicide Blues," in which he sang that he will "blow my brains out just for fun." A religious number, "There's a Light Guiding Me," sat alongside "Big Ball in Town," about dancing in Brooklyn, and "Cross-Eyed Nancy Jane" lay opposite another of his old songs that would become a signature number, "Pretty Polly." Rounding out the selections were "Call Old Rattler," "Free Little Bird," "You Can't Do Wrong and Get By," and Bill Monroe's "Rose of Old Kentucky."

Along with the songs appeared a biographical sketch, photos, and jokes. "Someone wanted you at the Railroad Station," one joke begins, answering, "The Train. It couldn't leave without a jerk." Another claims, "Your left eye must have a wonderful personality," the reason being, "Because your right eye is always looking at it." Yet another asks, "What was you doing standing on the corner with a pair of scissors in your hand and a gun in the other?" The answer: "I didn't know whether to cut across the street or shoot up the alley." Stringbean would recycle these jokes and more like them throughout his career.

A particularly special gift in this book comes in the form of an early example of one of Stringbean's famous "letters from home." In this humorous bit, String would read a letter from his "loving family" that comically insulted him and other family members while also offering bafflingly illogical news. The return address is "300 Miles Outside" and "60 Minutes Past." Addressed "Dearest Son," it opens with, "I was glad to get your letter saying you wouldn't be home for a long time." Going into detail, the family assures String, "The old cow that was sick ain't sick no more. She's dead." Along the same dark lines, "Uncle Jim got bit by a dog and the dog is not expected to live," while "Pauline got her tongue twisted around a yodel and died last year." One wonders if perhaps David was not writing some truth of his relationship to his family, especially when the family asks, "What do you do to keep from doing nothing?" The letter closes, "Well I will close and if you don't get this letter let me know and I'll mail it to you." This routine and the many letters Stringbean wrote for it became a major fan favorite and a staple of his comedy.

Touring with Stringbean in 1950 was seventeen-year-old Roy Clark. He had won the USA Country Banjo Championship, which brought $500 and an opportunity to perform on the Opry. When he arrived in Nashville, contest judge and Nashville promoter A. V. Bamford signed him up with Stringbean and Lonzo and Oscar, who headed out for a two-week tour through Colorado, Texas, and Oklahoma. Roy's name appeared at the bottom of the bill as "Extra Added Attraction: Musical Wizard Roy Clark." As Roy later wrote, "I had to keep the look of awe off my face, because out of the chute I was playing with the biggest stars, right up there with country music performers who were my heroes."[38] The young instrumentalist formed a tender admiration for Stringbean.

It may have been during one of these tours out west with other Opry performers that Stringbean appeared in Las Vegas's Last Frontier Village. Established in
1942 by R. E. Griffith and William J. Moore, the Last Frontier was the second-
oldest resort in the city, built to the theme of the American West.[39] Standing
four miles south of downtown and one of the first resorts that drivers from Los
Angeles encountered, the Last Frontier touted a lovely pool right along Highway
91 that brought promise of cool freshness in the desert. The village featured an
Old West town where tourists got photographs of themselves on wagons, with
cowboy figures, or standing by saloons. There was a wedding chapel, two mu-
seums, a shooting gallery, the nine hundred tons of western antiques amassed
by Robert "Doby Doc" Caudill, and a restaurant named the Silver Slipper.[40]
Stringbean performed either in the six-hundred-seat Ramona Room banquet
hall or in the equally large showroom.

GOOD-BYES, HELLOS, AND FARM: 1952

In January 1952, David went to Radio Station WHIN in Gallatin, north of Nashville, where he recorded as a backup player with Mac Wiseman on the Dot label.[41]
Wiseman was making an effort at a solo career after playing with the Foggy
Mountain Boys. Oscar Sullivan joined them in the studio playing mandolin.
The group recorded four numbers. Stringbean's halting style provides a striking counterpoint to Wiseman's smooth vocals on "[I'll] Still Write Your Name
in the Sand" (the A-side of 45-1091), cutting off on a solo that harks back to the
rhythm he had used with Bill Monroe on "True Life Blues." The same goes for
the B-side, "Four Walls around Me." On "Georgia Waltz" (B-side of "Dreaming
of a Little Cabin), String plays only rhythm.

These recordings offer some surprises too. On "Dreaming of a Little Cabin"
(A-side 45-1092), String plays unusually bluesy licks. And on "You're the Girl
of My Dreams" (A-side 45-1115), String's picking sounds surprisingly similar
to Earl Scruggs's style, including a nifty melody on the E and A strings amid
what sounds quite a lot like three-fingered picking. It is an unusual moment in
Stringbean's playing, and one wonders if he had been practicing the Scruggs
style, perhaps in an effort to change with the developments in music.

These were the last days of Uncle Dave's life, and David remained a true and
loyal friend and acolyte. Looking back on the final years of his time with his
aging mentor, David recalled, "I tell you, in older years when he wouldn't be
feeling good but he'd get out on that stage and he'd just light up like a Christmas
tree, you know. And I'd think he wouldn't be able to work. He looked like he felt
bad, but when he got ready to go on that stage he just lit up, looked like. Just

lit up like a Christmas tree."[42] Uncle Dave died on March 22. He left one of his Gibson RB-1 banjos to David. Serial number F614-1, it had been manufactured especially for Uncle Dave and shipped to him on June 10, 1940.[43] Along with the lightweight open back and wooden dowel, it used a simple nickel-plated brass tone ring rather than the die-cast Zamac ring, and the rim featured sixteen hook-and-shoes instead of the one-piece Zamac twenty-four hook flange. The tailpiece was a simple, extensionless Grover model rather than a Grover Presto or First Model. Its mother-of-pearl inlays had simple fleur-de-lis and bird shapes on the fretboard, while the peghead featured an inverted fleur-de-lis, a tiny inverted teardrop, and a cursive "Gibson." The banjo was not nearly as dolled up as the Vega No. 9, but as second instruments go, it was historically significant and dear to David Akeman.

Death struck close to home again on July 16 when Blanche died in Owensboro at age forty-two. The death certificate listed coronary occlusion as the cause of death, but the family tells a story that she had eaten watermelon during the day and had gotten to feeling bad and died later that night.[44] The *Owensboro (KY) Messenger-Inquirer* carried the obituary, noting that she "died suddenly at her home, 1927 Frederica Street, at 1 a.m."[45] Her body was scheduled to be moved to Winchester the next morning, with the funeral and burial to take place the next day. No mention was made of her having been married to Grand Ole Opry star Stringbean. Stringbean was moving on in his new life, but, assuming news of his first wife's sudden death reached him, it surely saddened and shocked him, especially coming on the heels of Uncle Dave's passing.

These losses found counterbalance in the return of the Joneses that summer and a move, finally, to the country. When Grandpa and Ramona arrived, David informed them that he and Estelle had picked out a 143-acre farm in the Ridgetop community north of Nashville with two houses on it for $10,000. "He didn't have that kind of money at the time and neither did I, so he suggested we go in together and buy it," Grandpa remembered. "We did, and those were some of the best years of my life."[46]

The land lay among lovely hills and fields. They put Estelle's brother to work fixing up the houses, David wryly claiming that "every time he went out on a tour, when he got back he just handed over the money for repairs on those old houses."[47] David and Estelle chose to live in the smaller of the two houses, a red cabin-like edifice with just a few rooms. The floors were of oak, and one wall was paneled in warmly varnished pine that framed the fireplace, which quickly became David's particular pride and joy.

The Akemans had no indoor toilet, using their outhouse instead. Their water source came from a cave on the property. Inside the cave ran a waterfall, and piping was run out from it through thirty feet of low crawl space. A cistern was built in the cave, as well.[48] That water source may have played a role in previous labor on that property, for there is a claim that former owners had been moonshiners. In fact, there is a story that the original house on the property burned down from a fire that got out of hand with the still and that an infant perished in it. The tiny house the Akemans chose to live in and the big white house the Joneses moved into were apparently built at the same time in the 1920s.[49]

Those houses stood very close together, and the two families met often. "Many an evening," Grandpa remembered, "we would eat out on a picnic table that sat between the houses. I remember once we were having corn on the cob. String would eat all the corn off, throw the cob back over his shoulder, and say, 'This is a handy old place.'" It was a classic David Akeman/Stringbean gesture and humor, and it typified the kind of camaraderie the families enjoyed. Also, as Grandpa put it, "the hunting and fishing started all over again."[50]

As the year progressed, Stringbean continued to perform on the Prince Albert Opry and was making appearances in late summer through fall with Ernest Tubb and others in Florida, Arkansas, Oklahoma, and Kansas.[51] A show in Kansas City, Missouri, that drew a crowd of twenty-five hundred received a review in the newspaper, citing Stringbean as "a droll Kentuckian who is heard every Saturday night on WDAF and who sings the genuine old folk songs almost exclusively."[52] The designation of singing "old folk songs" foreshadowed what was to come in Stringbean's developing image. Interestingly, the paper specifically cites his playing "Crazy War" and even included some of the lyrics:

> I run all over Europe
> Trying to save my life.
> But if there ever come another war,
> I'll send my darling wife.

Stringbean may have been giving expression to sentiments connected with the military stalemate in Korea, reviving the song to try to catch a mood of suspicion about war while not clearly crossing the line into protest.

Markedly absent from that show and other Grand Ole Opry performances was Hank Williams. He was dismissed from the Opry in August for his drinking, and he died in the early hours of New Year's Day, 1953. His death struck a sad note for the end of a year that had brought David and Estelle a mixture of sadness and joy. Both endings and beginnings had taken place. And some of the beginnings were set to bring yet more endings, for the country music industry itself was about to face major challenges that would affect the career of Stringbean.

HERDIN' CATTLE IN A CADILLAC COUPE DE VILLE
1953-1959

STRINGBEAN ON SCREEN: 1953

As country music fandom came to grips with Hank Williams's passing, String-bean was continuing his steady career on the Opry. He appeared in a Prince Albert ad in the February issue of *Farm Journal* that year. Dressed in a dark shirt and a white sport coat sans tie, he looked a far cry from his Stringbean character. Smiling as he packs his pipe with Prince Albert tobacco while standing among leafless woods, he says in a dialogue box, "There just isn't any smokin' experience compared to lightin' up a pipeful of cool, rich-flavored P. A." Underneath this writing is signed "Stringbean Akeman," and beneath that, "Banjo playing comic and star of 'Grand Ole Opry.'"

Hatch show prints from that year reveal Stringbean performing in numerous Opry package shows. Venues included Shelbyville, Tennessee (April 15); South Pittsburg, Tennessee (June 26); Memphis, Missouri (July 22); Rapid City, South Dakota (July 30); Billings, Montana (August 2); Centerville, Iowa (August 12); Lewisburg, Kentucky (August 14); and close to home at the Breathitt High School Homecoming in Jackson (September 7), which featured an "All Day Barbecue on the Ground."[1] Despite their no longer being an official duo, Stringbean and Lew made an appearance together at the Bean Blossom Festival in Indiana on July 26.

When not traveling to these show dates, David spent his time with Estelle, Ramona, and Grandpa and their children, which now included Mark. The two families planted a garden in the spring and particularly enjoyed picking black-berries for jam to go on biscuits, which David ate practically every morning, with the jam heated up. In the warm months, the families went fishing and took along Estelle's brother, Big, who used only a jitterbug. Estelle, it seems, could throw a plug almost as well as her husband. Grandpa remembered one time when the two families took a fishing trip up to Jackson County in Nash cars equipped with a "Bed-in-a-Car" feature.[2] David had been telling Grandpa and Ramona about "blue holes" he would fish back home. When they arrived, it rained so hard the "blue hole" had grown muddy. Grandpa and Ramona would kid him for years for taking them to a "yellow hole."

Estelle did the driving in those Nash cars. One of the most consistent claims about David is that he never drove and that he may not even have known how to operate an automobile. "I never did know of String driving a car for a single mile," Grandpa wrote. The comment contradicts Grandpa's claim that the two of them drove their respective cars out to float on the Harpeth and Stone Rivers, and there is some question about whether David *could not* rather than *would not* drive. Grandpa related that "Lew Childre, who used to partner with String, claimed that he got him to drive for about 30 miles once somewhere down in Alabama; Doc Lew just said he was tired, crawled into the back seat, and went to sleep. String wanted to get on home, so he drove." The story sounded suspicious to Grandpa, and he followed it up with, "At least that's what I've heard; I'm still not sure I believe it." Apparently strengthening Grandpa's suspicion was the fact that when he and Stringbean bought a tractor together, Stringbean did not know how to drive it and wanted Grandpa to take the wheel. When Grandpa insisted he would have to learn to drive it himself, "he got on one day and put the tractor in gear, and when he let out the clutch, it jumped about three feet. But he finally caught on and did a lot of work with it."[3]

Whether Stringbean knew how to drive a car or not, Estelle's driving pointed to the fact that, unlike David's marriage to Blanche, he and Estelle were insepa-rable. Curt Gibson, who would later play guitar with Stringbean and also serve as his driver, claimed, "String confessed to him that by remaining dependent on his wife to drive him everywhere, he never had to leave home without her. He really wanted her company all the time, and it was his way of insuring that they spent maximum time together." Before long, there would be an affectionate running joke about Estelle being Stringbean's chauffeur. Along with driving, she helped him with his grooming: he may have put on his rubbing alcohol for deodorant himself, but it was she who shaved him with the apple vinegar he preferred because he claimed anything else would cause him to break out.[4] Re-vealing of their grounding intimacy, although even Stringbean's closest friends called him by his stage name, Estelle always called him David.[5] One of the most endearing images of the two that Grandpa paints is of the couple sitting together in the mouth of the cave during thunderstorms, the tall man sitting with his dark-haired wife as steel-blue clouds break into crashing rain and lighten into fresh newness once the storm has passed.[6]

While sadness struck on March 4, 1953, when David's sister Lizzie died at the age of forty-seven in Hamilton, Ohio, Bill Carlisle's joining the Opry brought joy.[7] The high-strung "Jumpin' Bill" loved to joke and prank, and he later told of one running gag in which Stringbean would call him on the phone and tell him, "Bring your ax on up, and we'll throw that ax on some of them." What exactly Stringbean meant by that was not clear, but they enjoyed the joke of having a go at their best friends on the Opry. On one occasion, Stringbean called and simply said, "I've got my ax good and sharp" as his summons. When Bill got to the house, "String was sitting by the fireplace sharpening his ax, and he said, 'Who we going to ax first?' I said, 'I don't know, who do you think?' And he said, 'I think we ought to get little Jimmie Dickens first, he's little.'"[8]

If life appeared to be running in greased grooves for David and Estelle, the reality is that massive changes were taking place in American culture. This was the year, 1953, when Marilyn Monroe burst into top billing with a trio of films and Marlon Brando sneered as a motorcycle-gang antihero in *The Wild One*. A new kind of division was growing between the likes of Monroe and Brando and the so-called squares, the boring folks who might even square-dance. The divide was generational too, pitting the youth against the adults who had survived the Depression and war. The unrest bristled beneath society's surface, but it could also rear up into full view. Meanwhile, television was gaining more and more traction. This technology had been developing prior to World War II, and since the war's end that magical box of moving pictures was steadily making its way into American culture.

Stringbean and other Opry stars would need to navigate these new times and this new form of media. He displayed a deft ability to adapt while staying the same, bringing old-time music into a new technological age. Local Nashville television was struggling, but the Grand Ole Opry had actually picked up and gone to New York as a whole, a broken but brave Hank Williams included, the prior year to appear on *The Kate Smith Evening Hour* on March 26 and April 23.[9] It may have been these broadcasts that inspired producer, screenwriter, and songwriter Al Gannaway to put the Opry on the television screen.

Gannaway was not interested in the kind of grainy black-and-white broadcasts typical of this new medium at the time. Instead, he wanted to bring the Opry into lively full color. A barn-interior stage was set up on the Vanderbilt

University campus (for whatever reasons, the Opry refused to allow filming on its stage) and five cameras set up to shoot Opry performers in 35 mm, full color. His son Gary explains that Al turned the cameras "on and off from a little control panel he built himself. He called it 'Gannavision'."[10] Gannaway filmed a series of performances by the Opry cast from 1952 to 1954 and pieced them together to create the beginning of a television program, *The Country Show*, that began airing in 1955.

Stringbean was filmed on that stage sometime from the fall of 1952 to late 1953, and he emerges in full iconic form. He wears a long-sleeved orange gingham shirt that stretches well below his waist and is sewn onto short blue jeans with a leather belt in place unnecessarily. A keychain loops over the right hip pocket, while a white handkerchief sticks out of his back left pocket. His tiny black coachman hat looks too small for his head. For this occasion, he has not painted on the sad eyebrows. He is playing the Vega No. 9, which presents its own personality as it rings its bright sound and beams its ornate gladness, the distinct inlays flashing in antiquated loveliness.

In these performances, String showcases his unique acrobatics. When he is playing the melody and being "serious," he frails deftly. But when he sings, he starts clowning, gliding his right hand up the neck as high as the ninth fret to brush the strings. When playing an open chord, he lets go of the neck altogether and swings his left arm and hand or brings it up to the twelfth fret or higher and flutters his fingers as if he is playing a fancy run (in fact, he does not even touch the strings). The latter move might have poked gentle fun at Scruggs's playing fancy triads high up the neck. When Stringbean finishes a number, he grabs his hat by the front of the brim, flips it, and sets it back down on his head backward. The gesture is both funny and endearing, an almost-doff dignified and ludicrous at the same time, reminiscent of Chaplin. After this move, Stringbean breaks into a series of nods and arm-and-hand waves combined with an expression that conveys that, yes, he really is good at what he does and now he has done it and it is time to go and he appreciates your attention but he did not really need it anyway. He walks away as if glad he has gotten this over with.

There are three clips featuring Stringbean. In one he plays "Cripple Creek" as musicians play behind him and other people on the stage clap in rhythm, while Ernest Tubb stands aside, svelte and swarthy, looking on. In another clip, Tubb introduces Stringbean, saying, "Well, friends and neighbors, if you have any doubt about this being a country show, you won't in just a minute or two when I introduce this next *character* that comes out here." At that point, Tubb breaks into a wide grin, a genuine affectionate amusement that he cannot fight back, for all his professionalism. Regaining his composure, Tubb says, "All joking aside, he's a wonderful entertainer, so let's bring him out right now. Here he is, the old Kentucky Wonder, Stringbean!" Stringbean lopes in, left arm swinging, looking around as if he is a little peeved he has to be here, his expression dead serious. "Thank you," he says to Tubb. "Much obliged to you." Then he announces the song, "Little Liza Jane," and calls out, "Hang on, chil'ren!" and sets in playing, his left toe tapping the time. He occasionally rocks his upper body in time, and he plays some of the melody higher up the neck than usual. In his second solo break, he steps side to side in time and utters his favorite midsong spoken line, "Lord, I feel so unnecessary."

In the third clip, Stringbean goes ahead and does his hat flip when he makes his entrance amid onstage crowd applause. He walks to center stage and then turns back to Ernest Tubb and says, "Thank you, Ernest, thank you. Hold that mule 'til I get back, and I'll give him to you." "I'll do it, boy, I sure will," Tubb replies, smiling, as Stringbean adjusts the crown of his hat and puts his hand on his hip as he looks around at the crowd. Then, straightening first his right and then his left arm as he pulls up the sleeves, Stringbean announces, "Every time I do this song, here, I have a fit. And I feel one a-coming on, right now. Hang on, chil'ren!" The song is "Hillbilly Fever," and he rears back, looking right and left during the introduction. This time, though, he ups the ante when he plays a bridge, revolving in short steps that accentuate his short jeans, sending Ernest Tubb scurrying back out of the way and laughing with wide-open mouth.

After playing the melody, Stringbean takes his hat off and fans the banjo neck while he sings the second verse and chorus. Then he waves his hat around in time to the music and plops it back on his head to finish the verse. This time, playing a bridge, he high-steps in a circle, handkerchief flailing. "I'm a-getting hot, now," he says when he gets back into position and then offers up his "Lord, I feel so unnecessary" line. Singing only the chorus this time, he breaks into a flutter of tiny running-in-place steps, barely able to get the breath to say, "Lord, I feel so unnecessary" again. Then he finishes the song as everyone laughs and claps. This time he waves his right hand over his head and moves his left hand, elbow bent, wrist limp in a crabbing motion as he walks away shaking his head.

It is all quintessential Stringbean, humorous in a dry way, mixing the expected and unexpected, and, above all, entertaining.

There is a striking irony in Gannaway's using such technological innovation and fidelity to high quality in order to record and present so traditional an entity as the Grand Ole Opry. That irony heightens in the case of Stringbean, who would have left the Vanderbilt campus downtown to return to a tiny home, with no running water, an outhouse, and a wood fireplace for heat. Whether he was conscious of it or not, Stringbean was beginning to represent the past in country music. He had not yet reached even forty years of age, but already he was being transformed by cultural developments into an old-timer. Elsewhere, his birth-year brother Frank Sinatra was reviving his slumping career through transformation, first with his acclaimed performance in the August-released film *From Here to Eternity* and in his finding a new, bold, destined-to-be-iconic sound in collaboration with Nelson Riddle. But, while Stringbean would continue to add to his act, he stayed fundamentally the same, digging in as a person rooted in the rural culture into which he had been born. And he was bringing the past into the sparkling present, the Kentucky Wonder fitting in just fine in a time of technological wonder.

Stringbean may have been successfully entering the television age, but he continued his regular old-fashioned ways. As fall came on, Stringbean and Grandpa took to walking out along the railroad that ran in front of the farm to hunt quail. Neither of them had a bird dog, and so would whistle the "bob-white" notes to find and raise a covey. Grandpa remembered Stringbean always using "a little Stevens 20-gage double with the barrel cut off about an inch."[11] Meanwhile, Stringbean continued making his performances on the Opry and in person, with appearances in Scottsville, Kentucky (October 16); Jonesburg and Augusta, Missouri, with top billing (October 29 and 30, respectively); and in a particularly big show along with Lonzo and Oscar and the "Nation's Newest Sensation," Marty Robbins, in Orlando, Florida (November 11). Hank Snow introduced Stringbean's playing "Lonesome Road Blues" on the November 21, 1953, Prince Albert Opry.[12] A month later, Stringbean sang the new Arlie Duff hit, "Y'all Come," on a Christmas Day WSM radio program called *Noontime Neighbors Radio Show*.[13] New Year's Eve found him at Washington, Missouri's City Park Auditorium for the "Big New Year's Eve Dance."[14] With the new year arriving, however, Stringbean prepared to undertake a new yet retro adventure that reunited him with an old friend.

TOMMY SCOTT'S SHOW AND REVOLUTION: 1954–1955

Tommy Scott's closest friendships had formed during his time with Charlie Monroe's Kentucky Partners. After his wife, Frankie, Tommy listed Curly Seckler and Stringbean as tied for second place in his hierarchy of relationships.[15] Whenever Tommy, Frankie, and their daughter, Sandra, visited Nashville, they made their way over to visit with Stringbean and Estelle. In early 1954 (or possibly late 1953), the Scotts visited the Akemans with a proposal to join them on the road.

After his stint at the Opry, Tommy had experimented with multiple entertainment approaches, including circus, film, and television performances. In 1952 he created the Tommy Scott Hillbilly Jamboree and Circus Revue. This show marked a turning point. He had continued bottling and selling his Herb-O-Lac, Vim, and other medicines, but now he "began depending on the admission we charged to keep the show on the road, playing indoors at schoolhouses, theaters, and armories across the country. We traveled to over 350 towns each year."[16] Tommy still sold medicine, but he focused more on selling entertainment. Part of his tactic to infuse variety for the show's annual appearance in those towns was to bring in big-name entertainers on a revolving basis. These included Red Sovine and the singing cowboys Monte Hale and Jimmy Mack Brown. For the 1954 season, he wanted to bring on Stringbean.

Sitting down with String and Estelle, Tommy laid out his proposition. Whereas past stars had been brought in according to an agreed-upon fee, Tommy offered his old friend a far more lucrative arrangement. "I thought of a more effective way to make it for both us," he later wrote, "was to not pay String his flat but give him a 50 percent split of the door and let him sell whatever he wanted, pictures and the like." Stringbean may have hawked copies of his joke and song book and may also have had photographs printed up to sign and sell. Given the less favorable financial arrangement with the Opry, it is not surprising that Stringbean accepted this offer. According to Tommy, they went to the Opry management that very night so String could inform them he was leaving to join Tommy's show. "Let's just say that his decision to leave to go with me didn't set too well with the Opry," Tommy wrote.[17] It is one of the few times any mention has ever been made of Stringbean upsetting anyone. Incidentally, Red Foley left the Opry later that year for Springfield, Missouri, to host the Ozark Jubilee.

With such a massive tour before them, Tommy had an idea that would come to define the Akemans. As Tommy put it, "The first thing we went and did when he joined was to go purchase two brand new Cadillac Coupe De Villes so that we had reliable cars for the trip. I think they were both tan. I knew a dealer where we could get them and just pay $100 over invoice." Thus it was that David and Estelle began a practice they would continue throughout their lives of buying a work car fitting for an Opry star. It was to be practically their only splurge, their single fancy purchase. It may seem a contradictory move at first glance, given that they chose to live in such a rustic and simple way otherwise. But the move was not one of pride or vanity so much as an embracing of a high-quality car and of their place in life, at least from a public viewpoint. Even this extravagance was not so extravagant, for not only did they pay a lower price, but, according to Tommy, "Stringbean didn't want heat in the car; I had to work to convince him it was going to be cold in Canada, and he finally gave in to have heat, but I'm not sure if they ever turned it on."[18] In fact, the Akemans would come to take a practical approach to this luxury, as dealer Goebel Bunch explained that they traded in for a new model each year and simply counted all the miles on the speedometer as work miles to take off their taxes.[19] They kept a second, humbler, vehicle for nonwork driving.

Before long, Stringbean would play up the humor of the contrast between his country ways and his driving a Cadillac, writing one of his funniest self-referential songs, "Herding Cattle in an Air-Conditioned Cadillac Coupe de Ville." This hard-driving humorous number tells of String living in a valley as "rich as cream" where he has the "finest neighbors you have ever seen." More than that, even though he spends only three cents a week, he is doing well herding cattle in his fancy car. He would not say he was rich, exactly, but he was leading the life of Riley, who himself never actually had it this good. In the closing verse, String explains:

> Well, I've got science baffled, also the blue-eyed world.
> I fish when I got ready, and I love to hunt them squirrels.
> You'll find me ever' morning when the sun comes over them hills.
> Just a-herdin' cattle in an air-conditioned Cadillac Coupe de Ville.

Tommy gave his friend free rein in the show. Stringbean did his letters-from-home routine with troupe member Sam Baxter as straight man. Freddie Harper, part of Tommy's band, remembered Stringbean's singing and playing, recalling that "Sam used to stand next to him on the left, playing the old bull fiddle, and Gaines Blevins on guitar was on his right." Tommy shared his own memory of one particularly painful night at a VFW hall in Arkansas (yet another mishap in that state for Stringbean). No advertising had been done for the show, the result being a crowd of not more than fifteen. Tommy remembered overhearing the few in the audience puzzling how entertainers who drew such a small crowd could afford new Cadillacs. Nevertheless, Tommy said, "We did the show just like the places was full, and I will never forget what Stringbean said when he finished his numbers. He kissed the banjo and said, 'Mine and your shadows will never grace this stage again.' Did his little hand wave, and walked off."[20]

Offstage, the Akemans and the Scotts had the time of their lives as they trekked together across the country. "Frankie loved having Estelle Akeman around too," Tommy wrote.[21] Tommy and Frankie's daughter, Sandra, remembers the show's entire cast and crew descending on diners, especially for breakfast. When traveling north of the Mason-Dixon, including in Canada, the Akemans bemoaned the lack of grits, Estelle saying often, "I wish I could get good grits, and if I just had them I would cook them."[22] A photograph presents the Akemans and the Scotts having one of these meals together. They sit together holding plates. Tommy and Estelle grin broadly away from the camera at someone who has tickled them, while Frankie and Stringbean smile at the camera. Stringbean is dressed in a dark shirt and suit. Estelle has her right arm over his shoulder. The image projects simple, pure happiness, with no sign of lurking anxieties.

But there was reason to worry. On July 5, 1954, Elvis Presley recorded "That's All Right" in Memphis's tiny Sun Studios. He followed it with a recording of his rocking version of Bill Monroe's "Blue Moon of Kentucky." Stringbean may not have heard about the record right away, for he was busy at work, having ordered Hatch posters that were sent out on July 21 to Tommy's Hollywood address.[23] But on October 2, Elvis made his first and only appearance on the Grand Ole Opry. The Opry crowd was not impressed, and, like Hank Williams before him, Elvis headed off to the Louisiana Hayride. Stringbean may have scoffed at Elvis along with the rest of the Opry cast, but a musical revolution had started.

This revolution veered close to String. Tommy Scott actually tried to hire Elvis but refused to pay the forty-dollar fee per week the young man demanded. Tommy found another way to capitalize on Elvis's fame, however, in Freddie Harper, one of Scott's own band members. Harper had been performing as "Tex" after T. Texas Tyler, but now he grew his sideburns out, shaped his hair into a pompadour, donned pink and black, and became Rudy Preston. Tommy had posters printed announcing "In Person Elvis Presley Type Rock and Roll Show," with "Elvis Presley," "Rock," and "Roll Show" all in bold letters.[24] Tommy's show thus featured two polar-opposite exotic figures. The two characters—Stringbean and Elvis—differed in many ways, the one conservative, quiet, and backward looking, the other progressive, raucous, and forward looking. Yet they both keyed into the appeal of iconic appearance and style.

There is something to learn of the impact of the Elvis iconography in the iconography of Stringbean. Just as Stringbean had donned blackface and played his rube role in ways that worked deep in minstrel modes, so Elvis now crossed racial boundaries in his performances. Just as Stringbean's costume exaggerated him beyond normal human appearance and his painted-on eyebrows gave him his mournful expression, so Elvis installed a bottle in his pants as he gyrated, while his shining pompadour leaped uncontrollably in the air and his eyes glared under eye shadow in a way that made him seem another kind of being. It was an era of fascination with exotic, iconic, outlandish, even freakish characters, especially on television, and Stringbean fitted in well with the likes of Vampira, Pandit, and Liberace. Although not conscious or direct, Elvis's image drew from the same well that produced Stringbean.

SCROUNGING: 1956–1957

It was at that unfortunate point, when rock and roll was crushing the country market, that Stringbean's run with Tommy Scott came to end. There was no bad blood, and Tommy hated to let String go. The entire show was like a family: String and Estelle had been around when Sandra learned to drive on dirt roads in Canada, Estelle worrying mother-like about how she fared in her lessons.[25] But the model of revolving in big stars and keeping the show fresh demanded turnover. "It was a sad day when I said goodbye to String on our show, but like everything else, it was time," Tommy wrote. "He had played all our venues, and I needed to get something else going to keep the show fresh."[26] When David had set off on the adventure with Tommy, he likely expected either to return to the Opry later or to strike out on his own as a purely solo act. But the seismic shifts in the culture toward new, rebellious, youth-oriented music posed massive problems. The far-less-staid Tennessee city Memphis had gotten out of hand, and Nashville had *its* hands full trying to wrestle this new movement down.

Stringbean's first obstacle was getting back on the Opry. He had not made enemies among his colleagues. In an endearing mention by the man who would lead the charge in helping country music to survive rock and roll's attack, Chet Atkins in a 1955 article had predicted that young musicians adopting finger-picking of the guitar would soon, "as my friend Stringbean says, . . . 'Baffle the blue eyed world.'" But the man in charge of booking artists on the Opry felt differently. "Jim Denny didn't want to let him come back," Tommy remembered, "and almost didn't until Roy Acuff found out what was going on and interceded on our behalf, getting Stringbean's place in the Opry cast re-instated."[27] This was not the only time Denny would act ugly—at one point, Ernest Tubb actually threatened to shoot him.[28]

Nevertheless, Stringbean resumed his Opry appearances, although apparently not so often in the Prince Albert segment. The beleaguered Opry carried on as best it could, the singing cowboy and film star Tex Ritter joining. A February 1956 package show in Sedalia, Missouri, presented Stringbean in second billing under Moon Mullican but in equally large letters and with the added tag "King of the Banjo." Opry package shows, in general, continued to include him, and Stringbean also performed on Red Foley's Ozark Jubilee. But, overall, show dates were hard to come by.

Stringbean had dealt with crisis before and went to work surviving this one. Journalist, musician, and longtime owner and publisher of the *Sparta (TN) Expositor* Bobby Anderson remembered meeting Stringbean just after he returned to the Opry.[29] At the time, Anderson was a staff writer for central Kentucky's *Times-Argus* and the radio station affiliated with it, WMTA. One night, when covering the Opry, Stringbean approached him. "I understand you're from Kentucky," Stringbean said. "I am, too." Without further introduction or small talk, Stringbean began instructing the young man: "Here's what I want you to do for me, boy. I want you to go back up there to Kentucky and books some shows for me in some of your schools."

Citing the fact that rock and roll had reduced performance opportunities to almost nothing, Stringbean gave details. "Book me into two or three schools up there where you live. Tell them to charge a dime for admission to my shows," he detailed. "Those kids in school had rather pay a dime any day to see me perform than to have to sit in the classroom all day!" Before heading to the stage to play on the Ryman, Stringbean asked for the radio's staff band and explained that he played every song in A. In another insight into how Stringbean operated, he mentioned that he particularly needed a bass player. "Have him stand close to me," he said. "I take all my rhythm from the bass." That put the pressure on Anderson—*he* was the bass player, and he "faked more of my efforts than I played."

Nervous though he may have been about his bass skills and playing with the Opry star, Anderson booked shows at three schools in Kentucky. He remembered the gymnasiums being full. The admission was a dime when only a year before Tommy Scott's show tickets were 65¢ for children and $1.25 for adults.[30] Anderson captured the moment in tender detail:

> At the end of the day I divided up the receipts. Each band member was given a few dollars for his three-gig effort that day. I gave Stringbean the rest, while he and his wife, Estelle, were enjoying a snack of tuna salad and pimento and cheese sandwiches in our dining room. His share amounted to less than $100. He carefully folded the money, as if it had been a thousand or more, placed it in his billfold and returned the wallet to the bib pocket of his overalls. You would have thought the amount had been a million dollars by the profuse helping of homespun appreciation he showed us.

Such penuriousness was needed at that time for performers, but it was business as usual for String. Years later, Stringbean recalled that struggling during the Depression and war years had taught him to save. "I learned to lay a little bit by every time I made some," he said. "Then in the '50's when rock-n-roll come along and hurt country music, I won't bad off. I had enough laid by not to go hungry so I took to fishin' fulltime. To be right honest, I sorta hated to give it up and go back to work."[31]

He and Estelle were determined to stretch each dollar and each penny. "Now those folks lived and ate simply," Tommy Scott remarked, the Akemans' spartan living sticking in his mind. "A common home meal with them was cornmeal mush and beans with a little bit of whatever String caught or killed that day while hunting or fishing."[32] With no water bill, cutting their own wood for heat, and growing, catching, or killing much of their food, David and Estelle kept their personal costs at rock-bottom minimum. They may have already run electricity into their house by this time, however, for David had taken note of Jackie Gleeson's line "How sweet it is!" and would use it as part of his performance, giving it his own Kentucky country emphasis.

David was also saving money on clothing. Taking note of George Morgan's nice suits and their being about the same size and build, David got an idea. Bill Carlisle explained:

> [String] used to see George Morgan with a new suit on. I remember one time he walked up and looked at that suit. And he felt it, and [George] says, "String you'll have that before long." George furnished him. George would wear a suit a couple of times, and if he didn't like he'd just give it to String. String would bring him a few squirrels. And String had suits in that closet he never wore. You know, he'd rather wear his overalls. Yeah, he never did wear them, but he had them.[33]

The Akemans' severe saving had a goal that went beyond survival, or perhaps it might be more accurate to view that goal as defining their idea of survival. As Tommy put it, "String had one main goal in life that was unusual when you consider how meager their existence was for a major country music star. He wanted a million dollars. That was his goal just to physically have one million dollars in cash." By the time Stringbean was playing Tommy's show, he seems to have been freely making proclamations of this goal within the industry. A letter from Hatch tells String they "hope that you are having a big success and will make a million dollars." It is difficult to read his tone or purpose in these statements. There could be levity in them, and Tommy Scott saw it as a joke when Stringbean would say, "Me and my five string are going to make a million."[34] Stringbean would convey this "goal" as the years passed with continued ambiguity that contradicted his otherwise humble style. If it was meant to be a joke, it succeeded with some, but the possibility that it might be taken seriously would worry others.

Making a million must have seemed an especially big joke in 1956 as rock rolled over the country. March saw the release of Elvis's debut album. To his original Sun group, RCA added Floyd Cramer on piano, Chet Atkins on guitar, and backup singers. The smoother, more polished sound of these recordings not only contrasted with the rawness of Elvis's Sun records in his debut album released in March, but also signaled a new approach to recording in Nashville that would soon divide the country industry further. That technique of creating a uniform backup to vocalists played by excellent and amazingly versatile performers, with Chet Atkins one of the principal movers and shakers, would come to be called the Nashville Sound.

As the holiday season approached, David's mother, Alice, came down with pneumonia. A week later, she died, on December 18, 1956. The death certificate lists her as having had heart disease and that her death was caused, in part, by cerebral thrombosis.[35] The doctor had been attending to her heart problems for almost a month prior to that time, so her death may not have been entirely a surprise. She and James had moved back to Jackson County. The family would have had to gather from various points for the funeral, David from Nashville; Robert, Joe, and Sallie from Indiana (possibly Alfred, too, although he may have already begun his trek westward, where he spent much of his life); and Nora from Campbell, Kentucky.

Another loss appeared on the horizon with the coming of 1957. Grandpa announced that he and his family were moving out of the house next door. Connie Gay had a new young star in Jimmy Dean, who was finding success in television with a show called *Country Style* on WTOP-TV in Washington, D.C. In the spring, CBS picked up the show, changing its name to *The Morning Show*, and Gay invited Grandpa to be on it. Grandpa informed String that he would sell him his part of their farm. As they signed the paperwork to seal the deal, Stringbean told him, "You'll be back in a year."[36] In testimony to how close Stringbean felt to Grandpa, he wrote him a letter and sent it to Virginia from "The Producing Old Farm."[37] According to Estelle, it was the only real letter she ever knew David to have written, despite all the gag letters he wrote for reading onstage.

It was Estelle, herself, who kept up correspondence with friends and family. In one undated letter that has survived, she addressed "Dear Folks" on stationery from the Sunset Motel in Winchester, Illinois, although written from home.[38] It offers a personal glimpse into the Akemans' lives. She related that she has been feeling puny with a bladder problem and that David (no "Stringbean" in this letter) had been fishing every day and catching "some real nice bass." Estelle did confirm that today, at least, he would not be able to fish because he had to mend a fence to keep in their twenty head of cattle, which was probably not a problem because a cloud was coming up. The letter was apparently written early in June, for Estelle explains that she and David are headed to Kentucky and then Evansville, Indiana, before heading to North Carolina for shows on June 15–18. "Let us hear from you," she concludes, and signs off, "Estelle and David."

Meanwhile, the Opry carried on in the face of fracturing that hit close to home when Flatt and Scruggs became Opry regulars over Bill Monroe's objections. Bill refused to speak to Lester and Earl, which made for painful moments backstage at the Ryman. Stringbean, however, remained friendly with both the Blue Grass Boys and the Foggy Mountain Boys. When the latter started their own television show, he accepted invitations to appear on it. In one segment, Lester introduces Stringbean in his laconic voice, "Here's our favorite cowboy around the Grand Ole Opry. Want you to meet him right now. Our good buddy, Mr. Stringbean."[39] Stringbean makes his arm-swinging walk up to the microphone and tells Lester he is glad to see him and that he is looking well. In this clip, Stringbean wears a shirt with vertical stripes that accentuate the false length of his torso. Also, he wears a beige-colored hat with the narrow brim and crown that rounds up over the otherwise top-hat shape. This was the hat he would wear most often for the rest of his career. For this appearance, he had painted on his sad eyebrows.

He rips into the intro of "Run, Rabbit, Run," on the Vega, while Earl plays the *guitar*, looking strangely benign. Stringbean also plays "Herdin' Cattle" on the episode, and when he breaks into his solo after the first verse, Earl, who stands behind his right shoulder, says something inaudible to him, which prompts String to say, "Play it, Earl Scruggs!" The usually stone-faced Earl smiles brightly. For a moment, one might wonder who the major star is—the exotic-looking man who plays and sings with such gusto or the nondescript, bland fellow playing along in the background who looks up to the taller man?

In fact, these two both bore themselves with becoming humility and held each other in respect and affection. Earl's affection for Stringbean shows especially in another appearance, this time with both men playing the banjo, Stringbean with his Vega No. 9 and Earl with his famous Gibson Granada Mastertone. "Here's a song been a-bafflin' the world," Stringbean says as he keys up to play, bringing uproarious laughter from all the Foggy Mountain Boys. Earl's face lights up, and he laughs with a wide-open mouth. The two men pick together this time, String in his two-finger style and Earl in his three-finger style. This time, Earl stands to Stringbean's left and leans forward, looking up *at* but also *to* the older performer. The song, "Twenty Cent Cotton and Ninety Cent Meat," lays out the dreadful math that leaves poor folks unable to eat, taking a droll view of the kinds of terrors Stringbean and so many in his generation had faced during the Great Depression. His later recording of the song would be one of his most often rereleased. At one point, after playing a bridge, Stringbean announces, "Keep that up fine, and you're headed for Broadway," bringing more laughter from Earl and the group. It is an endearing moment for both performers, the banjo genius playing behind the old-time entertainer, never taking a solo and enjoying every minute.

A distinct lick appears in Stringbean's playing on this number. In talking songs such as this one, Stringbean tended to set up the vocal parts by picking a bridge that ran into his fretting the third string (in his tuning, the A string) at the fourth fret. Doing so created an unresolved suspended chord that makes the C# dominant. It is a nifty move, perhaps not wholly unique to Stringbean but distinctly his and effective in the higher tuning.

Those clips also feature Stringbean's increasingly common left-hand gestures. To his already established antics, he now began to use his left hand for emphasis as he sang lyrics, while his right hand clawhammered the open strings. The maneuvers had a grace about them, often involving his extending his hand below the neck and turning from palm up to palm down and back again. Then sometimes he would lift his hand higher, above the neck. In the "Twenty Cent Cotton and Ninety Cent Meat" performance, he reaches high to show the difference between high prices and low cotton. But in other performances he would lift his hand to just above shoulder length, and it looked, for all the world, like the Babe calling his own home run that day now going on twenty years ago, back long before David had even begun his long road to stardom.

That stardom continued despite the threat of Nashville's new pop style. Chet Atkins was working with recording producers such as Steve Sholes, Owen Bradley, and Bob Ferguson as well as recording engineer Bill Porter, and they were fighting for the survival of their industry. Certain vocalists fitted perfectly in this new style; Jim Reeves led the way, and Patsy Cline's legendary voice excelled. But this Nashville Sound offered no room for Stringbean's style of singing. And the banjo was not to be heard among the strings and piano of the city's recording A-team of studio musicians. That old-time music now began to be categorized, for the first time, as "bluegrass," the name derived from the Blue Grass Boys.

The atmosphere must have felt strangely mixed up to David. The March 9, 1957, Prince Albert Opry illustrates the conflicting forces of the moment. In that broadcast, the Jordanaires take off on a rocking "Sugaree," with electric guitar backing, which sends the crowd cheering and clapping in rhythm. Following that number, Hank Snow welcomes young traditionalist Porter Wagoner to sing "A Satisfied Mind" in a clearly country style with the increasingly passé steel guitar. After a commercial for Prince Albert, Chubby Wise breaks in with "Sally Gooden" for a square dance, and for a moment it might be 1942 again. Hank Snow follows with "(The Angels Are Lighting) God's Little Candles," which sounds very close to the Jimmie Rodgers style that first inspired him. Then Snow introduces Chet Atkins, who glides into a smooth-trotting "Tennessee Blues," full of ribbony picking and perfectly placed diminished chords and tremolos. After that mesmerizing performance, out come Minnie and then Porter again with "I'm Day Dreaming Tonight," another old-time waltz. Hard on the heels of that number comes Stringbean with his original radio offering "John Henry," and the crowd responds with outbursts as energetic as those during the Jordanaires' singing.

Amid all this musical variety appears yet another style that at the time obliquely signaled a veering back to Stringbean's roots. Snow had begun the program with a Caribbean-rhythmed number, "Calypso Sweetheart." It was not unprecedented for the musically open-minded Canadian to venture outside of country, as one of his earliest hit singles was the shaker-filled "Rhumba Boogie" (1951), and his hero, Rodgers, had gleefully recorded in Hawaiian style. But in "Calypso Sweetheart," Snow's inspiration seems rather to have come from Harry Belafonte's 1956 album, *Calypso*, especially "Jamaica Farewell." That number by Belafonte, with its gentle Caribbean rhythms and harmonies, represented a genre finding a large and enthusiastic audience. It was being called folk music, and it reached into the very roots of cultural expression. Among the songs on Belafonte's *Calypso* album, "The Banana Boat Song—Day O" captured the hearts and imagination of many young people. One group based in San Francisco, however, latched onto the line "I had to leave a little girl in Kingston town" from "Jamaica Farewell" when naming themselves. With their success came a new wave that would bring String to unanticipated audiences.

OLD PATHS, DIFFERENT PATHS: 1958–1959

The Kingston Trio released its debut album on June 1, 1958. When it showed up on the *Billboard* charts in October, it began a steady climb, and with it came the folk music that soon began to be recognized as a marketing genre. The album's cover featured a photograph of the trio. Right in the center, flanked by Bob Shane and Nick Reynolds with guitars, stood a thin young man named David Guard playing a banjo. In this time when major recording labels showed little interest in banjo music, Dave Guard stood tall holding a banjo, its round white head of the banjo forming an enormous omphalos as though grounding it in the traditions the album's music celebrated. It is almost eerie to see another lanky Dave appearing on the music scene with his image tied to a banjo. It would have made for a wonderful story if he had been inspired by David Akeman. But this Dave's inspiration came from another banjo player and singer who might as well have been David Akeman's alter ego: Pete Seeger.

A comparison of Seeger and Stringbean helps illuminate the latter in the context of American roots-music preservation, for they represented opposite sides of the same coin. Pete Seeger stood about the same height as Stringbean. He sang many of the same songs Stringbean sang. He played clawhammer but would also dip into other styles. Like Stringbean, Seeger would most often be associated with Vega, fashioning his own banjo neck out of lignum vitae and fusing it to a Vega Tubaphone pot. Similar to the Akemans, Seeger and his wife chose to live simply in the country. Just as Stringbean's long and lean body complemented the banjo, so famed folk musicologist John Lomax said of Seeger, "He just *looked* like a banjo."[40] Viewed through a lens that highlights these parallels, the two men were practically identical.

But they were also bracingly dissimilar, even in their odd points of near resemblance. Whereas Stringbean was born in 1915 in the heart of Appalachia, Seeger was born in 1919 in the heart of Manhattan. Both men's fathers were musicians, but whereas James played the mountain banjo almost certainly by ear, Seeger's father, Charles Seeger, had studied musicology and composition at Harvard, conducted the Cologne Opera in Germany, and taught at Berkeley, Julliard, and the New School. Stringbean likely knew little about his family's history beyond his grandparents' generation, but the Seeger family had rubbed shoulders with Astors and Roosevelts and had made a fortune in sugar refining in Mexico. Where Stringbean made it no further than the eighth grade, Seeger was boarding-school and Ivy League educated. While Stringbean pursued his goal of amassing a million dollars, Seeger embraced poverty out of a suspicion of the material wealth he had been born into.

The point of unconscious intersection between these two performers came via Charles Seeger's love of what he conceived to be the music of the folk. Inspired (along with John Lomax) by Harvard professor George Lyman Kittredge, Seeger instilled a love of folk music in his son. In 1936, when David Akeman was playing on WLAP and with multiple bands in Kentucky, Charles took his seventeen-year-old son to a folk festival in Asheville, where he fell in love with the banjo. Pete dropped out of Harvard in 1938 and went to work with John Lomax's son, Alan (born six months to the day before David Akeman), at the Library of Congress's Archive of American Folk Song project. While performing live and on radio with the likes of Burl Ives, Lead Belly, and Woody Guthrie, Pete published his instructional book *How to Play the 5-String Banjo* in 1948. In 1955

Seeger, who had been a member of the Communist Party USA in the 1940s, was called to testify before the House Un-American Activities Committee. Despite his success with the Weavers, he, that band, and folk music, generally, went underground. Now, in 1958, the Kingston Trio not only revived that music but made it mainstream.

It was Pete Seeger's playing and his book that inspired Dave Guard, but strangely that source failed to acquaint him with Stringbean directly. While Guard would have learned about many old-time banjo players in Seeger's book, it made no mention of Stringbean himself or of his distinctive style. Stringbean's omission, although surely not intentional, nevertheless signaled the strange medley of points of connection and disconnection between himself and the folk-music movement. Given Seeger's deep fascination with Appalachian music and culture's honesty, how could he have not taken note of Stringbean, who was actively preserving the very same music? Added to his playing and singing, String's costume and comedy tapped deep into American culture, and he appealed to the audiences made up of the people who fascinated Seeger. Ironically, if Seeger knew about Stringbean at all, he may have found his contemporary's costume and performance style to be undignified, hillbilly stereotyping for commercial purposes. The 1962 edition of Seeger's book included a photograph of Grandpa with a caption identifying him as a "well known musician in the commercial 'country music' field . . . who sticks strictly to the oldfashioned frailing style of banjo picking."[41] The caption also mentions Grandpa's writing "a good instruction book," which Stringbean had not. Perhaps Seeger saw Stringbean as just too over the top, appealing to the masses with his comical look and having nothing to offer for ethnological study.

But, of course, Stringbean was *thoroughly* authentic. If anything, he found himself caught up in a kind of ideological blind spot in 1958. The country audience knew him, and the hard core of that group revered him precisely because of his authenticity. However, that audience had shrunken in size and buying power compared to the audience that embraced rock and roll and the Nashville Sound. Folk enthusiasts of the previous decades were not interested in commercial music. Where Ralph Peer had gone to Bristol looking to make money, these intellectuals sallied into the mountains with the "purer" goal of preserving culture and finding something exotic in relation to mainstream northern urban culture. Seeger and Stringbean may have been playing the same melodies and singing the same lyrics, but they did not understand them the same way or sing them for the same reasons. For Seeger, this music represented an already past culture that had happened to survive in mountain pockets. For Stringbean, this music was part of everyday living and breathing that not only was happening in real time but must negotiate its world in its own ways. The music touched Stringbean within the immediate realm of family, friends, home, and work. It touched Seeger as an alien expression of people who lived very different lives from his own but who offered perspectives that rang true.

Despite the initial disconnects, though, the folk audience would come to love and appreciate Stringbean. As for the Kentuckian himself, he decided to embrace recording, perhaps sensing an opportunity among folk record–buying enthusiasts. In September 1958, working with producer Hal Smith, Stringbean cut four songs: "I Wonder Where Wanda Went," "Short Life and Trouble," "Run Little Rabbit Run," and "You Can't Do Wrong and Get By." Cullman released a single of "Run Little Rabbit Run" / "You Can't Do Wrong and Get By" (Cullman-456408) in 1959. Even as that record was released, Stringbean recorded and saw released on Cullman another single with "Barnyard Banjo Picking" and "Train Special 500" (Cullman-6416). "Train Special 500" features Stringbean playing in a minor tuning, using the banjo to capture the driving rhythm of a train, the song taking its place in the grand tradition of train music. "Barnyard Banjo Picking" especially marks out important territory for Stringbean. In the recording, he rakes the banjo strings and bellows out to "boys" to come down to the barnyard and play. He then starts into descending notes on the low E string (normally the D string in standard G tuning) in his two-finger style and launches into the lyrics of "Hot Corn, Cold Corn," which he may have gotten from Asa Martin. The number was traditional, but Stringbean's version (for which he claimed authorship) was memorable and perfectly suited to his style. Many artists would go on to play it, including Jerry Garcia.

While Stringbean was making his first foray into solo recording, danger exploded at home. When Grandpa, Ramona, and the kids moved out of the big white house, David and Estelle decided to rent it out to Mr. and Mrs. Fred Burdette and their son, Fred Jr. On Thursday afternoon, December 11, the Burdette family was sitting around drinking with Mrs. Burdette's brother Charles Strickland, who had driven up from Atlanta, bringing Fred Sr. back with him.[42] The family began arguing because Fred Sr. was having an affair with a younger woman. The argument escalated to the point that Fred Jr. pulled out a .22 caliber pistol and shot his uncle, who, aged thirty, was actually two years younger than he. Fred Sr. grabbed his twelve-gauge shotgun and rushed out of the house, covering the seventy-five feet from there to the Akemans' house. Stringbean was away on a hunting trip, but Estelle was home. Fred Jr. gave chase, using his mother as a shield. As he walked behind his mother, he took a shot at the house, aiming at his father but actually hitting Estelle. Fred Sr. returned fire with the shotgun, hitting both his wife and his son. Stringbean later reported to the newspaper that Estelle was "just nipped a little" in the leg and did not know if she would press charges. The paper said the Burdettes were "still too drunk" to provide their own version of the story.

In retrospect, the event appears as a grim foreshadowing of the Akemans' deaths, but Stringbean downplayed it to the press. Whether the Akemans terminated the Burdettes' rental agreement at that point is not known, but good news came that the Joneses were moving back to Tennessee. Grandpa would later write that, while he had enjoyed reconnecting with Joe Wheeler for hunting with his return to Virginia, the television foray just did not work out. Maybe it was rock and roll, or maybe it was, he admitted, his poor performance doing commercials during live broadcasting. Whatever the reasons, String's prediction turned out to be correct, and the Joneses were moving back eleven months after leaving. They did not move back into the white house, though. Instead, they purchased ninety acres very close to the Akemans.

One thing Grandpa noticed on his return was that String, with all his time at home during these lean years, had found a new revenue stream that fitted perfectly with his passion for spending time in the woods. This new profitable activity was hunting not for animals but for ginseng. It was something that took David back to his boyhood in Jackson County, and perhaps now that he had reached age forty-three memories and yearnings for home and his youth filled his mind and heart. "He taught me how to spot ginseng 30 yards away," Grandpa wrote, "and we spent many a day hunting it together; of course, it was a good excuse to just get out and walk the woods, which we both liked to do." Bill Carlisle later explained that String sold the ginseng to Opry musician Joe Edwards "for about sixty dollars a pound." Bill commented that "he'd go out and dig that stuff all the time and sell it just like he had to."[43] A decade later, Stringbean might not have had to, but in 1958 the money was probably welcome.

The decade closed out with relative calm. In far-away New York City, Billie Holiday passed away on July 17, 1959, and the heat of the initial rock-and-roll craze burned out. Stringbean saw his Cullman singles released that year. Cullman also released a single by Curt Gibson on the Cullman label.[44] Gibson had moved to Nashville in 1958 and started playing backup on the Opry, quickly becoming another of Stringbean's friends.[45] David also formed connections with the Wilburn Brothers, Teddy and Doyle, and a new comic from Knoxville, Archie Campbell.

Entrenched though he was on the Opry, Stringbean may have wondered if he was doomed to slip into obscurity as the very definitions of music genres continued to shift. The October 1959 issue of *Esquire* featured an article by Alan Lomax titled "Bluegrass Underground: Folk Music with Overdrive" that gave a serious nod to the music tradition Stringbean had been a part of. Lomax saw bluegrass as "a sort of mountain Dixieland combo in which the five-string banjo, America's only indigenous folk instrument, carries the lead like a hot clarinet." David would have sat up at first in the unlikely event that he read the article expecting to see his own name. But, scanning down, he would have seen the following: "Bluegrass style began in 1945 when Bill Monroe, of the Monroe Brothers, recruited a quintet that included Earl Scruggs (who had perfected a three-finger banjo style now known as 'picking scruggs')."[46] Thus was Stringbean written out of the narrative of bluegrass history, just missing its origin and, by implication, representative of the style Scruggs moved the music beyond. In reality, Stringbean's banjo playing had been a crucial step along the way and Earl's another.

While the error would be righted later, for the moment String found himself cut off from an audience that should have naturally appreciated him. Neither he nor Bill was much interested in what some intellectual ethnomusicographer had to say, but Earl Scruggs's wife saw an opportunity in that article and went to work promoting her husband's career. Progressivist leaning, Earl gladly accepted the opportunity to play at the inaugural Newport Folk Festival in July 1959. The effect devastated the audience, framing their concept of the banjo and their worldview in an entirely new way. This kind of performance spoke their language in a way Stringbean did not. Even Stringbean's humor would have hit the wrong notes with audiences attuned to the sly, demure wit of Seeger and David Guard.

Thankfully for Stringbean, as 1960 got under way, the audience that already knew and loved him was making a resurgence. Following a classic story arc, in a moment when his career may have seemed to face defeat, fortune turned back his way. He was about to enter the most profitable and successful period of his life.

CHAPTER 6
PRETTY POLLY
1960–1965

NEW ERA, NEW PROGRAMMING: 1960–1962

February 1960 was a cold and dry month in the Nashville area.[1] As the short gray days steeped into chilly blue gloamings, increasing signs of social and political radicalism appeared on the Akemans' television. The first day of this month saw four African American North Carolina A&T students protest segregation nonviolently by way of a sit-in at the Woolworth Store on 132 South Elm Street in Greensboro, North Carolina. It was the city where Stringbean had spent most of his time with Charlie Monroe back in 1940, sponsored by Tommy Scott and Charlie's patent medicine. Stringbean had appeared as a blackface performer to help sell patent medicine then. Now, this drugstore in this drug-producing town became the site of a larger effort among African Americans to achieve integration. Their sit-ins inspired students in Nashville to do the same, reviving efforts they had already begun the year before at Harveys and at the Cain-Sloan department stores.

While these activities geared toward improving Black life appeared on news programming, on February 15 a television occurrence portended a new kind of programming that would cater to white rural audiences. In that evening's episode of *The Danny Thomas Show*, the world got its first glimpse of the small town of Mayberry and its sheriff, Andy Taylor.[2] Taylor, portrayed by Andy Griffith, issued Thomas a ticket for running a stop sign over Thomas's protest that there was no road there. When Andy tells Thomas the amount of the fine, Thomas pulls out a wad of money, provoking Andy to exclaim, "Whooee! That's quite a roll you got there!"

Given how Jackie Gleeson's television quip "How sweet it is!" had inspired Stringbean's onstage performance, it is tempting to think that this Danny Thomas episode may have played a role in inspiring String to start his practice of carrying a large wad of money. What fun to reverse the roles, with the country rube carrying the wad instead of the city slicker? It is not clear exactly when Stringbean began to carry a large roll of money on his person, but it may have started as a gag. Tommy Scott claimed, "A lot of folks didn't really know he actually just had big bills on the outside, and that wad was stuffed with dollars."[3]

Ironically, although in the episode Danny Thomas says he is sure people have not heard of television in "these parts," the episode spawned a beloved series and built momentum toward a blitz of rural-based programming that would dominate televisions throughout middle America. The first episode of *The Andy Griffith Show* aired on October 3, 1960. Almost exactly a year later, *Mr. Ed* hit the screen. And a year after that, in September 1962, CBS began airing *The Beverly Hillbillies*. That program hit especially close to home for Stringbean because Flatt and Scruggs played the theme music, taking them into living rooms across the nation and further solidifying their profile as *the* premier bluegrass performers.

In parallel to this rural television programming, certain new artists embraced more traditional country music. One of these was another Kentuckian, Loretta Lynn. She had already worked with Buck Owens, who disliked the Nashville Sound and the establishment that purveyed it. Lynn hit it off with String right away. "Stringbean was one of the very first friends Doolittle, my husband, and I made when we first came to Nashville in 1960," she remembers. "He and his wife Estelle were some of the nicest folks you could find anywhere." Loretta rode in on the success of her hit "Honky Tonk Girl," which reached fourteen on the *Billboard* country-and-western chart. She signed a contract with the Wilburn Brothers' publishing company and made her first appearances on the Opry. Of Stringbean and his wife, Loretta says, "He was also kinda like a gentle giant. And his wife made everyone feel so welcome." Loretta's fond memories get at the particular joy Stringbean brought. "You know, it's funny I remember always thinking that he was older than he was because he was always in character. He was funny, always making everyone laugh."[4]

Just as Loretta and Stringbean were bound to hit it off, so Stringbean grew close to Porter Wagoner. The two got to be pals at the Opry, and Porter became one of Stringbean's favorite people to ride with on occasions when Estelle did not drive him. "Porter Wagoner is the safest driver in the world," Stringbean would say. "I'd rather drive with him than anyone." One of their engagements was at a Catholic monastery in Kentucky. "When they arrived, a priest walked up and said, 'Are you Mr. Wagoner?' 'Yes.' 'Is Mister Bean with you?' Stringbean rolled down the window, and the priest said, 'Mr. Bean, if you're in doubt about any of your material you're going to use—any smutty material or anything that's the least bit shady—please refrain from using it here.' String said, 'Okay, Chief.'"[5]

When Porter started his television show, he wasted no time booking String. The debut episode aired on September 14, 1961, and in the September 19 episode Porter welcomed Stringbean, who sang "Twenty Cent Cotton and Ninety Cent Meat," "I Wonder Where Wanda Went," and "Barnyard Banjo Picking."[6] Porter brought Stringbean back shortly after in episode 22. The two talk and joke, and Stringbean breaks into "String and His Banjo" followed by "Herdin' Cattle."[7] It was the third of the songs he played, however, that was becoming a signature one for him. He had learned the old ballad "Pretty Polly" when he was still very young back in Kentucky and had included it in his joke book in the early 1950s. Played in modal tuning, the haunting number well captured String's native Appalachia. It was the kind of song that could appeal not only to country audiences but folk ones, as Stringbean would soon find out.

The year 1962 saw String back on Porter's show again, this time with "Stringbean's a-Fishin'," playing Uncle Dave's Gibson. "Give me a rod of steel with a bamboo feel," String says, setting up this number about his favorite pastime and the jitterbug, especially. He returns later in the episode to play "Suicide Blues," this time on the Vega. In a comic bit after, Porter reminds String that he owes him five dollars, and Stringbean pulls a coin out of his breast pocket and gives it to Porter. When Porter complains that it is only a nickel, Stringbean replies that the coin is five dollars with all the income taxes taken out of it.

Porter's affection for the older entertainer is clearly genuine. The host treats all of his guests well, and he laughs with the show's regular comic Speck Rhodes. But there is something extra in Porter's interactions with Stringbean: he cannot help but smile and laugh at Stringbean's dry style. Porter's reaction illustrates the peculiar appeal of Stringbean. "Stringbean" inspired hilarity and affection via a spark that lay deeper in his persona than his playing, singing, jokes, or antics. That spark spread throughout those songs, jokes, banjo playing, and entertainment styles and quirks, illuminating them with his special, utterly unique glow. Something about Stringbean allowed Porter to be more boyish than usual, probably because he had been a character the young singer had grown up listening to but also because Stringbean emanated plain, simple goodness that inspired wholehearted sympathy and outright love.

STARDAY: 1961–1962

Also, in that 1962 episode, Porter brings out something for the audience to see—Stringbean's new album. As Porter holds it up for the camera to capture, String nods humbly and nonchalantly and makes sure to tell Porter and the audience there are fourteen songs on there. This album took its place in a blitz of recordings String was making with a label in Nashville that was fighting the good fight with all its heart.

The Starday Record label began in Beaumont, Texas, in 1952, the brainchild of Jack Starnes and Harold W. "Pappy" Daily.[8] Starday first made its name with the original Arlie Duff recording of "Y'All Come" that also entered Stringbean's repertoire. In 1957 Starday moved to Nashville under the directorship of Don Pierce and set itself against the trends of both rock and roll and the developing Nashville Sound, committing instead to traditional country music. Studying the rural market for old-time and bluegrass music, Pierce came to realize that the country audience was made up of older adults who preferred long-playing albums to singles.[9] Accordingly, Starday focused on producing LPs of old-time and bluegrass music from established stars and young traditionalists. Pierce compiled these albums from in-house recordings and already existing ones from smaller labels.

A key element in these Starday productions was the packaging. Pierce designed distinct covers tailored to the market. As he later remembered, "Whether posing the artist holding a pig, sitting in front of a barn, rocking in a chair with a rooster on his lap, riding a horse, or just going fishing, Starday albums screamed 'Hillbilly!'"[10] However hillbilly-ish the covers were, Pierce's extensive write-ups on the covers carefully avoided the pejorative term "hillbilly" that might offend his buyers. Pierce also resisted boxing this old-time music into the category of "bluegrass," instead stressing the roots of authentic mountain music. While Starday's direct marketing through mail order aimed at the rural audience, the records managed to get to the urban folk audience in Greenwich Village. Although Pierce was slow to realize the potentials of the latter market, it would provide a new lifeline for old-time musicians such as Stringbean.

Being a long-standing Opry star whose singing reached into the very roots of the country music industry without exactly falling fully into the bluegrass genre, Stringbean made sense as one of Starday's recording artists. An October 1960 issue of *Music Reporter* carried a notice, "Sessions Mount at Starday," relating that "September sessions either already held or scheduled include those for Benny Martin, Cowboy Copas, Dottie West, Ray Hendrix, Paul Wayne, Lonzo and Oscar, Stringbean, Red Sovine, Willis Brothers, Oak Ridge Quartet, Old

Hickory Singers and others."[11] Also joining the group of Starday recording artists would be Stringbean's friend Bashful Brother Oswald. True to form, Pierce not only made original recordings but also worked out deals to acquire recordings Stringbean had made for Cullman. With this material in hand, Starday released its first Stringbean records the next year.

Two of these Stringbean releases were seven-inch extended-play records with four songs each. One, titled *Stringbean "the Kentucky Wonder" and His Banjo* (SEP-152), featured on its A-side "20 Cents Cotton and 90 Cents Meat" and "Working on a Building" and on the B-side "Forgetting to Forget You" and "Give Me Back My Five Dollars." The cover of the other record, *Stringbean and His Banjo* (SEP-131), presented a photograph of a rural scene, including a split-rail fence with the roof of a cabin barely seen behind and a mountain rising above in the background. The back of the cover bears a photograph of String in his long-shirt, short-pants costume accompanied by liner notes written by Pierce: "Stringbean, the 'Kentucky Wonder,' is the banjo-playing wizard heard every Saturday night on the coast-to-coast Grand Ole Opry program." Pierce goes on to say that "David Akeman" is "a very nice-looking fellow when 'out of character,'" and "Everyone agrees he is a great showman and a wonderful guy." On the A-side were "Stringbean and His Banjo" and "Herdin' Cattle." The B-side bore Uncle Dave's old number "Don't Bob Your Hair, Girls" and "Wake Up, Little Betty."

Pierce combined these recordings with others to create Stringbean's first LP, *Old Time Banjo Picking and Singing, with Stringbean, the Kentucky Wonder, and His Five String Banjo* (SLP-142), released in July 1961. The front of the cover gleamed in the kind of full Technicolor Starday specialized in. Split almost directly in half, the left side featured String on the Opry stage, wearing his older black hat, a red-and-black-striped shirt, blue jeans, and cowboy boots. He plays the Vega No. 9 as he stands at a microphone with the iconic "WSM Grand Ole Opry" placard on its stand. His head is tilted to his right in his classic pose. The right side of the cover is bright yellow, with lettering in blue, red, pink, and green, announcing "The Kentucky Wonder and his Five String Banjo" and underneath that "14-Most Requested Songs-14."

The cover's back again sports a write-up by Pierce, outlining Stringbean's biography. In addition to being a wonderful guy, "'Bean', as his Opry comrades call him, is an easygoing quiet, friendly fellow with a host of friends." Pierce presents the story of Stringbean trading a couple of chickens for his first banjo, recounts his working at WLAP and Bill Monroe, and mentions Uncle Dave's willing him a banjo and that some of the songs on this album were Uncle Dave's. Pierce continues, "He combines comedy with his authentic banjo work and is a favorite with audiences with his sad, puzzled expression and ridiculous getup."

Revealing that Stringbean lives on a "beautiful 134 acre farm near Goodlettsville, Tennessee," the write-up affirms that he "understands farming and country people" and "is an expert fisherman and hunter." As a country man himself, Stringbean plays "old songs having originated from England, Scotland and Ireland dating back to the 16th century." Pierce concludes by observing of the record, "This is a part of our American heritage and Stringbean, the Kentucky Wonder, is a living legend in our times."

The record itself sports the trademark Starday yellow label. To the eight tracks previously released on the EPs and the Cullman import "Barnyard Banjo Pickin'" were added five new recordings. Two were Uncle Dave numbers, "Keep My Skillet Good and Greasy" and "Kentucky and Tennessee," the latter played similar to Uncle Dave's style, maybe even on Uncle Dave's RB-1. Also new were "Georgia Rose" and "Birdie." And there on the A-side appeared the song gaining more and more traction for String, this time simply labeled "Polly."

In terms of sales, this record likely ranked in the middle to lower end of the pack for Starday. It appealed to longtime Opry fans, who were surely happy finally to see an LP from one of their heroes. But String was not a made-to-order type of recording artist. Unlike stars who fitted into clear categories, Stringbean pursued his own path, in keeping with his personality. His greatest power lay in the immediate impact of performing in a live setting, and live shows provided his strongest record-selling venue. Pierce later reminisced:

> Now, with String, we had a very personal thing. He would come by frequently, and he'd always call me "Boss," like he does just about everybody else. But he'd come in with his bib overalls and his pipe, and his wife would be driving the car, since he never attempted to do that himself. He was the most appreciative guy to get a small royalty statement that I ever saw. He just always would thank me, you know, for recording him and for putting out his records, and he would buy a tremendous amount of albums that he sold on personal appearances, and sell them.[13]

String's personal appearances, where he could sell records, included dates in North Dakota and Florida in 1961. Whispering Bill Anderson recalls sharing the bill with Stringbean in West Palm Beach, a decidedly non–country music place at the time. Few people bothered to leave the beach on the Saturday afternoon in autumn, and even that small audience hardly responded. Instead of getting mad, as Anderson expected, String simply wiped down his banjo, put it in the case, lit his pipe, and told the fresh-faced entertainer, "Billy Boy, they took me serious." It would not be the last time he would use that quip. Meanwhile, Anderson was getting the crash course in Stringbean's way of doing business.

In one of his first Opry appearances, Anderson, not knowing that Stringbean always played in the key of A, asked the older entertainer what key Anderson's band should play in backing him up. "He looked at me as though I had lost my mind," Anderson says. "He held out his right arm, rotated the palm of his hand up and then down, and then back up again. As if I had just asked him the dumbest question in the world he simply replied, 'Is there any other?'"[13]

Meanwhile, Stringbean also started making more independent moves. It was probably in this time that he signed on with the Wil-Helm Agency that the Wilburn Brothers and Don Helms had established in the late 1950s.[14] This connection may have led to his hiring the former manager of Elvis Presley, Bob Neal.[15] More independent bookings could mean more direct record sales. Apparently, the strategy worked for him, as Pierce added, "He always seemed to be amazed that he could do so well, but he was always so grateful to everybody. I never heard him say a bad word about anybody. And the guy, he sold some albums for us, too. He really did."[16]

Stringbean's new manager, Neal, likely arranged the article on him in Nashville's *Tennessean* on April Fool's Day 1962.[17] By this point, Starday had released two singles drawn from the 1961 releases, and the article's author, Phil Sullivan, had gone out to the Akemans' farm for an interview. The accompanying photograph is refreshingly candid, featuring a relaxing String sitting back in a leather armchair in front of a blazing fireplace, his left arm up over his head, his right hand cradling the Gibson RB-1. He seems to be in midsentence, his pipe curving from his lips. Taken from a high angle, it is the closest any public photo ever came to capturing what it was like visiting with David Akeman at home.

Stringbean, Estelle, and their quiet country home and lifestyle cast their spell over Sullivan, for the tone and content of the article are filled with warmth and nostalgia. "The life [Stringbean] lives is the envy of every farm boy who ever followed a mule down a dusty corn row and wished he was on the creek bank fishing," Sullivan writes. "It has been described in books as the idyllic life. It is the true wonder of Stringbean." Sullivan using the word "wonder" well corresponds to Stringbean's other cognomen, and it also describes the aura surrounding him that Sullivan identifies and that was becoming increasingly evident in the responses of other entertainers around Stringbean.

Sullivan rhapsodizes about the Akemans' "300 acre farm" (it appears to have grown), which he romantically identifies as being in "a cove near Goodlettsville." Describing the environs, Sullivan explains, "A thick mat of grass covers the floor of the hollow, and Stringbean's white-faced cattle push and tug through the grass." Sullivan continues, "At the base of a steep hill sits Stringbean's small, brown house, which can almost qualify as a cabin. Behind the house a huge cave in the side of the hill pours out a stream of sparkling water and gusts of cold air." That the cattle might need tending to now and then seems not to have crossed Sullivan's mind, as he describes a lifestyle in which "nearly every morning" after breakfast, coffee, and pipe smoking, Stringbean invited his wife to go fishing, often with such Opry buddies as Grandpa Jones and Bill Carlisle. "He's a good fireplace sitter and likes to talk about wood," Sullivan writes, and he quotes Stringbean saying, "I guess I've got 4,000,000 cords of firewood on these hills" and adds the pithy line, "A fireplace man needs a lot of wood."

Stringbean also enjoyed sitting on the porch watching trains go by on the nearby railroad. But, Sullivan wrote, "Occasionally the placid flow of String-bean's life is interrupted by the necessity of work." Sullivan then tells about Stringbean's recent album and singles and that he is recording more songs for Starday and will likely need to travel away from his placid life more. "This might seem a threat to Stringbean's way of life, but don't bet on it," advises Sullivan, for Stringbean had told his new manager, "I told him I didn't want to work too much."

While this article was not a major piece, buried in the second half of the newspaper, it marks a significant point in what Stringbean had come to mean as an entity in that moment. The times were a-changing in the outside world, as a young Bob Dylan would write a couple of years later, having just released his debut album in March 1962. That fall saw James Meredith become the first African American student at the University of Mississippi amid rioting and the presence of the National Guard. The young president who ordered federal assistance in the incident, John F. Kennedy, imagined an ideal world based on the Camelot of the musical he and Jackie adored, but he faced severe trouble with the Cuban missile crisis in October. In August the fifties sex icon and one of Kennedy's lovers, Marilyn Monroe, died of a drug overdose. Meanwhile, the United States had sent Alan Shepard into space the previous year, and now there was talk of rocketing people up to walk on the face of the moon. Amid all of this change, both terrestrial and extraterrestrial, Stringbean stayed the same, his home an idyllic bubble untouched by the machinations of increasingly dramatic times.

What did David himself think of where he now stood in the world as he approached the half-century mark of life? He may have begun to feel old and out of step with the young people of his moment. But, like Grandpa, the Stringbean persona possessed the ability not only to age well but to become even more appealing with time's passing. Nothing confirms the old-timeyness of old-time music than the performer being old. There is power in being a relic, and Sullivan's article represents the first harbinger of who fans and industry insiders alike were coming to see Stringbean as being.

The spring Starday recording sessions Sullivan referred to produced a new album released in 1962: *Stringbean: More of That Old Time Banjo Pickin' and Singin'* (SLP-179). This follow-up LP was the album Porter Wagoner presented to his live and television audience. It features the same Stringbean photograph as his 1961 album but cropped from the waist up and thus not revealing Stringbean's string-bean-y physique. The photograph is centered on an otherwise white background, which announces "14 Native American Mountain Folk Ballads," making an even clearer bid for the folk audience. The writing on the back is practically identical to the previous album but features three small photographs. One was the earlier-mentioned young David with the Vega, another one of a young David and of David and Uncle Dave also described previously. To these are added a third of Stringbean in denim, pipe in mouth, smiling, with a safari-style fishing hat on, holding up a mess of good fish with Estelle at what looks to be a grocery and bait shop.

Again importing recordings from Cullman, this record offers a cornucopia of the songs that had endeared Stringbean to so many audiences. These included "Opry Time in Tennessee" and "Stringbean's a-Fishin'" as well as the Cullman recording of "Train Special 500." String picked his way alongside a Dobro through the gospel number "Sinner Man, Where You Gonna Hide." "Pluckin' the Bird" featured him taking a rare trip up the neck in his banjo solo. His rendition of "Chewing Gum" surpasses Uncle Dave's recorded version of the song, String offering up an invitingly humorous series of chewing sounds. "I Intend to Make Heaven My Home" introduces String's employment of mandolin-style tremolo on his banjo in slower waltz numbers. "Here, Rattler, Here" starts off with a memorable spoken-word reminiscing about fox and raccoon hunting in his youth in Kentucky. "Lord, I'm Coming Home" combines with "Goodbye, Sweet Thing" and "Suicide Blues" to introduce shadows of loss and death that now sound heartbreakingly prophetic. Particularly interesting, in his rendition of "Mountain Dew," especially, Stringbean smooths his sound out with a brisk bluegrassy pace and harmonizing vocals that transform the song from a comic number into a mesmerizing summoning of mountain atmosphere. That sound coincided with his restoration into bluegrass history and his official entrance into the folk scene.

FOLK AND BLUEGRASS: 1963–1965

With the onset of 1963, Stringbean was finding his groove in recording, television, and personal appearances. Some of these in-person performances were in package shows that included Patsy Cline. She may have represented the Nashville Sound, but she got along fine with old-timers such as String. On one road trip from Nashville to Hendersonville, North Carolina, she sat in the backseat with him and Bill Anderson, Darell McCall, and Cowboy Copas and fell into the floorboard laughing at Copas's tales about Ma and Pa Kettle.[18] Anderson remembers, "I realized for the first time how totally unflappable [String] was when he said in a soft voice, 'Billy Boy' (which is what he always called me), 'everybody in this car is crazy except me and you.' He paused and I smiled. Then he continued, 'And I'm not too sure about you!'"[19] Tragically, not long after that, Patsy, Copas, and Hawkshaw Hawkins died in a plane crash. A young reporter named Larry Brinton covered the event for Nashville's other major newspaper, the *Nashville Banner*. Brinton would later play a role in the Akemans' murder trial. In another foreshadowing, Copas and Hawkins were buried in Forest Lawn Cemetery, where String and Estelle would later be laid to rest. For now, the couple befriended Hawkins's wife, fellow Opry cast member Jean Shepard. Following hard on the heels of that tragedy came the November 22 assassination of President Kennedy.

Amid death and turmoil, Stringbean went about recording another album, *Stringbean and His Banjo: A Salute to Uncle Dave Macon* (SLP-215). The full-color photograph that fills practically all of the cover's front brings us into Stringbean's home as Sullivan's article had. String's green armchair complements the warm reds in the varnished pine paneling and wood floors. A fish is mounted on his wall, perhaps a prize catch of his or Estelle's. A pipe holder full of briars sits on the mantelpiece along with a smaller framed image obscured by the album's lettering. A shotgun and fishing rod lean against the wall beside the hearth, and the small broom for sweeping out the ashes hangs on the wall. The ashes themselves lie in a white heap in the fireplace.

The man sitting in the chair is more David Akeman than Stringbean: no makeup, no long shirt, no short pants, no hat. Instead, he wears a white and red gingham button-down, blue jeans, and boots, and his pipe swoops down from his lips. He seems almost to be smiling as he holds the Gibson RB-1. Inserted to his left is a black-and-white photo of Uncle Dave with his leg over one of those Gibsons, in the middle of one of his antics. Although this photograph is clearly staged, it resembles the one in the Sullivan article from the year before and captures a more intimate and everyday side of Stringbean.

Pierce's write-up on the back of the cover outlines Uncle Dave's and Stringbean's biographies. It reveals that the recordings were all made at Starday Studios, with Tommy Hill directing, Jack Drake playing bass, Hoss Linneman on Dobro, and Eddie Wilson on guitar. The photograph was taken by Terry Tomlin of the *Tennessean*; a different photographer, Jack Corn, contributed the photographs to the Sullivan article. Pierce also thanks Vito Pellettieri, the (then) recently retired music librarian at WSM. Pellettieri had been a friend of Uncle Dave's and "felt that an album of this kind would be well received, and he suggested many of the great old song favorites that were included." Apparently, it was not actually Pellettieri or even Stringbean himself who conceived the idea of doing the record, for Pierce later explained, "I remember I was the guy that encouraged him to do the album on Uncle Dave Macon. He had some reservations about that, but he knew all the old Dave Macon songs. It came off well, and we had a unique album cover there, with that picture of Uncle Dave, so that it looked like he was reminiscing about him as he was picking his banjo there."[20]

As for the songs, themselves, side A tears off with renditions of "Ida Red," "Tennessee Farmer," and "Pretty Little Widow" that stick very closely to Uncle Dave's playing and singing style. Listening to "John Henry," one might recall its being the first one Stringbean played on the air at WLAP back in 1935. "There'll Be Moonshining in Them Old Kentucky Hills" may be Uncle Dave's, but Stringbean makes it his own, claiming in a spoken-word introduction that his brother in Kentucky ("back where I come from," he added) had a still to which revenuers might go but would not return. "Hesitation Blues" falls back in line with Uncle Dave's style, and Stringbean again used his tremolo in "Take My Hand, Precious Lord." The B-side offers, after the classic "How Many Biscuits Can You Eat," the sensitively rendered love song "Over the Mountain," maybe Stringbean's most melodic and exquisite recording. After all the foot-stomping numbers Stringbean usually pounds through, in "Over the Mountain" his singing reveals surprising control and intimacy. As per his usual approach to waltzes, he uses his tremolo, which works in lovely combination with delicate Dobro picking along with carefully placed lead-guitar flourishes. "Bully of the Town" has a wheeling kind of joy about it, Stringbean's vocal and frailing both strong. The next number is the quasi-religious "I'm the Man Who Rode a Mule around the World," a traditional bragging number sometimes called "I Was Born about Ten Thousand Years Ago." Along with String's take on the traditional "Cripple Creek," the record rounds out with "Free Little Bird," which Wilson's Lester Flatt–like G runs give a bluegrass feel to, and the hauntingly modal didactic number "You Can't Do Wrong and Get By."

As this record made its way out into the world, another television-venue opportunity came for Stringbean in the form of *The Wilburn Brothers Show*. Loretta Lynn remembers, "When the Wilburn brothers started their television show, I was their female singer and Stringbean was a big guest star and was on the show a lot. That's when we all really got to know each other as everyone became a big family." The show ran for eleven seasons, and Stringbean became an important person in the lives of Loretta's twin daughters, Peggy Jean and Patsy Eileen, who were born in 1964. "He would play with my twins and watch them for me many times while filming my part of the show," Loretta explains. "My girls loved him."[21]

Meanwhile, an echoing roar across the Atlantic arrived with four young men from England in the United States in February 1964. By the time Beatlemania struck, Stringbean and his old-time music had been shoved so far to the periphery of mainstream American culture that it had little impact on his career. The British invasion crushed the folk-music scene the same way Elvis and company had devastated country music. But just as Stringbean survived in the niche remainder of country music, so he now found a home in the embattled folk fans still devoted to the likes of Dylan and Seeger. As invitations came from colleges, the unlettered Stringbean quickly found these audiences to be different. They wanted his authentic music played as a native of Appalachia.[22] The new scene buffaloed him, but he embraced it. As Don Pierce said, String "would never cease to be amazed at how much he would get on personal appearances with the rise in popularity of bluegrass and folk in the colleges. You see, he had the flogging type of banjo player, which really was not bluegrass, but he was included in many of those shows. And all of a sudden he got real busy."[00] As multitudes marched for freedom and violent conflict arose in the 1964 Freedom Summer's voter-registration campaign and Americans troops continued to fight in Vietnam, Stringbean brought traditional music to often left-leaning students.

Pierce had this audience in mind but also wanted to make sure Stringbean did not lose his established country music audience when they released the 1964 album *Way Back in the Hills of Old Kentucky, with Stringbean and His 5-String Banjo* (SLP-260). This time the cover sports a photograph of Stringbean beside a creek. As he waits for a bite, he looks off into the middle distance, massive pipe in mouth again, wearing a plain blue shirt, rolled jeans, and brogans along with a straw hat. He holds the Gibson RB-1.

The back of the cover presents the usual Stringbean biography and explains that the songs on this album Stringbean learned as a boy in Kentucky. Tommy Hill again gets credit for directing the record, but this time Hoss Linneman is listed as the engineer. On fiddle on this record was Tommy Vaden, who recorded with many major artists and is most often remembered for his playing on Hank Snow's "I'm Moving On." Pierce adds the following verbiage attesting to Stringbean's authenticity:

In recent years an entire new generation of folk singers has sprung up. Some are amateurs, some are students some are arty types, and some are folkniks and beatniks. None of these descriptions fits Stringbean because he is a pure and authentic Country Music singer who learned the art as a child and who has performed as full-time professional throughout a lifetime career in the Country Music field. We think there is a worthwhile difference that fans of real Country Music will appreciate. The tremendous popularity for folk music finds Stringbean performing on stage at colleges and in the big cities; however, his heart will always be with the Grand Ole Opry in Nashville, Tennessee, and he will always be singing the songs that he learned "Way Back In the Hills of Old Kentucky."

With the opening tracks, "Little Pink" and Bill Monroe's "My Rose of Old Kentucky," this record offers a different feel much closer to bluegrass. Stringbean's banjo rings as always, but now comes with it Vaden's deft fiddling. The energy of the music overcomes Stringbean in "Big Ball in Nashville," driving him to roar "Yeah!" and "Come on, Five!" to exhort his banjo—a phrase he used often. "Poor Ellen Smith" is hard to listen to with knowledge of what was to befall String and Estelle:

> Poor Ellen Smith,
> And how she was found
> She was shot through the heart
> Lying cold on the ground.

Stringbean returned close to his birthplace in "Old Cumberland Gap," with more two-finger picking and Vaden fiddling. The western-style "Little Adobe Shack" and the cavalier ballad "The Roving Gambler" strike rather different notes from the other tracks, but the B-side resumes with more familiar Stringbean music in "Black Eyed Suzy" and the Cullman import "Short Life and Trouble." String mixes picking and brushing of the banjo's strings to create arrestingly punctuated rhythm in his take on "Little Sally Goodin.'" "Banjo Pickin' Girl" seems particularly made to order for the folk audience, with it's a–a–a–b/a structure of singing one line three times, then inserting an extra phrase in the final repeat. Instead of his tremolo approach to a waltz, String employs pinches and reeling picking in "Rye Whiskey" that conveys drunkenness as effectively as Heinrich Biber's "Battalia à 10." After driving through "Honey Babe, I'm Bound to Ride," Stringbean returns to his tremolo for the closing gospel number, "Hold to God's Unchanging Hand," adapting it, this time, to a popping four-four beat.

February 1965 saw Stringbean back in Chicago, but under different circumstances than when he recorded with Bill in that city twenty years before to the month. Now he was here for the fifth annual University of Chicago Folk Festival. A photograph in the university's magazine pictures Stringbean in a sport coat, sans hat, his profile handsome and rugged, a look that appealed to folk audiences.[24] He later explained that the festival organizers did not want him dressing in his famous costume. "No, they wouldn't let me, no," he said. "They didn't want no foolishness there. They wanted it straight." He played "Pretty Polly" three times over the course of two days.[25] He was included in the evening performances, which were filled to capacity, being "the heart of the Festival."[26]

.   Despite the bluegrass-style sounds of his 1964 record, Stringbean had not yet made significant headway in the bluegrass crowd. After enduring the narrative that the "true" bluegrass sound started with Earl's joining the Blue Grass Boys, Bill Monroe finally warmed to the idea of reaching the folk and bluegrass audiences and asserting himself as the genre's true founder and leader. Bill's first college concert was the 1963 University of Chicago Folk Festival, and he worked with ethnographer Ralph Rinzler to make further inroads. The month after that engagement, Rinzler published an article in *Sing Out!* titled "Bill Monroe—the Daddy of Bluegrass Music," which restored Bill to that lofty position.[27] That summer of 1963, Bill and his Blue Grass Boys played the Newport Folk Festival for the first time.

Two years later, on Labor Day weekend, 1965, the Blue Grass Boys were the centerpiece of the first-ever multiday bluegrass festival held at Fincastle, Virginia. For the finale of that event, the festival organizer, Carlton Haney, presented "The Story of Blue Grass Music, with Music and Narration by the Artists Who Recorded and Performed the Songs for the Last Quarter Century."[28] This sequence went all the way back to the beginning of the Blue Grass Boys, with representative former band members stepping up to play songs indicative of their tenure and corresponding stage of the development of the bluegrass sound. Stringbean did not come in person, but his importance became clear. "Then came the banjo," Haney said after demonstrating how Bill had developed harmony. "The man who first played banjo with Bill Monroe is not here today. He's known throughout the world as Stringbean today, but he's not here. But on some of the sessions and some of the records—the first ones—that used the banjo, you heard very little. But if you'll listen, back in the background, you will hear Stringbean."[29]

With that Bill and the boys broke into "Rocky Road Blues," Lamar Grier picking the banjo but not making it sound much like Stringbean's two-finger style. Haney later mentioned Earl Scruggs but merely included him and Lester Flatt as one of the many musicians who had played in the band, emphasizing Bill's mandolin in "Bluegrass Breakdown" rather than Earl's banjo playing. Grier had clearly trained in the Scruggs style, robbing listeners of the actual sound Stringbean brought. In "Rocky Road Blues," the audience was hearing Scruggs playing, if not his name, which inadvertently confirmed his style's being the bluegrass style. But it was a triumph for Stringbean because the five hundred listeners that day went away knowing he had first brought the banjo into the bluegrass sound. It was yet another signal that David Akeman, at age fifty, had come into his own, and it surely paved the way for String's invitation to the Chicago Folk Festival and other such events.

Stringbean with the Bar-X-Boys, circa 1938. (Courtesy of Mark Kelsay Royse)

Stringbean/David Akeman dressed smartly with his newly acquired Vega banjo, circa 1943. (Courtesy of Phillip Akemon, founder and coordinator, Stringbean Memorial Bluegrass Festival, www.StringbeanPark.com)

Stringbean's Vega #9 Tubaphone banjo. (Courtesy of Country Music Hall of Fame and Museum)

String Bean's joke book, published circa 1950. (Taylor Hagood personal collection)

String and Estelle newly married, 1945. (Courtesy of Phillip Akemon, founder and coordinator, Stringbean Memorial Bluegrass Festival, www.StringbeanPark.com)

Stringbean at home, 1962. (© Jack Corn—USA TODAY Network)

Stringbean at ease in his leather chair, 1962. (© Jack Corn—USA TODAY Network)

Stringbean with a big catch, date unknown. (Courtesy of Phillip Akemon, founder and coordinator, Stringbean Memorial Bluegrass Festival, www. StringbeanPark.com)

Stringbean at the Opry in his classic arm-extended pose, 1973. (Nashville Public Library, Special Collections)

Stringbean lies dead in front of the fireplace where he so often sat, 1973. (Courtesy of Tommy Jacobs)

Estelle dead in the field the morning after, 1973. (Courtesy of Tommy Jacobs)

Packing away the Vega #9, 1973. (© Jack Corn—USA Today Network)

John Brown, 1973. (Courtesy of Tommy Jacobs)

Doug Brown, 1973.
(Courtesy of Tommy Jacobs)

Stringbean's empty
costume, 1974. (Nash-
ville Public Library,
Special Collections)

Stringbean Memorial Festival billboard, 2017, Jackson County, Kentucky. (Photograph by Taylor Hagood)

Stringbean and Estelle's grave, Forest Lawn Memorial Gardens, Goodlettsville, Tennessee, 2018. (Photograph by Taylor Hagood)

ME AND MY OLD CROW
(GOT A GOOD THING GOING)
1966-1973

PROTESTING, RESISTING, MANAGING MONEY, AND ARRIVING AT LAST: 1966–1968

Towering on the stage with his comical physique, Stringbean remained stalwart and largely nonpolitical in a time when change and politics screamed with intensity. He *did* flirt with making a political statement in 1966, however. That year, as Louisville native Muhammad Ali proclaimed that he would refuse to serve in Vietnam if drafted, String recorded "That Crazy Vietnam War." The core of the song was not new—Stringbean simply updated it from "Crazy War," which he had been performing for at least thirty years. It was undeniably more a personal protest than a cultural one, and it was not hard-core radical. Nevertheless, the song made it clear that war was not for Stringbean. And when it was released as a single (Starday 752), its B-side's "Hey Old Man (Can You Play a Banjo)" offered an up-and-back-down-the-scale refrain that rhymed "banjer" with "gander" combined with hard-driving frailing to make the record one that surely appealed to sophisticated folk-music devotees. He may not have been the next Bob Dylan or Joan Baez, but the record came as close as Stringbean ever would to embracing leftist politics and style.

Whatever inroads he made into folk and bluegrass, Stringbean remained squarely in the field of country music and basked in the glow of performers who appreciated him. Stringbean's appearance on *Those Stonemans* is particularly memorable.[1] He makes his way onto the stage with arm extended Babe

Ruth style. His tan hat has lost its black band somewhere along the way. Also notable, he wears pink pants with rhinestones. These pants he had acquired from Little Jimmie Dickens, who later recalled:

> I had the rhinestone suits, you know, the Nudie rhinestone clothes. And String says, "Ever get tired of some of those old pants you got? I'd like to have a pair with the rhinestones on it." And next week I brought him a pair. I brought him a pair with rhinestones all over them. And he had it fixed with the shirt on it with his costume, and he wore those little rhinestone pants there for two or three years.[2]

Although firmly rooted in traditional country music, the Stonemans for this show have donned a distinctly rocking look, Patti, Roni, and Donna all wearing miniskirts and white go-go boots. But Stringbean is all old-time in his look and music choice, announcing that he will play "Pretty Polly," which he simply refers to as an "old folk song." Then magic begins as he looks down at Roni to say he will sing it to her, responding to her flirtation. She mimics his hand gesture when he stretches his arm out while singing, and he turns back toward her on seeing her and actually allows himself a half smile and shake of the head. It is a surprising and endearing moment when this man known for his stone face cannot help but smile at this young woman.

There is something extra fun about the performance as Roni continues her antics. The chemistry between her and Stringbean is perfect. After the number is over, Roni asks him, "Have you ever done any acting, String? I think you'd make a fantastic Romeo." String replies, "I appreciate it," and shakes his head, bringing audience laughter. "I'd make a good Juliette," she says, and he retorts, "Stick with me, kid, and we'll make a fortune." It is not just Roni but the entire family that adores him, though. When String talks about his playing in the folk scene at college campuses, Donna says, "He was in original folk. He was like Daddy, you know. Daddy was original folk, and he is. And I just love it." Donna refers to their father, Ernest "Pop" Stoneman, born in the 1893 and "the only country musician to record on both Edison cylinders and modern stereo albums."[3] Through it all, Stringbean stands tall in new glory, surrounded by young people who recognize and appreciate him as timeless, entertaining, unique, and inextricably tied to the banjo.

These were much-deserved laurels for a man who had endured so much and stayed true to himself the whole way. The year 1967 must have felt like a particularly transformative and sad time for David. On April 25, his brother Joe died, followed shortly by his father, James, on June 1, in Scottsboro, Indiana. Whatever friction had existed between father and son had apparently diminished by that time. With his father dead and his own career and position seemingly secure,

David came into an awareness of himself as being part of the elder generation. He told Grandpa, "You and I are about the last of the real old-timers. When we are gone, that'll be it."[4] Stringbean embraced his being a figure out of a lore-filled past, and, like Grandpa, he wore it well. He did much better than Frank Sinatra, who the next year on his television special *Francis Albert Sinatra Does His Thing* donned a glittering Nehru suit with a long frilly collar and tried to remake himself singing "Sweet Blindness" with the 5th Dimension. Stringbean, on the other hand, rather than trying and failing miserably to be part of a new wave, gave free rein to the uncanny mix of comedy and, in its authenticity, cool blend of being among young people who, themselves, embraced new musical directions while preserving their musical heritage.

In fact, Stringbean had become a bridge from the earliest days of country music's history until here in the psychedelic sixties. Grandpa bridged the eras too, as did Minnie Pearl, Roy Acuff, and others. But Stringbean had the unique honor of having been mentored by Uncle Dave, which tied him all the way back to the nineteenth century before there even was a Grand Ole Opry. String accepted this new status with quiet, becoming grace. He modeled stability, even when catastrophe struck. For example, when a promoter made off with concert money without paying any of the entertainers, String made up a jingle about it, singing, "Mr. Brown . . . has left town . . . with the green."[5] To be sure, he displayed signs of stardom, which included flashing that wad of money and riding in a new Cadillac. But that Cadillac was a work car, and String had worked hard for that money. Biff Colley related a story about Stringbean's car and its meaning in relation to his persona:

> You remember a story. . . . Backstage at the Opry, the guys, I think some of them may have been talking about the salary, the Opry salary, and some of them were saying we're going to have to talk to them about giving us more money to work on the Opry. And they were trying to get some support, and they stepped out the back of the old Opry house and String was passing by in that Cadillac. . . . A couple of three of them, some of them says, "String hold it, hold it let's go to the bosses at WSM and talk to them about raising our salary or we're going to quit. What do you think, String?" String said, "Boys, I came here a-walking."[6]

Just as the Stonemans saw Stringbean as an industry treasure, so Porter Wagoner continued to fawn over him. In a 1967 appearance, String enjoys a response from Porter similar to that on the Stonemans' show. Porter announces Stringbean as his "special guest," who is "one of my favorite friends in country music, my favorite entertainer." Porter explains that he even keeps a photo of String on his desk. He can hardly get through the introduction without laughing, even as he calls Stringbean "one of the greatest people I know" because the Kentucky Wonder is standing in a mouth-gaped pose across the way, causing audience laughter. String wears the same outfit of predominant pink, with glittering pants, he sported in the Stonemans' show. After Stringbean performed "Pretty Little Widow," Porter puts his arm around his shoulder and tells him, "We all love you on the show, and it's really a lot of fun anytime that you come to see us, believe me." At that point, in walks Roger Miller with two other musicians; as String throws his hand out in silent emphasis, Miller cannot help himself, laughing and also mimicking String's gestures. When Porter mentions that String gets better all the time, Roger adds, "Oh, I swear, and his music's improving. I really like it." Stringbean breaks in to announce that he will do "a heavy," Johnny Horton's "The Battle of New Orleans."

By this time, String was known around the country music family not only for carrying cash but also for his distrust of banks. The rumor began to spread that the couple had amassed a small fortune through their frugal living and kept it hidden at home. His friends worried. Jean Shepard remembered,

> Grandpa Jones come up to me right here at the Ryman Auditorium one Saturday night, and Grandpa said, "I want you to talk to him about carrying all this money around," and this—I didn't know anything, you know, and Grandpa said, "He'll carry thousands of dollars around on him," said, "He won't put no money in the bank," said "He don't trust banks."
>
> So String was sitting over there and he was puffing on his old pipe, you know, and [said] "No, I don't believe in banks. Banks will take your money." And I told him, I said, "Bean, banks are a lot different nowdays." I said, "You need, uh, you need to put your money in the bank," I said, "You know, the government insures money now." And he said, "Oh, is that right?" I said, "Yeah, they'll insure bank accounts, you know."
>
> So about two or three months later, something like that, we was sitting backstage here at the Ryman, and I walked over and sat down by String, and he was puffing on that old pipe, and he said, "Went to a banker today." I said, "Oh, did you?" [He] said, "Yeah," said, "I opened a couple of bank accounts."[7]

Shepard's story and subsequent revelations complicate the idea that String and Estelle refused to put money in banks under any circumstances. In addition to opening bank accounts, with a known one being the Bank of Goodlettsville, the couple put cash in bank strongboxes.[8] That said, both Stringbean and Estelle continued to carry large amounts of cash, and if flashing that wad had begun as a gag for String, as he grew wealthier he now began to populate that roll with authentic big bills. As for how much money the couple kept at home, current owner Brian Buchanan describes one high room back in the cave on the property with nails driven into the rock walls and wonders if the Akemans may have kept bags of cash hung up there, safe and dry. Tommy Scott was convinced that String and Estelle had multiple hiding places for their cash. The idea that the couple was squirreling away a lot of money grew more widespread in Nashville.

Despite their legendary frugality, the Akemans did splurge around this time. In their shared love of fishing, they acquired a cabin on Center Hill Lake about an hour and a half's drive from Nashville. Formed by the 1948 construction of Center Hill Dam by the Army Corps of Engineers, the lake spread like fingers of a hand around the middle-Tennessee hills. Grandpa and Ramona had bought a cabin there already. Bobby Anderson—the reporter who had gotten String some school show dates ten years earlier—had also now moved to Sparta, near the lake, as the new owner and publisher of the *Sparta Expositor*. When he heard about the Akemans buying the cabin, he went out to visit them. He was struck by the couple's continued daily thriftiness despite having the money to buy a second home. "You would have thought, by the act that Stringbean continued to play out, that they were near penniless and down to their last meal," Anderson recalled about watching them eat breakfast that morning. "He reached out for a napkin and tore it in half. After winking at Bill and me, he handed one-half to Estelle, keeping the other half for himself, then remarked in his own dry Kentucky drawl, 'Poor man's got to cut every corner he can, if he expects to get by.'" Anderson was not buying it: "Stringbean was indeed a thrifty individual," he allowed, "but he would never be considered needy."[9] Indeed, money was coming in at a steady rate, and Stringbean was about to be making bigger money than ever.

HEE HAW: 1969–1972

Canadians John Aylesworth and Frank Peppiatt got their show-business start in the radio-television department of the MacLaren Advertising Agency in Toronto. They transitioned into television with the Canadian Broadcasting Corporation's weekly television comedy show *After Hours*. They then went on to write for *The Jimmy Dean Show*, where they discovered the U.S. market for country-themed programming. The program they envisioned was a rural version of *Laugh-In*, and they joined forces with Sam Lovullo to make it a reality. They paired Buck Owens with String's friend and fan Roy Clark to cohost the show they called *Hee Haw* and set their plans to shoot it in Nashville at the CBS affiliate WLAC to be aired in 1969. While the show would introduce new young comics such as Lulu Roman and Junior Samples, it was anchored by veterans Archie Campbell, Minnie Pearl, and Grandpa Jones. It only made sense that Stringbean should be a part of the cast too.

The proposed show faced challenges that raised doubts for many in the cast, including String. Grandpa's son, Mark, remembered riding in the backseat while his dad drove Stringbean to go downtown to buy clothes for the new show.[10] The 1969 fashion did not quite fit the two men's signature looks, but they picked out what clothing they could, including a number of shirts with long collars. Looking at their new acquisitions, Stringbean told his old friend, "Well, if the show don't go, we sure got some nice big collars." While *Hee Haw*'s corniness presumably did not bother the likes of String and Grandpa, other cast members, including Buck and Roy, worried about the show demeaning country music and its fans. But the money was good, and they gave it a go, even if they too considered it something of a lark.

If many in the cast were unsure about the show's prospects, the writers at first could not figure out how best to use String. He certainly was funny looking. Lulu Roman, encountering these country stars for the first time, saw Stringbean dressed in his famous costume and thought, "What is that?" Laughing, she remembers, "There was a period in my life I was eating LSD, honey. And I remember I saw him, I thought, wow, one of them came to life. One of those people I thought I saw."[11] As wild as Stringbean looked, though, for whatever reasons, he did not easily fit into the writers' vision for the show until they struck on the idea of dressing him up like a scarecrow and putting him in the cornfield.

The cornfield segment was one of *Hee Haw*'s touches of creative genius, and String's role was unique. This recurring routine threaded through episodes in a fast-moving mash-up of jokes that the cast and visiting guest stars often botched. Anchored in the field, Stringbean stood in, rather ironically, for a kind of voice of reason as he critiqued the others' jokes and gaffes in his dry way. The very first episode in 1969 set the tone. After the introductory sequence, the next clip features a crow puppet cawing, while sitting on top of a scarecrow's hat. Stringbean is not visible at that point nor during rapid zooming clips that follow, even though the scarecrow itself looms in the background. But then, after a few of these clips, the scarecrow comes to life, Stringbean saying, "There's more corn around here than the whole state of Kansas," with perfectly pitched comic timing. No sooner do the words get out of his mouth than the crow puppet on his shoulder caws loudly in his ear. String dips his head as though the crow is pecking at him, the scarecrow *scared of the crow*. In a later visit to the cornfield,

String says, "That joke ain't nothing to crow about," again bringing the crow's screeching and then another quip: "I wish it'd rain, maybe this bunch would go home."

Stringbean's screen time is short in that opening episode. The other famous Opry comics get far more. Archie Campbell appears throughout the episode. Minnie Pearl gets an entire segment to herself in addition to skits. Likewise, Grandpa gets multiple speaking parts, including bits on the porch surrounding by demijohns and girls in Daisy Dukes, an extended scene sitting around the woodstove telling jokes, and his "Grandpa, What's for Supper?" But Stringbean got his name listed in the closing segments, and that sad-faced, dry-delivered scarecrow performance, along with that cawing crow, caught on immediately. Delivering his lines in his sad-faced, dry style, he became an instant icon. The crow on his shoulder did too, its caw provided by director Bill Davis, who said, "The thing I'm most proud of is to have been the voice of that angry crow on Stringbean's shoulder in the cornfield."[12]

When the opening season met with success, Stringbean went to work writing a song to celebrate—"Me and My Old Crow (Got a Good Thing Going)." "I used to hunt them old crows," String admits in the song, but things have changed because "now he helps me out on *Hee Haw*, he's the best friend I ever found." The refrain assures, "Me and that old crow, got a real good thing going. He helps me get a lot of laughs, my pocketbook's growing." String and the crow got to be such good buddies String took him fishing, only to see the crow "catch more fish than me." Still, when asked what he would take to do a show, Stringbean now demanded "Five hundred dollars for me, five hundred for my old crow." It is a number filled with almost childlike exuberance, a comic tune in which String laughs at himself while taking pure and genuine pleasure in finding success in such an unexpected way. The single was released in 1970 on the Nashville Nugget label (NR-1049), the B-side sporting his classic "Twenty Cent Cotton and Ninety Cent Meat." Pierce had by this time sold Starday to LIN Broadcasting, and while Starday-King (Pierce having merged Starday with King Records) continued releasing albums, including a compilation of previously released Stringbean recordings titled *Hee Haw Cornshucker* (NLP-2100), the company made fewer and fewer recordings and soon was liquidated.

String followed the success of his scarecrow bits on the show with his letters from home, which further cemented his iconic status. When the crew and cast gathered in the fall to record the next season, Stringbean went to John Aylesworth with a proposal. Hailing him as "Bossman," the scarecrow explained, "I sure do appreciate being on this show. I like bein' the scarecrow in the cornfield well enough, but I was wonderin' if I could do a little more than that. There's a routine I do called 'Letter from Home' that gets some good laughs, and I'd like to do some of 'em on *Hee Haw*."[13] Aylesworth agreed to see the routine and declared it "manna from heaven." It made a great complement to Grandpa's "What's for Supper?" routine. At first, String simply did his usual letter routine, but then he added something new. A cast member would ask if he had a missive. Thus prompted, String would reply, "Yeah, I've got it right here next to my heart, heart, heart," patting all of his pockets, starting with the one over that organ but winding up finding the letter often in his back pocket. It was pure gold.

High times had come to Stringbean, and he was enjoying every minute of it. His joy comes across on-screen. While he maintained his famous woe-is-me look and delivery in his scarecrow performances, he loosened up in his letter-from-home sequences. In an October 16, 1971, episode, Archie, Grandpa, Junior, Cathy Baker, and other cast members gather around as String delivers his "heart, heart, heart" catchphrase and reads his letter.[14] As had become common for him now, String wears glasses, the thick frames sometimes raised high above his ears, the lenses obscuring his eyes. Reading the salutation to "Stringbean," he confirms, "That's me." The news is that his uncle Frank is celebrating again, "celebrating the fourth with a fifth." Another revelation is that String's cousin Euell is a track star, so fast "he can turn off the light and jump in the bed before it gets dark." Euell was his real-life nephew's name, and Sam Dood's name also appears in String's letters. In this clip and others like it, String sits loose and relaxed, dressed in his overalls, the normally stern face smiling easily. Thin and bespectacled, his bad teeth showing, he comes across as more endearing than ever. More than ever, he seems the favorite easygoing uncle who teaches you fishing and makes you laugh and whose house you always want to visit.

In that clip, Stringbean is flanked by two of the program's famous beauties, Lisa Todd and Gunilla Hutton, and the presence of the *Hee Haw* women furnished a memorable story from Stringbean's time on the set. A perennial challenge for the program was finding the right way to dress these long-legged, buxom women. As Grandpa Jones put it, "The fans don't like to let the show get too risqué; every so often the producers get letters from people complaining about the girls' short shorts or low-cut blouses, and sure enough, the next taping session they'll raise the necklines and lower the hemlines. But gradually things start creeping back to where they were—until another bunch of letters comes in."[15] At one point in response to the public outcry about the women showing too much skin, Sam Lovullo ordered the wardrobe designer, Ed Sunley, to design more conservative clothing, and Sunley responded by dressing them in outfits that "were practically turtleneck sweaters."[16] The move brought a response from String.

"Boss, I need to talk to you," String said.

"What is it?"

"Holy Moses, boss, but the only thing I had left in life was that there 'Pickin' and Grinnin'." I'm always standing in the back 'cause I'm so tall, which gives me an opportunity to look down into them beautiful girls' bras whiles I'm doin' my lines. Now you've gone and taken this last pleasure away from me."[17]

While he may have intermittently lost the pleasure of eyeing *Hee Haw* women, Stringbean was enjoying life with Estelle both around Nashville and at their Center Hill Lake cabin. A postcard promoting Holmes Creek Boat Dock on the lake includes a photograph of String standing on the dock fishing, dressed in overalls and wearing his safari hard hat. The back of the card proclaims Center Hill Lake the "Bass Capital of the U.S.A." and identifies Stringbean by name. By this time, deck fishing was no longer necessary, as David and Estelle had bought a sixteen-foot Sea Devil Pro-Bass boat with a 65-horsepower Mercury motor for fishing excursions on the lake. Grandpa's son, Mark, remembered fishing with Stringbean there. At that time, String typically used a Hula Popper, a lure first invented in the 1940s. Poppers have cupped mouths that make a popping sound in the water, and the Hula Popper was so named because it wore what looked like a hula skirt. This popper worked best when swept side to side, and Mark remembers the bubble trail String left in the water. String was mainly after bass, and he believed in his maxim, "You can't catch fish without the line in the water."

String's fishing buddies continued to expand. He took Hank Williams's son, Hank Jr., out to the water, showing particular kindness to the young man in the difficult position of filling the shoes of the legend whose name he bore. Porter Wagoner became another fishing pal. Porter regularly experienced Stringbean's gag of calling and pretending to be the person on the other end of the line. The call to go fishing might come early, but only for the purpose of delay, as String would say in Porter's voice, "String, I don't believe we can go. It's a little too windy and a little too cold this morning. I will check with you later, String."[18] Grandpa got the same treatment: he recalled that during *Hee Haw* filming times, the phone would ring and he would answer only to "hear myself talking back. It was like an echo, only it wasn't an echo. I could hear myself, or something that sounded just so much like me that it wasn't funny, saying, 'All right, I'll come by and get you, String.'"[19]

Stringbean reserved another phone gag just for Grandpa. Back in the 1940s, Grandpa recorded a number called "Going Down the Country" based on an old Carter Family song that said, "Jeff David knew, when the cruel war begun, that he wouldn't be a Union man, or carry the Union gun." With that song in mind, Stringbean would call and, when Grandpa answered, would say, without salutation, "Now *what* was it old Jeff Davis knew?" If the call resulted in going off on a drive somewhere, then Stringbean might keep Grandpa entertained by taking off his hard-shell safari fishing hat and playing it like a banjo while singing "every old song you can imagine, and then some."[20]

When not fishing, Stringbean continued to enjoy live appearances. He did an interview with Reuben Powell and Bob Hyland for the Renfro Valley Tape Club backstage at the Memorial Hall in Springfield, Ohio, on March 28, 1970. The interview was intended to contribute to a special hundredth anniversary of Uncle Dave, but it focused on Stringbean and his career as well. Stringbean reflected on his career, including his experiences working with Uncle Dave, Charlie and Bill, and also recently on *Hee Haw*. Then, thinking about the many people who adored old-time music, he commented:

> Reuben, it's sure a pleasure to get to talk to the fine folks all over the country. I believe in old-time music. I've kept mine old-time. It will never be nothing but old-time as long as I have anything to do. When I get to where I can't play the old-time I'll quit. Boy, you'd be surprised how many college kids loves that old music. I played the University of Chicago two days, and that thing was sold out two months before I went in there. You know what they wanted to hear? "Pretty Polly." I done "Pretty Polly"—had to do it three times, I really did. In Chicago . . . I was headlining that show. There was people there from everywhere, you know, kids. And they'd set there, and you could hear a pin drop while you was a-working. They'd just sit there and watch you. It was the greatest audience I ever worked in.

Addressing the current state of country music, String noted that many people, including college students, saw the Opry as becoming "too modern." They would have to listen all night to hear just two or three really country songs.

Stringbean mentioned in the interview that Nugget would be releasing his new album shortly, *Me and My Ole Crow (Got a Good Thing Going)* (NRLP-102). Nugget took a different approach to marketing Stringbean than Starday had, and it promised an interesting future. Playing up Stringbean's cartoonish image, the album's cover sports artwork by Randy Mincey, with a caricature of "Stringbean Star of the Hee-Haw Show" in a boat with his crow fishing. String wears his signature hat but this time also wears overalls. He holds his banjo away from a fish jumping out of the water, shielding his instrument with his lifted leg. It is the crow who has hooked the fish, however. The crow holds a bamboo rod as opposed to String's more expensive-looking rod and reel. The crow smiles, its

legs crossed, a cigar held between its toes. The back cover sports an old photograph of Stringbean and with it a write-up by Hank Jr.: "I couldn't begin to
count the many times I've stood in the crowded wings backstage and watched
a long lean man wearing his britches round his knees, casually walk out, flip
his funny little hat, strike his faithful 5-string banjo and start an explosion of
applause and laughter from the audience, as well as me." Extolling Stringbean,
this son of a legend assures buyers, "I take special pride in not only being a fan,
but a collector, like so many others, of all the Stringbean recordings." After listing his favorite songs on the album, Hank Jr. writes, "They say we're living in
the space age but it sure feels good to have Stringbean to bring us back to the
earth age with his banjo and songs."

The recordings are arguably Stringbean's best. Naturally, it kicks off with "Me
and My Old Crow," but after that comes "Shake That Little Foot Sally Ann" and
Bill Monroe's "It's Mighty Dark for Me to Travel" before launching into String's
signature, "Pretty Polly," now renamed "Polly Are You Mad." Side 1 finishes up
with yet another appearance of "Twenty Cent Cotton and Ninety Cent Meat."
Side 2 begins with "Herdin' Cattle" followed by the rousing "Fire on the Mountain," which Stringbean makes his own with certain tweaks in the tune. With
"Going Up Sourwood Mountain," String offers up a fine take on a traditional
tune. Then comes "That's What I Like about the South," celebrating everything
from a southern drawl to candied yams and black-eyed peas. Stringbean fills
in with exclamations of "Come on, Five!" and "Earl Scruggs may be listening at
you." Next comes perhaps the most brilliant interpretation of Stringbean's career
in his morphing Little Richard's "Long Tall Sally" into his own style. String roars
out that Sally has *got* everything Uncle John needs, bringing this rock standard
into a whole new context. His bluesy performance of "Nine Pound Hammer"
is no less deft and entertaining. Hank Jr. got it right when he said on the cover,
"I believe this album tops them all." Given the direction Stringbean was going,
the best was yet to come with his recording career.

Even as he continued to push the boundaries of his music, Stringbean continued to carry the banner for old-time music on the Opry in the midst of the
Nashville Sound's chokehold on the city. The Opry cast continued to grow, with
1971 seeing the arrival of Jan Howard, still in deep grief over the loss of her son
in Vietnam. She quickly grew close to Stringbean and Estelle. Paul Hemphill,
capturing the Opry in that moment in his lyrical, tactile way, left us an evocative
portrait of Stringbean during this time:

> And in the runway leading from the dressing rooms to the stage, a popular old-
> time banjo picker named Stringbean (David Akeman, really) leans against the

wall in the costume he has worn on the Opry for 25 years: trousers sewn to the tail of an extra-long shirt, the belt just above his knees, making him appear four feet long from the waist up and two feet from the waist down. "Yah, it happened, all right," he was saying. "I was on this TV show in Chicago, and some engineer up in a booth looked at his monitor and said, 'There ain't no way.' When he tried to adjust the thingamajig, whatever you call it, he messed up a million TV sets." Jim Ed Brown was introducing Stringbean now, so he broke off his story and dashed onto the stage to do his first number of the night.[21]

Whatever trends may have reigned in Nashville, people loved Stringbean more and more. That affection shines forth in an appearance on *Dell Reeves' Country Carnival*.[22] After String plays "Me and My Old Crow," Reeves comes weaving over, laughing, cigarette in hand, telling String, "We look forward, each time, for your visit. All the boys and the nice folks, too." Reeves then asks String what he has been doing, to which String replies, "I've been watching television." String has been watching exercising, he explained, but his wife has been watching "them recipes" on her TV in the kitchen. The two televisions going at once had gotten mixed up, and String reads what he had written down while trying to take in recipes and exercise instructions simultaneously. The resulting "recipe" jumbles the two shows cleverly and also suggestively, leading off with, "Lie flat on your back and grease your pan well." As String reads through the list—"Inhale deeply one teaspoon full of baking powder" and "Pour two tablespoons of salt between the movements of arms and legs" and "Always sit in upright position so your batter won't spill"—Reeves cannot catch his breath for laughing. When String finishes, Dell tells him, "String, you been a-watching the wrong show, Chief." The show closes with Stringbean standing in his costume contrasting sharply with the other cast members in their sequin-festooned seventies-style clothing. It is a powerful visual that vivifies Stringbean as an acronym comfortable with any trend, including those not yet dreamed of in philosophy.

OPRYLAND: 1972–1973

Big changes were afoot at the Opry. Downtown Nashville had been growing increasingly rougher since before the decade had started. People standing in line at the Ryman on Fridays and Saturdays encountered prostitutes, drug dealers, and drunks. The Ryman itself was showing wear under the trampling of capacity crowds, and the lack of adequate parking and air-conditioning were concerns for the organizers. Plans began to be discussed for a new Grand Ole Opry house, a state-of-the-art building set far away from urban decay. In 1969 WSM president

Irving Waugh visited AstroWorld in Houston, Texas, paying close attention to the way the theme park brought crowds in every day to complement the programming at the Astrodome. Why should Nashville not do the same with the Opry? he thought. Shortly thereafter, WSM purchased Rudy's Farm along Briley Parkway, away from the urban scene. There would be built the new Grand Ole Opry House and, with it, a theme park called Opryland USA.

Opryland opened on May 27, 1972. Visitors were greeted with rides such as the Timber Topper roller coaster and the Flume Zoom log ride. But the real emphasis was on musical entertainment of many varieties, from bluegrass to old-time jazz to rock and roll. The performances were top-notch, the performers themselves drawn from the superbly talented pool of musicians drawn to Nashville in hopes of success in the recording studios on Sixteenth Avenue. Along with these daily shows, Opryland booked big stars, and Stringbean started making regular appearances. This brought him yet another revenue stream along with constant Opry appearances.

Mark Jones was seventeen when Opryland opened, and he too sought a position in a show there.[23] He practiced hard on his audition number, "Mountain Whippoorwill," a complicated piece on the banjo that used fancy playing up and down the neck. Before going to the audition, he decided to run it by his father's best friend. He went to Stringbean's dressing room, and the older man sat and listened quietly as the teenager moved his hand all the way up the neck, playing chimes and complex runs. When he finished, he asked his father's buddy what he thought. Stringbean replied, "Little man, you done well. But there ain't no money past the fifth fret."

While String performed live onstage in Opryland, in August movie screens across the country presented a portrait of an Appalachian space conspicuous for banjo playing in *Deliverance*. The banjo-playing kid on the porch, portrayed by Billy Redden, bore a distant resemblance to Stringbean when he smiled, showing a similar set of teeth. Redden also captured the mysteriousness Stringbean evoked, a distance that Stringbean softened by making it inviting but that carried the whiff of Appalachian secrecy and aloofness. In a scenario reminiscent of the one that precipitates the action of *Deliverance*, Grandpa and String discussed how land prices skyrocketed when slated for flooding by damming rivers. When String commented he wished he had bought some of that land to sell to the government, Grandpa quoted Alexander Pope's line, "Hope springs eternal in the human breast: / Man never is, but always to be, blessed." Stringbean replied, "Yeah, and he's a turkey all the way."[24]

The *Hee Haw* cast continued its twice-a-year filming. The set stayed lively, with the men playing pranks on each other, the most common being flicking Bic lighters against each other's rears and running away before the burning sensation hit. For holidays, especially, cast members would gather at Grandpa's or Stringbean's house, where Ramona and Estelle would cook and cast members would bring dishes from Kroger, since they were typically staying in hotels. "Those were really precious days," Lulu Roman says, recalling those occasions, "because at the end of it, it would always end up being us singing. We'd be sitting and sing, sometimes for hours. Talk about precious memories, it was precious memories." For Lulu, who had grown up in an orphanage, String and Estelle seemed like what she imagined favorite aunts, uncles, or cousins to be. One of those holiday gatherings especially stays with her: "I remember one time, we were all having such a good time singing and carrying on and eating, we looked up and realized that it was just snowing everywhere! Everybody was like, 'Hey listen, how are we going to get back to the hotel?' Grandpa and String are going, 'You are!'"

The *Hee Haw* cast was known to party hard, but Stringbean did not. "String wasn't a drinking man," Grandpa wrote. "He would drink a little beer, but never Canadian beer; he thought it tasted too much like home brew, and he had gotten sick on home brew once when he was a kid up in Kentucky."[25] According to Grandpa, they would sometimes pick up Old Tankard on their fishing trips. But just one beer would get Stringbean drunk and set him talking your ear off, which put him totally out of character. In his normal sober state, Stringbean could ride in a car for hours without saying a word, more likely to start singing than actually to talk. A 1964 photograph of Stringbean with Earle Rose may capture one of his rare drunk moments, his face twisted in unusual expressiveness in midspeech while he holds up a can in his right hand and a sandwich in his left.[26] But it is unclear what the can is, and he could have been just fooling around in front of the camera with a soft drink.

As 1973 progressed amid continued social and political unrest, fashions now ironically favored the Stringbean look. Cars had lengthened into lean bodies with sharp edges, and the Akemans' new 1974 model Cadillac that year was green, with a fancy green interior done up in "Jasper" Maharajah–style upholstery.[27] Men's and women's styles followed the same pattern, with tight shirts and pants that fell in sharp, straight tightness to the knees where they flared out. The fashionistas may not have been wearing Liberty overalls, as Stringbean now often did, but they had turned toward greater informality than ever, with suits even seeming less dressy. Long and lean was attractive, perhaps nowhere better captured than in the illustrations of Robert McGinnis, whose poster design for *Live or Let Die* released in July epitomized what the moment said was sexy in Roger Moore's first go at portraying James Bond.

To the cast of *Hee Haw* now came Roni Stoneman. String got her playing banjo on the show, introducing her as "My little friend from woman's lib, Roni Stoneman!" Fond of the show's older comedians, she noticed String and Grandpa reading the *Foxfire* books.[28] She also grew close to String and Estelle, and Estelle told her about how they would fill empty cans with cash and put them in the refrigerator's freezer. Roni took note that Stringbean went about armed, carrying a cowboy-style .22 revolver with the ironic name Colt Peacemaker. Roni remembers him patting his pocket to indicate "my friend."[29] She claimed Stringbean now was carrying large amounts of cash, as she remembers Roy Clark jokingly asking how much he would take for his britches, String claiming to have as much as $75,000 in his pocket. Aware of this wealth, Roni urged String to take Estelle to the French Riviera, explaining, "From what I was told, they don't wear bathing suits over there," which brought a grin.[30]

When not working, Stringbean found opportunities to visit friends. Over the years, String and Estelle had often gone to Toccoa, Georgia, to visit Tommy and Frankie Scott and hunt and fish with Tommy's father. String especially liked to bring game he had caught or killed, hoping Frankie could cook it for him. "Tell Frankie I sure would love some gravy and biscuits to go with this meat," he would tell Tommy, calling ahead to let them know what he was bringing.[31] Scott remembered the last time he saw String and Estelle. The visit was particularly sweet because the Scotts' daughter, Sandra, now married, had kept her children home from school in order to see Stringbean and say good-bye as they left. The Akemans got into the car to leave, but then something unusual happened, perhaps a premonition.

> His wife pulled the car out of the driveway, and then she stopped, and Stringbean got out. To the surprise and delight of all of us, he did one of his performances right there for the kids. When he was finished, he tipped his hat and said, "I usually get paid thousands of dollars for that act, but for you it is free!" He got back in the car, the shimmer of tears in all our eyes, as they drove away.[32]

At home, String and Estelle continued to enjoy their time together, with Opry family, and with the people in their vicinity. The fishing with Grandpa, Porter, Bill Carlisle, and others continued both on rivers and at Center Hill Lake. For these excursions, String and Estelle took their nonwork vehicle, a 1972 Ford Torino station wagon. Sometimes the Willis brothers would come along, and Skeeter provided fresh vegetables from his garden, about which he was especially passionate. Bashful Brother Oswald (Pete Kirby) remained a constant friend, as did Archie Campbell, and Tex Ritter joined so many others in having irrepressible affection for the Kentucky Wonder. String formed an especially close connection with one of their neighbors, Laurence Burnette, who went by the nickname "Bear." He and his wife, Ruby, lived about five hundred yards north of the Akemans, their names strikingly similar to the former renters who had had a shoot-out years before. Helping String around the farm from time to time, Bear thought of him as a father figure. He started calling String "Pa," and String started calling him "Son."

As a testament to Stringbean's becoming an institution, his likeness was being preserved in commercial representation. A chalkware figure of String-bean was produced by Harry Wright of Cave City, Kentucky, taking its place among statuettes of other Opry stars such as Grandpa Jones and Roy Acuff.[33] In a similar vein, a Madisonville, Tennessee, company, Topsy Turvy Toy, Inc., started manufacturing a Stringbean limberjack doll. String was one of a select number of country stars, including Grandpa, Acuff, Archie Campbell, and others, whose likenesses were silkscreened onto wood and a stick stuck in their backs. A child playing with them could manipulate the sticks so that the jointed legs danced.

In yet another sign of success, Stringbean found himself the attention of a journalist named Genevieve Waddell, who interviewed him for a piece in *Country Song Roundup*. Speaking to her of his life and career, String related some recent occurrences that he believed confirmed that his fame crossed racial lines. He told of driving into Nashville one day and encountering two African American little girls who saw him and Estelle and mimicked his "heart, heart, heart" routine. String also told Waddell that in Houston, he had checked into a hotel that Isaac Hayes was leaving. Hayes shook String's hand, and String said, "He knowed me right off from *Hee Haw* and said he was a big fan of mine. Loves the show and we talked about it."[34] Bill Anderson recalled String's pride in African American audience members, prompting the Kentucky Wonder to declare, "Chief, I am hot in all fields." String described the diversity of his audience in rural and urban terms, too. "And big business men," he said. "Doctors and lawyers just love us." Even local Vanderbilt University hosted String along with a number of bluegrass acts that fall, the Nashville elite that had once looked down on country musicians having changed. "Now they can't get enough of us!"[35]

In the article she was writing, Waddell also focused on the fact that kids loved Stringbean. She saw part of the appeal being in his costume and persona, but Stringbean saw another reason. "Young'uns have gone crazy over banjo pickin'," he explained. "I reckon there's a million or more of kids under twelve with a banjo. Everywhere I go I run into 'em, wantin' to know how to play one." Stringbean knew that fascination with the banjo, having felt it from his own childhood. All these years later, Stringbean could see how the banjo drew people together. Pete Seeger got it, writing on his banjo head, "This Machine Surrounds Hate, and Forces it to Surrender." Stringbean's African American fans may not have been so keen on him had they known about his days playing blackface. But, then again, maybe the banjo's power is such as to bring everyone together, whatever their pasts. Like the instrument he loved, String invited people into his circle. He even revealed to Waddell that he had an interest in playing only venues where the crowd could be close to him. "That's why I like Opryland," he said. "Folks can come up close to the stage and make their pictures. Same way at the Opry house. I'll be hurt if that same feelin' ain't kept in the new Opry house. You don't get paid much for workin' either place but there' somethin' pretty special about the Grand Ole Opry and Opryland too."

String gave Waddell insight into where his life stood and where it was headed. His health was excellent, he told her. "I couldn't recommend a doctor if I had to. I ain't never had one and don't aim to get one if I can help it. I just plan to keep on eatin' and sleepin' and livin' like I do." He loved *Hee Haw*—"We're just like a family"—and he had just signed on with Don Light's talent agency because "Don knows which colleges want us and that's the best place to go right now." He and Estelle's marriage was great, he said. He joked that she was "the only woman I know that can swallow a banana sideways" but also commented, "I think marriage is a 50-50 situation. Can't have your own way all the time. I got to consider her feelings, too." After the interview, Waddell wrote the article, and *Country Song Roundup* put it in the pipeline for publication.

With all his success and visibility, Stringbean's carrying cash worried his friends more than ever. Mark Jones remembered his father constantly telling Stringbean not to carry that money. Lulu remembers Archie Campbell speaking sternly to Stringbean. "You need to stop that," Archie would say. "Somebody's going to hurt you." For all the great, extravagant lengths David and Estelle had gone to save money, they were not as careful to protect it. They had an attorney now, William Faimon, but they did not direct him to draw up a will or designate to whom their fortune should go upon their deaths. If they wrote a will themselves or had another lawyer write one, Faimon never knew of it. They thought their money safe in their bank accounts and hiding places on the farm.

There may have been some truth to the perception that the Akemans' fortune had grown to immense proportions. According to Tommy Scott, "Slowly but surely he and Estelle saved and saved until one day he called me and told me he reached his goal" of making $1 million. The typically cryptic String did not come out and say he literally had $1 million in cash now. "The main reason I know this is because Lonzo and Oscar once tried to get me to invest in a cave they were going to buy and develop into an attraction," Tommy wrote. "I passed, but suggested they call String. String passed saying he couldn't right now." But, Tommy went on, "It wasn't but a few months when String called me and said he now had exceeded his goal, and he wanted to invest some of the money above that amount and wondered if I thought the cave deal would be good and still open. I told him to give Oscar a call and see if the deal was already made."[36]

Oscar took String up to the cave in Park City, Kentucky, in the Mammoth Cave area.[37] By this time, the amusement park, called Caveland Country Park, was open. Looking the attraction over, String pulled out his roll of money, which included three $1,000 bills, jokingly implying he might buy a share of the park. Like a lot of people, Oscar worried about that wad of bills bearing Grover Cleveland's profile, but String laughed and assured him that if anybody tried to rob him, "I'll give it to them, Chief, before I let them kill me." Later, in the fall and possibly as late as the first week of November 1973, String called and said he was not interested in buying into the park, per se, but that he did have $17,000 in cash he wanted to loan. Oscar told him they could not accept that loan unless he had put it in a bank, and then he presented the proposal to the Caveland Summer Music Park corporate board. Stringbean went to the board meeting in person and showed his wad of cash.

Among the people present at that board meeting was a man named Charlie Brown. He was born Charles in 1944, but he would always go by Charlie, like the character who became famous in the 1950s when he was growing up. At age ten, Charlie had moved with his parents, Henry and Marie, and younger brothers, Roy, Doug, and Jimmy, whom they called Jimbo, to a farm on Route 3 near Greenbriar, a little more than three miles up the road from the Akemans' farm. As a boy, Charlie played with his brothers and their cousin John, whom they called Tootsie, in a pond on Walker Bloodworth's farm along Ebenezer Road. Charlie grew into young adulthood and opened a welding and steel shop in Greenbrier. Now, at age twenty-nine, his business concerns reached beyond steel fabrication to the country music industry.

Along with his investing in Caveland, another revenue stream for Charlie's household came from the All-Star Talent Agency, which his wife, Joyce, owned and operated.[38] This business brought him and Joyce into regular contact with country music entertainers.[39] Grandpa and Ramona were friends with Charlie, and Mark was in the same class at Greenbriar High School with Jimbo. Also in the circle of acquaintances were Bill Carlisle, and he and Oscar led Stringbean to sign on with All-Star.[40] While String and Estelle were not close to Charlie and Joyce, they did have a working relationship, the two couples at one point going out to lunch together.[41] It was common for stars to work with multiple agents simultaneously, so String may have been working with Don Light, All-Star, and others as well.

Another new addition to Stringbean's professional team was Curt Gibson. After years of working with George Morgan, Curt began playing guitar for String in early 1973. Curt could follow String's playing onstage consistently, which was not easy because String would often improvise, holding some notes longer than expected and others shorter while varying the rhythm. The connection between the two men surpassed music, for they had both grown up poor and made it to the Opry. "I guess they saw themselves in each other," Curt's son, Steve, observes. "My father was one of the few people that Stringbean really trusted. Stringbean considered himself a good judge of character, and he just had a good feeling about my Dad."[42] This sense of trust translated into String trying often over the years to get Curt to move his family into Grandpa's old house (the Burdette shoot-out had taught him the importance of having renters he did not have to worry about). Curt had always refused, wanting to live in the city.

Now that Curt was working for String, the latter went to work again trying to convince the guitarist to move next door. Steve remembers going with his parents out to take a look at the big white house next to the Akemans' in May and again in August 1973: "When we got there, Stringbean was sitting on his front porch, wearing a turtle-shell hat, shelling string beans." Thirteen years old at the time, Steve did not want to move out of their rented two-room house on Dickerson Road. In fact, he marveled that a big country star's home would be smaller than the one his family lived in. Steve objected to moving mainly because he had to live within the city limits in order to play baseball for Music City Mobile Homes and the Parkwood Men's Club. Stringbean, hoping to persuade the parents by persuading the boy, tried to find common ground by telling about his baseball-playing days. "He told me a tall-tale about a runner that tried to steal second-base," Steve recollects. "String claimed he threw the ball between the pitcher's legs and got the runner out at second, without even getting up off of his knees to make the throw. I think he was testing me to see if I would believe him, but he said it with a completely straight face."[43] Stringbean also took Steve around his farm, showing him his corn and other crops and extolling the virtues of farming.

One of the chief selling points in Stringbean and Estelle's pitch was that their home in the country was far safer than the Gibsons' current residence. Dickerson Road had become especially rough, with a heavy drug scene. The move to the bucolic countryside brought safety, String argued. "I think I could leave a bucket of money on the front porch and come back at the end of a summer tour and it would still be there," Estelle told Curt's wife.[44] They showed Steve the room he would have, but he was not interested. In the end, String and Estelle failed to convince the Gibson family, and they stayed in town. Stringbean scrawled Curt's phone number on the chalkboard hanging on the wall beside the phone so he could summon him.

With his new guitar player who also now drove him, String made several appearances at Opryland through the summer. More distant venues required staying in hotels, and on one of those occasions, in North Carolina, when a maid came early and saw Stringbean still asleep in bed, she found him familiar but could not quite recall who he was. "Your, your, your, your [*sic*] . . .," she said, and String opened his eyes and said, "Heart, heart, heart, heart." "Yes, that's who you are!" she exclaimed.[45] June 22–24, 1973 saw Stringbean at Lester Flatt's Mount Airy Festival in North Carolina, in an event that brought together a number of String's old friends: Mac Wiseman, Clyde Moody, and Howdy Forrester. Apparently, Stringbean's drop-thumb picking did not bother Lester anymore.

String and Curt performed at college campuses also that summer. At one college date, the crowd did not respond well, prompting String to tell Curt, "Chief, I believe they took me serious."[46] But in another show, the college-student audience took him just as he wanted. As he finished up the show, the crowd roared its approval. Feeling the adoration, String turned to Curt and said, "He who plays the five, rules the world."

GOODBYE SWEET THING

Stringbean's Final Day of Life, November 10, 1973

The best thing about cold mornings is wood burning in the fireplace.[1] *The wood pops, tossing sparks into the shadows of the hearth like hands thrown in praise that dissipate, swift and irrevocable. Wood smoke and pipe tobacco blend with the salty tang of country ham cooking in a cast-iron skillet for breakfast to form a fine aroma wafting mellow and thrilling in the cold, slanting sunlight from windows.*

This cold morning, voices sound from the TV in the kitchen, while the tiny white budget plastic RCA radio brings in voices from Nashville. The leather of what is now a brown armchair creaks as String stands up and walks to the phone. He lifts the phone receiver and dials: Zzzzip-tick-tick-tick-tick-tick; zip-tick-tick; zzzip-tick-tick-tick-tick. When Grandpa answers, String mimics his voice as usual.

"Hello."

"Hey, String, I'll pick you up in the morning."

"Yeah, I'll remember, String, in the morning."

"All right, String, see you at the Opry."

"Yep, we'll see you tonight, String."

The receiver sounds in metallic suspiration settling back in place.

*   *   *

After breakfast String calls his neighbor Bear to come over and help him cut firewood. Then String heads out into the cold on this Saturday morning. Stepping over the frosty ground, he carries a yellow McCullough chain saw, with an automatic oiler. A new Opry buddy gave him one just like it, but with a manual oiler, so String traded it in for this one. The buddy's name is Jerry Clower, from Yazoo City, Mississippi. A big man with a puff of hair, Jerry used to sell fertilizer and has only recently "backed in to show business," as he puts it, by telling stories funny. He has just joined the Opry's cast, and the McCullough company gave him a chain saw for promotional purposes because he tells a story about Marcel Ledbetter who carved up a county-line joint with a McCullough for not serving him. Like David, Jerry is true country, the only person countrier Jerry has ever met being Loretta Lynn.

"Hey, Pa," Bear says, arriving to help.

"Hey, Son."

They go to work cutting, fresh-sawn wood smell arising as chips and sawdust fly into the breath-smoked air while smoke curls up from the chimney at the house. Stringbean wears gloves to work on this cold morning.

*   *   *

Later in the day, Stringbean puts the case with his Vega No. 9 and some hotel stationery with songs written on them in the trunk of the Cadillac. After laying the case down inside, he sets beside it a satchel that holds his costume, some checks he has not gotten around to cashing yet, and one of his .22 revolvers. He wears a black jacket, striped shirt, and overalls with a wad of $3,182, made up of thirty $100 bills, nine $20 bills, and two $1 bills, a substantial roll. Estelle waits in the driver's seat, wearing a black-and-white-checked coat, black pants, and black loafers with red linings. She has $2,150 pinned to her bra.

String checks his Waltham watch as he closes the Cadillac's green door. Estelle presses her foot on the accelerator, and they start down the long driveway, gravel spitting from the tires. She spins the green steering wheel to turn right onto Baker Station Road and make the half-hour drive to downtown Nashville.

*   *   *

The excitement of the Opry never dulls, even after all these years. Tonight, the crowds pack in as usual at the Ryman amid a jumble of tuning strings, voices conversing, and microphones popping and ringing through checks. Stringbean and Estelle find a seat around the table backstage and talk with Grandpa and Ramona and other folks. While String and Grandpa discuss their hunting-trip plans, Estelle and Oscar Sullivan's wife talk about crime being on the rise in the city. "You never know when someone might knock you in the head or something just for your money," Estelle says.[2] String tells Grandpa he is not sure he really does want to go up to Virginia with the weather so cold.[3] He adds that he would rather leave at seven instead of five in the morning, as Grandpa does. They split the difference and agree to leave at six.

String talks with other folks backstage. He, Bill Carlisle, and Metro police lieutenant R. L. Ezell, who works security at the Opry, discuss the recent shooting of a patrolman, Ray Wheeler. "Hoss, nowadays you can't tell who you're turning your back on," Stringbean says.[4]

*   *   *

On the stage, Stringbean plays in the 7:00 segment sponsored by Rudy's and hosted by Tex Ritter. Tex takes a long time introducing String. String sings "Hillbilly Fever." Then he invites the audience of three thousand to sing "Y'All Come" with him. The crowd gets so fired up—especially the college kids who love old-time banjo—that Tex beckons String out for an encore.[5]

The first show of the evening ends at 9:00. A young freelance reporter named Stacy Harris makes her way backstage, trying to get an interview with Bobby Bare. She has no luck but does spot String "looking mournful." She does not recognize him. He surprises her when he tells her she can interview him; he even seems anxious for an interview.[6] *She agrees, learning his stage name and how he got it so many years back from Asa.*

Stringbean reflects on his career and tells Harris how happy he is about "Hee Haw." He may not have been sure about the name at first, but he is grateful for the money, which is more than he is worth, he says modestly. Concerning the new Opry building, he thinks that while it will be more convenient and comfortable, the Opry itself might "lose a little of the old flavor." He also tells about his playing to college-student audiences, mentioning Vanderbilt, Western Kentucky, and institutions in North Carolina, marveling that the students know "more about old tunes than I do, and I've been playing them all my life."

Listening to the older man speak, another question occurs to Harris: What does he want out of life? "There ain't too much, I don't guess," he says. "I don't want to just plumb retire. I could—but I enjoy it. I love people. I enjoy meeting the people and talking to them. Signing autographs." Then he adds, "I went a lot further than I ever thought I would. A thousand times. I accomplished more than I ever thought I could. I never did think I'd make as much money as I did. I just figured if I got along and made a living I'd be satisfied. But I've been lucky, I guess."

*   *   *

The second show starts at 9:30, and Stringbean's second appearance comes in the fifteen-minute segment sponsored by Union 76, starting at 10:15. Again, Tex headlines the segment, kicking off with his lilting song "There's a New Moon over My Shoulder." When the audience applause dies down, he introduces String. Again, Tex takes longer than usual with his introduction.

"Since being on 'Hee Haw,' his price has gone up and his pantaloons have gone down a little," Tex says, prompting laughter. "He's got Curt Gibson here driving him around now."

Waiting in the wings, String says to those around him about tonight's earlier appearance, "Tex finally got me on after fifteen minutes of introduction." It is getting toward 10:25, and String yawns.[7]

Finally, Tex waves Stringbean on. String does his funny waddling walk out to the microphone and swings his arm up into his Babe Ruth pose.[8] Even with the delay, String pauses at the microphone to say, "How sweet it is!" The crowd roars, flashbulbs exploding from cameras lined along the front of the stage.

String tears into a frailing intro of his oldie "Going to the Opry to Make Myself a Name." Then, he plays "Hot Corn, Cold Corn." String finishes with his famous hat flip and slinks off the stage in his nodding way.

Before heading to the dressing room, String calls Curt over and says why don't they run through one of the numbers for next week. String plays that tremolo he uses often for waltz-time church songs, the Vega's sharp, bright sound cutting over the soft buzzing of Curt's fingers sliding on the guitar's strings. The song is "Lord I'm Coming Home."

* * *

When they finish the run-through, String walks to the dressing room. He does not take long to change into his overalls and wipe down the Vega No. 9 before putting it in its case. Zipping the case up and grasping its handle, he heads out to join Estelle. They are heading on home on this cold night, since he wants to get rest before that early start in the morning with Grandpa.

Roni Stoneman and Little Jimmy Dickens join Stringbean as he walks toward the door to go outside.[9] Both feeling a premonition, they tell him to be careful. "I've got my friend," he assures them, patting the pocket holding the revolver. "Well, I'll be seeing you, boys and girls," he says. "String, please take care of yourself," Roni says and hugs him. "Yes, String, be careful," Jimmy says. String heads out the door, speaking to one of the usherettes, Deb Faulkner.[10]

Watching him leave, Roni and Jimmy feel danger in their bones. They are both mountain people, and they have a strong intuition born of their Appalachian heritage. "You know, Jim," Roni says, "I hate to see them go. I'm worried a little bit." Jimmy looks at her and says, "I am too."

Skeeter Willis wants to head home too. He played at the beginning of the second show and changed in the dressing room he has changed in with String for years. He could hear String playing onstage over the air-conditioner. Once dressed, Skeeter headed out to his car only to find that some wag had pasted a Grand Ole Opry sign onto his windshield.[11] It took him a good five or ten minutes getting that poster off.

Finally, he did, but with the delay, now as he pulls out of the alleyway, he sees String and Estelle getting ready to leave. "I hear you're going hunting in the morning," Skeeter says.[12] Stringbean confirms he is. "Have a good week," Skeeter says, and drives off. The time is about 10:40. When he gets to Fourth and Broad, Skeeter remembers he forgot to deliver some peppers and tomatoes he had canned out of his garden for someone at the Opry.[13] He turns around and heads back, noticing that String and Estelle have left.

⋆   ⋆   ⋆

A little more than an hour later, the final minutes of November 10 tick away. Outside, Estelle lies in the cold, shot in the back and the head, just like the poor Ellen Smith her husband has sung about. She lies facedown, her body twisted, her face delved in the grass, one shoe off, her traumatized body settling into the beginnings of its ultimate breakdown.

On the porch, quiet and still, the Vega No. 9 sits in its black case, the sable hue fitting for this night's deeds. Its wood grains and metal pieces have resonated with awful sounds antithetical to the instrument's purpose. Instead of ringing to joy and togetherness, the banjo has chilled to fear, violence, and separation.

Inside the house, David lies stretched across the floor in front of his leather chair and fireplace. The pocketbook his old crow helped him swell has been taken along with his costume, the very physique of Stringbean. His glasses lie on the floor, no longer needed to read letters from home, for a bullet has stopped forever the beating of his heart, heart, heart.

SINNER MAN, WHERE YOU GONNA HIDE
November 1973-January 1974

CRIME SCENE: NOVEMBER 11, 1973

Stringbean's murder cast him in a new, tragic role. After decades of navigating hardship through massive cultural, technological, and musical change, David Akeman's life was cut off brutally. But the Stringbean entity now had to adapt to a new identity in ways David himself could do nothing to affect. In a moment when David's music was reaching new heights and his star was burning brighter than ever, Stringbean instantly transformed from someone destined to be an Opry legend into an Opry legend remembered for being murdered. At the same time, the benign goodness and simple happiness Stringbean projected fueled his recasting into a symbolic character of innocence destroyed by characters symbolic of evil. The resulting dark fable resonated so powerfully that it threatened to overshadow Stringbean's achievements in and contributions to country music's history and development.

The sense of immense, cosmic wrong emerged immediately, its pathos laced through the unfolding of the murder's aftermath and investigation. Grandpa surely felt it as he stood over String's body that Sunday morning after discovering Estelle lying dead in the field. He also understood that something must be done. Flicking his blue eyes up to the phone on the wall, he saw that the wire had been cut. He ran back out to his car and hurried home to call the Tennessee State Highway Patrol. Sensing something amiss, Mark made his way downstairs in time to hear his father tell what had happened.

Once Grandpa gave the details, he drove to the intersection of Highway 41 and Baker Station Road where, after a twenty-five-minute wait, a state patrolman arrived. Grandpa led the way to the Akemans' home.[1] Seeing that the murder had taken place in Davidson County, where the state patrol did not have homicide jurisdiction, the trooper called the Davidson County Metropolitan Police Department. The department had been created in 1963 as part of Nashville's consolidation of the entire county government. It was underfunded and called upon to serve five hundred square miles, a daunting if not impossible task. Housed in the former city meat market, Metro had yet to increase the staffing to compensate for taking on the greater territory of the entire county. The detectives had to make their own evidence kits.[2]

Whatever its limitations, Metro swung into action. Leading the investigation was Detective Sherman Nickens, a burly thirty-eight-year-old, born the same year David Akeman acquired his stage name. Nickens had a sharp voice with a heavy middle-Tennessee accent. His thinning hair on top was counterbalanced by a longish waving swoop in the back. He could act decisively and was not afraid to use whatever methods necessary to get results. He and pudgy plainclothesman Bobby Green were the first to head to the Akemans' home after having already spent a long night on duty. Shortly behind them came Lieutenant Tommy Jacobs, a young man with watery blue eyes that mixed sadness and bright clarity. He recognized Stringbean's name because he had dressed up like him for a part in a third grade pageant. Also, Jacobs's ex-girlfriend came from the Ridgetop area and had pointed out the Akemans' house once. Detective Dave Roberts and Sergeant James Vaughn of the Metro Identification Division rounded out the core group of investigators.

This quintet faced a baffling crime scene that began a rapid and tense swelling of personnel. Roy Acuff had beaten the detectives to the scene, and more of the Akemans' friends would follow. Along with other Metro police came more state patrol officers and Tennessee Bureau of Investigation (TBI) inspectors, all of whose territoriality created an edgy situation.[3] Further adding to the tension, everyone knew that Nashville's two major newspapers, the *Tennessean* and the *Nashville Banner*, along with radio and television stations, monitored police channels and that reporters would soon arrive. Already now, around a quarter past eight, the radio stations were breaking the news of Stringbean's and Estelle's deaths.[4] Amid all the tension and activity, Estelle lay still in the field and String's lifeless body lay facedown on the floor.

The investigators rolled String over, and a .32 slug fell out of his clothing. They thought this bullet had killed him, and they took note of more firearm debris. Inspection revealed a .32 automatic casing under the living room couch, presumably corresponding to the slug in String's clothes. Another .32 casing lay in the driveway, suggesting that it may have contained one of the slugs that struck Estelle. Aside from these, the investigators located two .22 long-rifle casings, one in the bedroom doorway and the other in the woodpile next to the fireplace. There were also two live .22 short-hollow points on the bed. More .22 slugs were lodged in the walls and floor.[5] Taken together, this evidence suggested that at least one .32 automatic and at least one .22 rifle had been fired.

The presence of different calibers of ammunition raised a question of who all was firing and why. The investigators considered the possibilities that there could have been multiple murderers or perhaps even a shoot-out between Stringbean and his assailant(s). Noting that the index finger of Stringbean's right hand was hooked in such a way that he might have been holding a pistol when he died, the investigators thought it likely that there *had* been a shoot-out. They needed to know what weapons he had and might have shot. A search revealed a .32 pistol in his tackle box, but it was a revolver instead of an automatic and had not been fired.[6] Seeing an empty gun rack and knowing Grandpa and String had intended to go on a hunting trip this morning, the investigators asked Grandpa if he could remember what guns his friend owned. Grandpa said String kept a .22 revolver in his show bag, which was missing, and another .22 double-action Colt revolver in his tackle box. That double action was also missing as well as a single-action .22 Colt Western Peacemaker revolver, a sixteen-gauge sawed-off double-barreled shotgun, and two .22 rifles.[7]

Grandpa's list supported the shoot-out idea, but other evidence pointed to multiple killers, as well. Cigarette butts indicated the perpetrators because the Akemans did not smoke cigarettes, and the predominance of Marlborough and Raleigh cigarettes implied that there were at least two murderers smoking the two different brands. Although the total number of cigarettes was never determined, the sheer amount suggested that the murderers had spent some time at the house smoking and drinking beer. Some of the empty beer cans matched those in the Akemans' refrigerator, leading the investigators to suspect the killers had helped themselves while they waited for the Akemans to return from the previous night's Opry.[8]

The investigators envisioned String returning from Nashville and somehow knowing there were intruders in his house. He set had his show bag and Vega No. 9 down on the porch outside the door along with a box of *Me and My Ole Crow* albums, which still sat there now. He had taken his .22 pistol out of the bag, opened the door, and fired at the intruders. The detectives figured Estelle must have parked the Cadillac and then fled in fear upon hearing gunshots and was gunned down midrun with the same .32 that shot Stringbean. The perpetrators then took String's gun out of his hand as well as the others and ran off with them. This scenario had merits, although it did not explain the .22 long-rifle casings.

It was also difficult to figure out how and why the Akemans' everyday car, the Ford Torino station wagon, should be parked at a nearby rock quarry. Fending off a television camera operator, Jacobs and a TBI agent investigated the vehicle. They found a paper bag and a stocking on the ground and Pall Mall cigarettes in the glove compartment.[9] It is unclear whether the investigators thought the Pall Mall cigarettes indicated a third killer, but they definitely thought there could have been more than two killers. The stockings could serve as masks to hide the perpetrators' identity. But who drove this car out to this quarry, and why? Puzzling over the matter, the TBI agent dusted the car for fingerprints.

As the morning wore on, sorting the evidence became more and more challenging because of the many people converging on the scene. As helicopters hovered above, reporters on the ground milled about the scene, mixing with investigators. In a situation in which every clue counted, protecting the site was crucial. Unfortunately, Metro itself could not be trusted, its own limitations showing, for Tommy Jacobs "complained police brass stepped on and destroyed more evidence than the press."[10] The possible corruption of the scene and potential skewing of evidence predictably served the purposes of the defense in the trial that would come.

For now, however, the looming question was why had the murders been committed? Seeking answers, the investigators began questioning neighbors, friends, and fellow Opry stars who were steadily arriving. News had traveled quickly through the country music family. "I've got some terrible news; String and Estelle were killed," a teary-eyed Tommy Scott told his family in a moment his daughter still remembers with pain. Steve Gibson remembers the phone ringing that Sunday morning just as the family had dressed for worship services. His father answered the phone on a small stand in the hallway and listened. When he hung up, he stood in silence, then turned to his wife, who had gathered with their son in their sense of something bad having happened. "Mom, last night somebody broke-in and murdered Strang and Estelle," Curt said.[11] She stood in shock, then burst into tears.

Curt made his way to his boss's house to join Grandpa and Ramona. Also there were Pete "Bashful Brother Oswald" Kirby and Bill Carlisle. Roy Acuff was already pressuring the detectives to find the killers, saying, "I hope when you find them, they burn."[12] He meant to help, too, going with the police to the Burnettes' house to call Opry manager Bud Wendell to lay down a timeline for the night before, especially for when the Akemans left the Opry. Skeeter Willis helped fine-tune that timeline later, but for now the investigators discerned that the murders happened sometime around eleven o'clock.

As for the motive, none of these stars could think of the Akemans having any enemies, but practically all of them spoke of String's tendency to carry that big wad of money. They had warned him that doing so would get him hurt or killed, but he had kept on. Moreover, there had been rumors about money in the house, and Bill Carlisle revealed a story similar to Roni Stoneman's that Estelle had told his daughter they kept money around the refrigerator.[13] The absence of money-stuffed cans in the refrigerator might have supported the idea that the killers had stolen money from the house, but that was not the direction the investigators took. Instead, they hypothesized that the would-be burglars had failed to find cash while String played the Opry and so had waited for him to return in order to rob him. The problem came when String started shooting and they shot back, escalating the crime to murder. Grabbing up guns, wallet, and other items, including String's pipe, they rushed out the door, leaving behind the wads of cash in Stringbean's overalls and Estelle's bra.

That cash was a rub, though. Not only did it mitigate against a money motive since it was presumably what the killers came for, but it also raised the question of who would have known about the money being in a wad instead of in the wallet. Either the perpetrators or someone they knew would have had to be enough in the know. Logic implied that they must have been in some way connected to Stringbean, either a family member, a friend, or perhaps someone in the country music industry or connected with it. If the crime had been committed on the streets because robbers happened to see Stringbean flash his money roll, then it made sense to see the crime as being committed by people the Akemans had no connection with. But this crime looked premeditated, set up to go to the house with knowledge of the location of the Akemans' home. All the stranger that String's wad of money had been left behind.

As the investigators continued to question people, String and Estelle were taken away to Phillips-Robinson Funeral Home under the direction of Dr. T. E. Simpkins, who performed the autopsies. Stringbean had been killed by a single shot through the heart, with the bullet entering his chest. There were small abrasions on his knees and shins and a bruise on his lip. Simpkins also discovered abrasions on String's right knuckles, suggesting he had punched someone or something. Estelle's body bore three gunshot wounds: one through the right shoulder blade, one entering the back of her left arm above the elbow, the third entering behind her right ear and exiting out the middle of the back of her cranium (the posterior parietal). The entrance of the head shot was avulsed, meaning that it was raised by the explosion just before the bullet pierced the bone. The shots to her back and arm had felled her, and then the killers had shot her close-up and point-blank in the head.[14] It was actually Simpkins who discovered the cash on the bodies; the fact that the detectives overlooked the wads of money may have strengthened their idea that the killers accidentally did too.

Back at Ridgetop, although the investigators would work into the evening, the work at the crime scene rose to a crescendo. At around twenty minutes past eleven in the morning, the head of Metro Homicide, Lieutenant Tom Cathey, made a wordless statement.[15] He picked up the banjo case that had been sitting on the porch all this time and carried it to his car. There, with Roy Acuff, Pete Kirby, and Highway Patrol Major Seamon (an Akeman relative) flanking him, Cathey opened the case and lifted the Vega No. 9 out amid camera cacophony. The *Tennessean*'s Jack Corn (who had photographed String sitting happily by his fireplace years before) got the best shot, the banjo inscrutable yet uncannily alive. Despite the round, twangy joy the banjo conveyed, today, with its white head starkly darkened by Stringbean's frailing hand, that exuberance seemed turned to grieving photonegative. Cathey's left hand propped the instrument by the neck, while his right hand hung above the tenth fret, as though the banjo had possessed him and guided him to brush the strings there just as its former owner had so often done. Cathey put the Vega back in the case and zipped it. With that sound, Stringbean came to an end as a living combo of instrument and human.

MOURNING: NOVEMBER 12–13

On Monday, November 12, Stringbean's name appeared in more newspapers throughout the country on one day than in his entire life. Papers from the *Hamilton (OH) Journal News* to the *Ogden (UT) Standard-Examiner* picked up the Associated Press story. It was appropriate that small-town newspapers such as these printed the story, for it was in these places that Stringbean had entertained and where people had fallen in love with him. At the same time, Stringbean's reach proved to be international, for the *Calgary Herald* also carried the story, and news reached Sweden's country music fans with the *Kountry Korral Magazine*.[16]

In Nashville the morning paper, the *Tennessean*, filled its front page with the news. "Killers Missed $5,700" screamed the headline in bold all-caps, and underneath appeared Corn's photograph of Cathey holding the Vega. The front page also sported a photograph of Stringbean doing his Babe Ruth–like arm extension. Bill Carlisle was quoted describing the house being torn apart, Roy

Acuff cried out eye-for-eye, and even Bear Burnett made it into the news talking about String cutting only one rick of wood on Saturday because another would tire him out before the Opry.[17] The afternoon paper, the *Nashville Banner*, brought more articles, including one by Stacy Harris based on her interview with Stringbean. Stacy had felt gut-punched Sunday morning when she realized the man she had spoken to the night before was gone. It was a great scoop, but a tragic one.

Along with providing information about Stringbean and Estelle, their deaths, and the state of the investigation, the papers revealed that fear as well as grief filled country music stars. Jerry Thompson, who would go on to cover much of the investigation for the *Tennessean*, wrote an article for that morning's issue titled "Opry Stars Now under Pressure." Thompson explained that accidents and death had befallen many Opry stars and that many others had been the victims of burglary. Bud Wendell weighed in with a quote, explaining that Opry stars were vulnerable. The article signaled a swift change in the industry. Obviously, country stars knew Nashville was becoming more dangerous, but with these murders a new uneasiness and distrust stole into the hearts of the performers. Shock mixed with grief, and their world seemed terribly threatened. "I just . . . I couldn't comprehend it," Roy Clark later commented. "My mind just would not accept the fact that he was gone, first of all, and that he had been murdered. It really, really just hit me hard." Lulu Roman said it was difficult to think "this could happen to us, to our family."[18] Many set about immediately having fences built and surveillance systems installed around their properties.

Meanwhile, Metro investigators struggled to find a foothold. Their phones rang with tips, bringing floods of information ranging from the seemingly plausible to the utterly outlandish. Some patterns *were* emerging, though, the most significant one being people reporting seeing a light-blue car with its hood up parked alongside Baker Station Road near the Akemans' house on the night of the murder. There was also talk of a yellow truck at or near the house. Amid this influx of calls at headquarters, teams of investigators were dispatched to various locations. One team, headed up by Jack Rohtert and Wanda Uselton, searched the Akemans' home again, which yielded the paperwork for String's .22 Colt Peacemaker revolver, serial number G-47470. The papers noted its being bought in a hardware store in Sparta, and a call to the store owner confirmed String's buying it there during a stay at the lake cabin.[19] That serial number gave the investigators something solidly traceable.

A couple of suspects had been identified. One was actually Bear Burnette. His way of speaking in short, staccato sentences seemed "goofy" and suspicious to the investigators. He claimed not to have heard any gunshots, and when the police asked him if he knew Stringbean to carry a lot of cash, he said, "Nope. Never knew him to carry over just a few dollars." After hearing so much about that money, his claiming not to know of it sounded suspicious. Not only that, but Bear's calling String "Pa" led to questions about whether the Akemans had adopted him and he stood to gain money from their deaths, all of which he denied.[20]

The other suspect was a young man named Jimmy Carter. A Metro K-9 unit had followed a trail from the Akemans' home across a field to an empty house where evidence of recent activity was found, including .22 automatic casings and a Zippo lighter. As it turned out, the Burnettes owned this home and rented it to Carter, who admitted he owned the lighter and that he and friends had been at the house Saturday night around eleven thirty. They had heard gunshots but assumed somebody was raccoon hunting in the hills. Carter's friends told also of the car with the hood up, although they remembered it as being white.[21]

The inspectors worked into Tuesday. That morning, an ID team with a metal detector discovered a .32 slug a few inches deep in the dirt beneath where Estelle had lain, and the team believed this slug had passed through her head. At Metro headquarters, two of Carter's friends, Teddy and Sheila White, were questioned directly about their time at the Burnettes' rented house on the night of the murder. Sheila not only mentioned shots but also claimed they had heard a woman scream.[22]

That day Stringbean and Estelle were laid to rest. The funeral took place at Phillips-Robertson. Among the hundreds of flowers surrounding the two caskets, one arrangement was shaped like a steering wheel, commemorating Estelle's years of driving, and several were in the shapes of pipes and fish. The caskets stood side by side, with Estelle's head at David's feet. David lay dressed in a blue suit, with a striped shirt and tie. "I'd never seen him in a tie before," someone was heard to whisper.[23]

The tiny chapel could not accommodate the more than eight hundred attendees, so most stood outside, while as many as could fit inside sat in two adjoining rooms during the eulogy. Present were the *Hee Haw* cast and practically every country music star. Luddie was there with her parents. David's brother Robert attended, but Alfred was away on a mission trip in Rhodesia. The newspaper mentioned two of David's sisters attending, but did not name them. Along with the Akemans' family and kin stood many who simply had been touched by the music and humor of Stringbean—country people in overalls alongside men in business suits. A quartet sang "How Great Thou Art" and "Precious Memories." Maurice O'Neal, minister of the Wingate Church of Christ that Luddie attended, preached the service, bequeathing the memorable line that "String had a string of friends. Now there is a string of sadness."[24]

After the service, a procession of three hundred cars made the trip to Forest Lawn Memorial Gardens along Highway 41. The road to the cemetery was lined with people, including firemen standing at attention in respect for the Kentucky Wonder. Among the official pallbearers who carried the two caskets were Luddie's husband, Harold Sparkman, along with Lester Wilburn, Bear Burnette, Ben Smathers, Bill Carlisle, Oscar Sullivan, Leonard Jones, Vic Willis, Porter Wagoner, Mickey Smothers, Harold Rugg, and Ray Parham.[25] The honorary pallbearers were Roy Acuff, Ernest Tubb, Bud Wendell, George Morgan, Grant Turner, Ralph Emery, Whitey Ford, David Hooten, Pete Kirby, Jimmy Riddle, Skeeter Willis, Dr. David Strayhorn, Dr. John Tudor, and all the other members of the Opry along with Hank Williams Jr. String and Estelle were buried in plots near Hawkshaw Hawkins and Cowboy Copas in what was becoming thought of as a Music Row of the dead corresponding to the living one in town.

Some of the stars gave quotes. "He lived to make people laugh, and he did just that," Grandpa said. "There wasn't a finer, more respected person in the entertainment industry. Stringbean didn't have an enemy in the world," Roy Acuff observed. Roy also pushed back against the idea that Stringbean had brought on his murder by broadcasting his riches. "He wanted to live out there in that little cabin. He could have had a better place if he had wanted it. I don't go along with what people are saying about Stringbean flashing his money around. I think people would have felt he didn't have anything as to think he was rich." A reporter approached Bill Monroe standing quietly at the funeral, surely thinking back over the years with his first banjo player. "Stringbean was a wonderful man," Bill said. "I never heard him say a cuss word and he never had a cross word with me in the three years we worked together. Everybody will miss him."[26]

It was horrible to think of Stringbean and Estelle murdered and galling to realize the killers were roaming free and unpunished. The next day, the *Tennessean* announced $14,000 in rewards being offered.[27] "We want these murderers brought to justice as quickly as possible. And we hope this kind of reward will expedite the process," said William C. Weaver Jr., the chairman of the National Life and WSM board of directors. The investigators felt the pressure growing greater from the industry and from the city of Nashville.[28] "The community was demanding that this case be solved," Sherman Nickens remembered. "You know, it was . . . it was a horrendous crime, and they was wanting it solved. I mean the, the Christians and, and everybody was wanting it, that's what they were wanting."[29] Needing to produce results under such pressure, the investigators decided to give Bear and Carter polygraph tests. As the questions were being prepared, however, the investigation took a major and definitive turn when, at half past four, a call came into Metro from the district attorney general's office with news that someone being held in custody had what seemed to be solid, reliable information.[30]

A BREAK—FELIX ELLIOTT AND THE BROWNS: NOVEMBER 14–16

The district attorney general was Thomas Shriver, a fixture in Nashville's elite. His father, also named Thomas but with a different middle name, had been a chancellor judge in the Tennessee Court of Appeals, and his mother, Attie, was a Nashville socialite. Born December 27, 1931, Thomas's education had followed a path befitting his family's station: Walter Stokes Grammar School, Hillsboro High School, and bachelor's and law degrees at Vanderbilt. Upon graduating, he practiced law in the firm of Stephenson, Lackey, and Holman, and then, taking a political turn, was elected to the state senate.[31] Marrying Marilyn Gober in 1964, he was named U.S. attorney general in the Middle Tennessee District at age thirty-two.[32] In 1967 the Jaycees named him "Young Man of the Year," and the *Tennessean* printed a photograph of him, with his distinguished profile and dark hair.[33] By the start of the 1970s, he was a well-known figure in Nashville, one writer describing him as a "political liberal" who had "all the moves of a first-rate politician." Now district attorney general for Davidson County, his reputation was that of a "sympathetic man in a position that requires tough-ness" and whom the police considered soft on criminals.[34]

On Wednesday, November 14, Shriver got word that a man being held in Metro jail on an arson charge had information about the Stringbean murders.[35] The man's name was Felix Elliott. He lived in Greenbrier and drove trucks for the Cherokee Hauling and Rigging Company.[36] Elliott claimed he had heard some acquaintances talking about Stringbean days before the murder at the same time they spoke of robbing a Grand Ole Opry star. He was hoping to use this information as a bargaining chip to get him off the arson charge.[37] The names he mentioned were Charlie Brown, his brothers Doug and Roy, and their cousin John. Charlie Brown was the welder and investor whose wife's All-Star Talent Agency Stringbean had worked with.

With that information, Shriver took the extraordinary step of involving him-self far more deeply in the investigation than was common for an attorney gen-eral. Shriver had personal motivation, for he knew about Stringbean and was himself a mandolin player in the bluegrass band Outbound Freight. "It was a real case of passion for him because of his interest in country music," remembered Hal McDonough, who at the time was two years out of law school and had just joined the district attorney's office.[38] Shriver was surprised to find Stringbean credited with authoring "Barnyard Banjo Pickin'," which he knew simply as "Hot

Corn, Cold Corn." Just how much Shriver knew initially about Charlie Brown's involvement and connections in the country music industry is not known. But since the nature of the murder implied that the killers had some kind of access to industry-insider knowledge, Charlie's connection may have lent credence to the usefulness of Elliott's information.

The lead sent the investigators into action. Some went to Greenbrier to get Charlie and Roy, others to Doug's house at 126 Lucille Avenue off Dickerson Road, and others to East Nashville, where John lived in a trailer. They found that John had gone out of town, but on Lucille Avenue the investigators encountered Doug for the first time as well as his girlfriend, Darlene Powell. Doug told the investigators he did not mind their searching the house, and they found packs of Marlboro cigarettes, one of the brands at the murder scene. The Brown men were brought to headquarters, while Darlene was taken to Shriver's office.

As the questioning began at eight that night, the investigators learned that Charlie had called attorney Joseph P. Binkley, one of the most successful defense attorneys in the city, hiring him for $3,000 out of pocket. It was a savvy move, and one that suggested guilt. Also suspicious was Charlie's self-possession. He was openly defiant, only half answering questions if at all, delaying whenever possible, and playing dumb. Bad blood arose between him and Jacobs, especially. Charlie denied having any knowledge of the murders, just as Roy and Doug did. Over at Shriver's office after some convincing, Darlene took a polygraph test, the machine revealing that she told the truth when denying knowledge of the murders. In the meantime, as Binkley clamored that the investigators were approaching Tennessee's legal time limit for holding people for questioning, Charlie, Roy, and Doug's younger brother, Jimbo, was brought in.[39] He claimed he had heard Charlie and Doug talking about Stringbean and Doug claiming he was going to get $25,000 from somewhere. Binkley delivered an ultimatum either to charge the Browns or to let them go. The investigators released the men at one in the morning.

This development broke to the public when the sun rose the next morning. The front page of the *Tennessean* featured an article with a photograph of Green leading a cuffed Roy Brown by the arm and one of Nickens with Doug. It was the public's first glimpse of Roy and Doug, both unkempt in button-downs.[40] Aged twenty-five and twenty-three, respectively, Roy and Doug bore the appearance of their troubled generation.[41] Roy had dropped out of high school to join the Marines in 1964, going to Vietnam and receiving an honorable discharge in 1967. He returned to Tennessee and got a job with the Armstrong Rubber Company in Madison, making $245 a week.[42] He married Carol Alley that year, and they had a child they named Roy. They divorced in 1971. Since his return from Vietnam, Roy had been in trouble with the law. He was thin and wiry, with hard eyes.

Doug had a child in 1968, tattooing his son's name and birthday on his left arm and the words "Born to lose and lost" on his right.[43] He went into the army on July 9, 1970, and mustered out February 9, 1972. He returned to Nashville and began working at the American Marine Company, located at 201 Woodycrest Avenue, although he also welded for Charlie. Doug had a more substantial look than Roy, his brown eyes capable of hardness also but with a touch of vulnerability too.

The article claimed that the Browns were brought in because of a tip from James Hamlett, who lived across the road from the Akemans. Hamlett told investigators he saw an older-model yellow Chevrolet pickup truck leaving the Akemans' home on Saturday night between a quarter to twelve and half past. "I got up 'cause my dogs were barkin'," Hamlett told reporters. "I saw this pickup truck come down over the hill, (of the driveway) over at Stringbean's. It was driving real fast." When a call was put out for such a vehicle, Robertson Country sheriff Herbert Long supplied the information that Charlie Brown owned a 1970 yellow truck. Charlie denied being *brought* in by police, claiming instead that his mother had called him to say the police had come to Robertson County to arrest two of his brothers and that he went after them. "They wanted to take a picture of my truck, but then they wanted to take pictures of another truck up there too, so I think they're just taking a shot in the dark," Charlie told the paper. "It looks to me like somebody just wants the $22,000 (reward money)."[44] As for the truck itself, Charlie assured the paper it had stayed at his house all through Saturday night.

Later that same night, an anonymous call came in to the *Tennessean* around one o'clock. City editor Frank Ritter described the caller as being "not drunk" but "grief-stricken." The caller claimed the murder was "all a mistake" because he and his partner had thought Stringbean was on tour, and so they were surprised when Stringbean returned. The caller claimed his partner shot Stringbean "with one of his own guns," and he wanted to set that straight and that it was the partner who had done the shooting. "This shouldn't have happened," the caller said. "He (Stringbean) wasn't supposed to come back home."[45] Doug later revealed it was he who had called, and it is the first iteration of what would become the official narrative that put the blame of shooting on someone other than himself. The claim that the partner killed Stringbean with his own gun contradicted the idea of a .32 automatic being the murder weapon, but at the time the investigators had no way of knowing if the caller really was one of the perpetrators, and Doug never said anything else about it.

The next day, Friday, November 16, Oscar Sullivan gave a statement to the Metro police. He told of Stringbean's interest in Caveland and of Charlie Brown's being on the board of Caveland Summer Music Park. Oscar also testified about

String's "burglar alarm": "I noticed that he had a fishing line from one point to the other across the gap, cattle gap leading to the house."[46] This alarm offered a possible explanation for how String and Estelle could have known there were intruders in their house, leading Stringbean to draw his gun and shoot it out with them. Like other Opry cast members, Oscar reported warning String about the dangers of robbers and that String simply laughed and rejoined, "I'll give it to them, Chief, before I let them kill me."

Also that day, John Brown returned to Nashville and turned himself into police headquarters, saying he had heard they were searching for him. When asked what he was doing the night of the murders, he said he had been "riding around on Broadway" just as Doug and Roy had said he was.[47] The investigators released him with the same plan of watching and waiting for him to make a mistake. John, it turned out, had the most violent history of the Browns. Born John A. Brown Jr. on October 12, 1950, in Greenbriar, he quickly grew into a cruel boy, who tried to cut dogs' tails off and drown chickens and ducks. In school John fought not only students but also the principal, the janitor, and gym teachers.[48] He moved to Detroit with his parents in 1966 and then to Pittsburgh, where he dropped out of Keystone High School in the tenth grade.[49] John then went into the Marines, where he was discharged after eighteen months, and returned to Detroit, holding jobs for only a few weeks at a time. During that time, he married a woman from Pittsburgh named Kathleen with whom he had two children.[50]

Constantly, violently jealous even as he carried on affairs with other women, John would often go into a kind of trance when he became violent and claimed to have no memory of his assaults afterward. As he collected a handful of convictions for driving under the influence and disturbing the peace, his mental state seemed to deteriorate. Finally, police had to talk him out of throwing himself from a bridge, taking him to Detroit General Hospital and then on to psychiatric treatment. Fed up, Kathleen moved to Pittsburgh with the children; their divorce was finalized on September 28, 1973. When John got out of the hospital without completing his treatment but taking pills that reduced his violence and wildness, he moved back to Tennessee to live in Greenbriar, and Doug got him a job at American Marine in Nashville.[51] Taken together, Roy, Doug, and John represented the kinds of long-haired, violence-prone, weed-smoking, whiskey-drinking characters the Opry was trying to escape by moving out of the Ryman.

That Friday evening saw the first Opry performance since the murders. The mood was grim backstage, where a large bulletin board on the wall was filled with cards and telegrams about Stringbean and Estelle. These missives came from all over the world. On the stage, Opry announcer Hal Durham opened with a statement:

> We could not begin the Friday Night Opry without paying tribute to the memory of a man who has contributed so much to this program and to country music everywhere. The death of Stringbean and his wife Estelle has saddened all of us who knew them and spent so many Friday and Saturday nights with them here in the Opry House.
>
> Nobody in our Grand Ole Opry family was better loved or will be more sorely missed. We know that thousands and thousands of people all over the country share our feeling of sadness and great loss.
>
> Last Saturday night we enjoyed and vigorously applauded Stringbean's final performance. Tonight we ask you to join us in observing these few moments of silence in tribute to the memory of Stringbean and Estelle.[52]

During the show, Roy Acuff could hardly control his emotions. "We're going to carry our program a little different tonight," he told the audience, his voice quavering with emotion. "I'm going to let the boys do most of it tonight." As the music played, Roy stood to the side with a long face. When time came for him to do a commercial, he had little joy to offer, giving the yo-yo he often played with onstage only a halfhearted toss. At the show's end, he gave his tribute, tears glistening in his eyes and declaring, "I hope there's some way that capital punishment can be brought back to the state of Tennessee, so we can punish the people who punish our people."[53] It was quite a statement, referring to the 1972 *Furman v. Georgia* decision that had ended the death penalty in a five-to-four U.S. Supreme Court decision. In Roy's eyes, the law should be changed back so that lives could be taken for lives taken. Many of the Akemans' friends would make similar pleas of vengeance and justice for decades to come.

STAR INFORMANT: NOVEMBER 17–NOVEMBER 29

Saturday, November 17, dawned with the investigators trying to firm up their hypothetical narrative of the murder. The Browns looked guilty. The investigators had established that on the night of the murders, John and Doug had left home at half past nine and returned at one or one thirty, that they smoked the kinds of cigarettes as those found at the crime scene, that John's blue car matched descriptions, that they had guns of matching calibers to slugs and casings at the scene (including .22 rounds being found at some point in Doug's house), and that Roy had deposited $200 shortly after the murders (apparently the first written assertion that any money at all had been taken from the Akemans).[54] These details combined with the investigators' instincts convinced them they were on the right trail, but they needed hard evidence in order to make arrests.

The core group of investigators set up headquarters at the Akemans' home. It was a haunting site that kept the tragedy fresh. The men unconsciously avoided stepping on the chalk outline of String's body on the floor whenever they put logs String himself had cut in the fireplace. Frustration was building within the team. Here, a week after the murder, they were a fractured group as they tried to build their case. The pressure intensified constantly, but in this moment of frustration, at ten in the morning, a man named James Morris appeared at the Akeman house with information that he hoped would garner him the reward to find the killers that now had built to $30,000. Morris worked at American Marine with John and Doug, and he claimed that Doug had been planning a home burglary for about a month not with John but with another coworker named Bill Downey.[55] He added that the job was to bring $20,000–$30,000 and that Doug had shown him a .32-caliber pistol he planned to use.

Downey showed up at the Akeman house of his own accord in the middle of the afternoon while Jacobs was trying to unstop the sink. He was dressed in work clothes, his hair long. He appeared to be very nervous. For whatever reasons, the investigators took to Downey, despite Morris's having said Doug had planned the burglary *with* him. They fixed him a sandwich and gave him a Coca-Cola to calm him down. Once he was a little more comfortable, they began to ask him what he knew. Downey confirmed that Doug had talked about robbing "a fellow who had a lot of money and who he said was with the Grand Ole Opry." When asked if Doug had said anything since the police had picked him up, Downey replied that he had not. The investigators then asked if Downey thought Doug would talk to him now, to which Downey said yes. They asked if he would cooperate with their investigation, and he replied, "I ain't no snitch, but them boys done wrong. They hadn't oughta killed them people."[56] Once he agreed to help, Downey asked for a glass of water, and Jacobs replied that he did not have a clean glass and needed to unstop the sink. Downey replied that he had done some plumbing. He fixed the sink, and that marked the beginning of an informing relationship.

That evening at six, WSM aired a special program just before the Opry in commemoration of String. It included interviews by Al Voecks with Grandpa, Tex Ritter, Roy Acuff, Buck Owens, Bill Monroe, and Bud Wendell.[57] The Opry show that followed was dedicated to Stringbean. Wendell opened with a statement:

> This evening's performance of the Grand Ole Opry will long be remembered in the hearts of all the performers. The Opry family is like every other family. We have moments of happiness, moments of pride, moments of anger and moments

of sorrow. Tonight, we are bound together in our thoughts by the sudden death of Stringbean and his wife, Estelle. String was loved and respected by everyone whose life he touched, whether it was in front of an Opry audience or a personal appearance on the road. We will understand if you applaud a little stronger here in the Opry House or if you sing along at home. Your life was also touched by Stringbean. The Opry performers here tonight may sing with more feeling and emotion, or the dancers may kick a little higher, or the musicians may pick with greater perfection. For it is their way of saying that all our lives have been enriched and we are better people by knowing String and Estelle. And their shadow will linger in our hearts forever.[58]

Following the statement, Wendell asked for a moment of silence. Although the show went on from there, Roy Acuff was too distraught to sing in the first show.[59]

In the investigation, with Downey on board and the target now squarely on the Browns, Metro changed tactics. From now on, the primary focus went to a siege and surveillance of the Brown family in hopes of a breakdown in their defenses. It was not all coffee and donuts for the investigators, though, especially when Charlie went on the attack, as he did on Tuesday, November 20, telling Roberts "to stay away from his brothers or he was going to 'do something about it'."[60] In fact, the investigators were probing into *his* life and finding that he loved gambling on horse races, which was illegal in Tennessee. There were other rumors of Charlie's involvement in and instigation of illegal and even violent activities.

While public updates on the investigation cooled off with the approach of Thanksgiving, Stringbean was still in people's minds, hearts, and eyes. He continued to appear in episodes of *Hee Haw* that ran nonstop as the decision was made to keep running footage of him on through the rest of the season. Grandpa recorded a clip for the show commemorating his friend. In Charleston, West Virginia, a notice appeared titled "Carry Money, Invite Death," citing Stringbean and Estelle and urging people to put their cash in safes. On Sunday, November 18, WAMB aired a radio documentary on Stringbean featuring interviews with Jimmy Riddle, Archie Campbell, and other Opry stars. Yet another remembrance appeared in a *Kansas City Times* interview with Buck Owens about the murders. "He was the kind of person I would like to live next door to and I ain't got no next door neighbors," Owens said. "That tells you what kind of guy he was." Tuesday, November 27, a dogwood tree was slated to be cut and removed from the construction path of Interstate 441 and relocated to the grounds near the entrance of the new Opry house to commemorate Stringbean and Estelle.[61]

In the midst of all the grief and newfound fear for safety among the country stars came another terrible, and at first seemingly related, blow on the evening of November 27 when another musician was murdered and robbed. James P. Widner, a guitarist with Hank Snow, had met up with a friend, Mrs. Mildred Hazelwood, for dinner at the Pitt Grill, and they were shot and robbed when he walked her back to the Holiday Inn on James Robertson.[62] The news hit the country music industry hard, and the press speculated about whether there was a connection between this double murder and that of the Akemans. Some in the country music industry thought Charlie the common denominator.[63] The murderers were quickly found paying for plane tickets with Widner's credit card at the Memphis International Airport. No direct connection was found between the two double murders, but the damage was done. An article on Monday, December 3, explained that country stars were taking greater safety precautions than ever, carrying guns, buying guard dogs, and installing alarm systems.[64] Porter Wagoner and Tex Ritter downplayed the situation, Porter saying robberies were "something that happens all the time and just recently happened to people in our business." But Bill Carlisle told the reporters, "Now, I ain't going to tell you what I've done, but you can bet I've taken precautions. . . . I did it immediately after String got killed."[65]

All the while, Downey informed to the police. His story presented Doug as wayward but not a killer. According to what Doug was telling Downey, Charlie had set up the Stringbean robbery job but had nothing to do with the actual killing. It was John who had done that. Stringbean had surprised them, coming in shooting. Appearing in the door in the midst of the shoot-out, Estelle ran away, but John downed her with a shot and then killed her execution style as she begged for mercy on her knees. The two men came away with just over $200, nowhere near the $20,000 they had expected. Roy, Doug, John, and Charlie knew not only where the murder weapon was but also about a will the Akemans had leaving their money to charity. Doug claimed to have put the will, Stringbean's costume, the gun, and $8,000–$10,000 worth of checks from Opryland and other venues all in Stringbean's leather traveling bag along with rocks and thrown it into a lake. Doug's .32 was the murder weapon, but it was John who shot them with Doug's gun because they had switched weapons, with Doug carrying John's shotgun. The story fell in line with the investigators' hypothesis.

NEW INFORMANT: NOVEMBER 30, 1973–JANUARY 14, 1974

On November 30, a possible path to finding the murder weapon and the Akemans' guns opened up. An anonymous tip claimed that a man named Jack Williams, who lived north of Nashville in Madison, had taken part in the disposal of the weapons. When questioned, Williams confirmed swapping firearms with

Doug and Roy and that he knew a place where Doug had shot his .32 before giving it away. The detectives went with Williams to the junkyard where he claimed the gun had been shot, but they found no slugs. Four days later, Williams agreed to have his car bugged, and the investigators listened as Doug got in the car and the two men talked. In speech slurred by pills and alcohol, Doug talked of being watched by Metro police and said he wanted to hurt them in some way. When Williams asked Doug why he killed "that woman," Doug said he had had nothing to do with the business.[66]

Nevertheless, Doug seemed to be breaking, for the very next day Downey reported that Doug had told him he wanted to make a deal with the investigators. The sense of guilt was getting to him, and he felt bad about depriving people of the charity the Akemans' will provided. If Doug really did want to make a deal with the investigators, that desire passed quickly under pressure from Roy because just twenty-four hours later Downey reported that Doug no longer sought a deal. Nevertheless, the investigators grew more confident that Doug was contrite, guilt ridden, and wanting to make amends, whereas John was a brazen killer.

Downey also now provided a path to evidence. He revealed that John had stolen String's electric blanket and pipe and taken them to Pittsburgh and left them with his ex-wife, Kathleen. Nickens and Green made the trip to see Kathleen, who did indeed have the blanket and talked to the investigators about John's past behavior.[67] Even as the noose tightened and perhaps because it did, back in Tennessee John married his girlfriend, Deborah, on Friday, December 7. The two had known each other since childhood in Greenbrier and had been dating practically since his return to Tennessee. Their timing was striking.

The pressure to find the killers remained taut as the pain of Stringbean's death continued. The December issue of *Country Music Reporter* dedicated two pages in memory of Stringbean. *Bluegrass Unlimited* did the same, including a brief biography of Stringbean and commenting, "If any member of the Opry could have been called 'a friend to all' it had to be String." As the holiday season drew nearer, Luddie and the rest of Estelle's family prepared for their first Christmas without their sister. At Greenbrier High School, Mark Jones felt uncomfortable sitting next to Jimbo in class every day.[68]

Feeling pressure, the investigators took aggressive action to try to break the Browns. Roy's girlfriend, Bonnie Duff, had seemed tenuous from the start, and they decided that with some extra pressure they might able to break her. They called her in for questioning on Monday, December 10, working to drive a wedge between her and Roy. When she said she was not involved in this mess, Nickens told her, "Oh, yes. You're involved when you know about it. You're just like Roy.

We know Roy didn't pull the trigger, but he's the same way." Not telling details made her guilty, Nickens pressed on. Bonnie did not break that day, but she did not long after, explaining that she had seen the Browns with a pillowcase full of stolen goods the night of the murder. When Jacobs lined up pillowcases in what he called "the first linen lineup in history," she picked out one Jacobs had retrieved from the Akemans' cabin.[69]

In the meantime, the Akemans' finances were discussed in the press. The *Tennessean* ran a front-page article on December 11 stating that according to the Akemans' family lawyer, William Faimon, and another attorney, Larry Westbrook, String and Estelle's estate had been largely determined to be worth $500,000, including the lake cabin and cash dating back to the 1930s.[70] Most notably, Faimon confirmed that neither David nor Estelle had left a will.[71] Continuing with this information, a December 13 *Nashville Banner* article proclaimed that, according to Bill Carlisle Jr., the Akemans' accountant, String and Estelle "were probably carrying their 'cattle trading money'" when they were killed. "Stringbean believed in banks and used them," Carlisle said, citing accounts in seven banks. "But they traded in cattle and always kept a fairly good amount of money around." However burned by the Depression Stringbean may have been, according to Carlisle, he believed federal insurance would step in if the banks folded. Despite these public statements concerning the Akemans' estate, questions lingered. The money Faimon accessed was not in accounts but rather was cash kept in safe-deposit boxes he counted by hand.[72] He counted enough that the ink stained his hands, but it was somewhat less than $500,000. Perhaps bills ate up the money in the accounts, but that would seem to run counter to the Akemans' famous frugality. Still, even if the estate amounted to $500,000, what should be made of Tommy Scott's assertion that String and Estelle had reached and surpassed their $1 million goal? Could it be that more than a half-million dollars remained unaccounted for? Could it be that the killers had made off with more than the mere $200 they claimed?

The investigators worked on toward the holidays. Another search at Ridgetop early in the week yielded more .32 casings.[73] Then Downey informed the investigators that John had traded his blue Buick in at Hollywood Motor Company on Dickerson Road. The police obtained the car and had a lineup of five witnesses to identify it as the one parked on Baker Station road the night of the murders. Three of the five confirmed it as the car. Christmas passed quietly; then on New Year's Eve, the investigators met with Shriver and his chief investigator, Charles Hunter. After being debriefed, Shriver told them they had a good case against the Browns but that they still needed "something physical to tie it all together." Shriver also told them to protect Downey at all costs.[74] As country music stars and fans mourned Tex Ritter's January 2 death, a diver who happened also to be a Metro policeman unsuccessfully searched a Ridgetop lake for the murder weapon and the Akemans' effects but found nothing.

There was hope for the case, however, as another chink opened up in the Browns' armor.[75] Charlie had recently hired a man named Jack Holt, who was suspected of transporting stolen motorcycles across state lines into Arkansas. The investigators brought this federal-level offense to the Federal Bureau of Investigation's attention, and on Sunday, January 13, the FBI issued arrest warrants for Holt. Convincing the FBI to hold off serving the warrants until they could talk to Holt, the investigators rushed to Charlie's welding business in Robertson County. Charlie immediately became belligerent, and as the investigators took Holt off to the federal courthouse for questioning, he said, "Don't worry Jack, I'll get you out." At the courthouse, the investigators told Holt they could get him out of the motorcycle case if he told them where Stringbean's weapons were. Holt denied knowing anything, so the detectives left him in jail to think things over. Within thirty minutes, Charlie arrived to pay his bail, but the jailers did not allow him to do so or to talk to Holt, who held out until the next day, Monday, January 14, when he finally said he would agree to take a polygraph test. That test revealed he was not telling all he knew about the murders.[76] When the police pushed Holt, he told them he would talk if he knew his family could be kept safe. When the investigators assured him they would take care of the family, Holt revealed that he had received the chain saw and guns from the Browns. The chain saw he lent to someone in Ridgetop but retrieved days before the arrest and threw into Ridgetop Lake at Charlie's orders. Stringbean's guns he had given to an ex-convict in Springfield named Thomas Lee Birdwell.

ARRESTS: JANUARY 15–17

On the morning of January 15, Holt took the detectives and two U.S. marshals to the lake, where a dive produced Stringbean's chain saw. The detectives then went to Birdwell's house, but he was not home. Sensing urgency that Charlie might know Holt had squealed, the investigators moved quickly to secure his family. While Roberts was in Holt's house helping Holt's wife pack, Charlie and his wife drove up. A tense scene ensued, Jacobs and Charlie facing off, Charlie apparently concealing a gun in his pocket. Roberts appeared on the porch just in time to defuse the situation. That night the investigators gathered at the Continental Inn and celebrated cracking the case. The next morning, they confronted Birdwell. Resisting at first, Birdwell broke when Nickens threatened to charge him as an accessory after the fact. Birdwell said he had given Stringbean's

Peacemaker to a man in Greenbriar named David Jones. They went to Jones's house, and he brought the gun in a holster out of the safe. The serial number, G-47470, checked out. The investigators had the rest of the guns by eleven that morning, and soon Grandpa confirmed they were the Akemans'.[77]

The investigators called Shriver with this new information. "Gentlemen, in view of the evidence you now have," he said, "I think you should go before Judge Boone and request warrants against John Brown, Jr. for murder of David Akeman and Estelle Akeman, and two warrants on Marvin Douglas Brown for the murder of the same people."[78] Jacobs asked why Charlie could not be arrested as an accessory. Shriver replied that state law prohibited a blood relative being an accessory after the fact the so-called Jessie James Law, allegedly originating to save the famous outlaw's mother from prosecution when he came to hide out in her home.[79] Jacobs pushed back, "Charlie planned the whole thing and took the chain saw and threw it in the water. And Roy helped him get rid of the guns through Jack Holt. John actually is the murderer. He killed them, not Doug, and John is only a cousin to the other three." At that point, the Vanderbilt-educated attorney general Shriver replied to the Metro detective, "You're right, by God, you're right. They can be accessories with a cousin. All right, on that basis, get two warrants against Roy and Charlie as accessories to murder for receiving and concealing stolen property."[80]

Upon attaining the warrants, the investigators drove to American Marine Company to arrest John and Doug, while others went to arrest Roy in Greenbriar. The media turned up en masse to cover the arrests. John was silent, but Doug seemed to be breaking and talking. Binkley showed up just in time to save the cousins from being separated and interrogated. The Greenbriar Police Department called to say that Charlie had turned himself in, and Jacobs and Nickens drove up to the county line to get him. They found Charlie sitting in the front seat uncuffed. Jacobs put the handcuffs on him with pleasure, "Y'all know you're making a big mistake, don't you?" Charlie sneered. "I didn't have anything to do with this." Nickens retorted, "You set the whole thing up. You knew Stringbean carried all the money." Brown replied with a threat: "I'd like to meet you out in the street somewhere without these bracelets." The whole business was finished at four o'clock. The Browns were installed in the Davidson County Workhouse to await a hearing scheduled for Tuesday, January 22. The four investigators were interviewed live on Channel 4 and then were treated by the television station to a dinner at the Captain's Table in Nashville's Printer's Alley.[81] It was January 16, 1974. The investigation had taken sixty-seven days.

News of the arrests hit the papers the following morning. The *Tennessean* called Holt a "star witness" and featured photos of Roy, Charlie, John, and

Doug being arrested. Charlie "joked and laughed with police officers" during the booking process. The article carried another component that had not been part of the story Downey had told. Where he claimed the killers had taken a mere $200–$250, according to the article, "police speculate that they took an estimated $17,000 that Akeman had in his possession only a few days prior to his death."[82] It was the one public mention that thought had been given to the possibility that maybe the cash was left behind because the murderers had secured far more money.

But police had caught their quarry, and the case now shifted into the legal forum. For the moment, in the deep, cold heart of January, a conclusion of sorts had been reached. The police had done their part to catch the killers. For a city rocked by troubles, it was time for catharsis, revenge, and justice. Against the sweet faces of Stringbean and Estelle loomed the leering visages of the Browns in stark, archetypal contrast. Evil had cruelly destroyed innocence, and the murders became a metaphor for Nashville itself, as a feeling spread through the city that it had lost its innocence, changed forever from a quiet, safe town into a vile, corrupt city.

CHAPTER 9
YOU CAN'T DO WRONG AND GET BY

January–November 1974

ESTATE SETTLED, LEGAL PROCESS BEGUN: JANUARY–MARCH 1974

On the morning of March 2, thousands of cars filled Stringbean's field as a throng of more than five thousand people dwarfed the tiny red house.[1] Clad in light jackets for the cool, cloudy morning, the majority were there out of curiosity and maybe a chance to be near the home of the man who in life had entertained them. Metro police worked to manage the traffic jam while a police helicopter hovered high above, the stuttering rhythm of its whirling blades droning amid the calls of birds in the brown hills all around. Roy Acuff, wearing a beret, made his way among the people signing autographs. Sixteen hundred in the crowd had registered to bid on the Akemans' estate.

At ten George P. Howell announced the beginning of the auction. "Colonel Billy," as he was called, began to work his way through the items, assisted by his sons, Hugh and Gwynn, and by James Thompson. After establishing preliminaries, Howell put up the first items, two of Stringbean's prize fishing rods, which promptly sold to his brother Robert, who paid $65 for one and $55 for the other. "I just wanted something to remember him by," Robert told reporter Jerry Thompson.[2]

As the wind gusted up to twenty miles per hour, the auction rolled through the day. More fishing tackle sold: String's straw hat he wore on the cover of *Way Back in the Hills of Old Kentucky* selling for $13, his tackle box with contents for $140, his boat for $2,200. A more unusual item was his wooden fishing-rod rack, which sported a whittled figure of Stringbean on it. Along with the fishing gear, the auctioneers presented the everyday implements of the farm, including hand tools, a 1972 Ford garden tractor/mower, and a classic red-and-gray Ford 8-N tractor with a bush hog. Then there was clothing, the Howells offering each pair of String's overalls as "probably the last pair Stringbean bought," bringing $7, $9, even $20. When Colonel Billy pointed out that a pair of glasses bore the letter S, implying it was monogrammed, it fetched $10. Closer inspection after the sale revealed that the S actually stood for Sheraton.

Naturally, the musical effects riveted the crowd's attention. Bidders were probably disappointed to hear that neither of String's banjos would be available. The Gibson RB-1 was being held at Metro headquarters, and the family had decided to donate the Vega No. 9 to the Country Music Hall of Fame. But one of the hats String wore onstage sold for $40, while a script for the Prince Albert Grand Ole Opry with Red Foley sold for $19 and another written with Minnie Pearl for $15. The albums Stringbean normally sold for $5 fetched more, with *Me and My Old Crow* going to bidders for $11. The Akemans' Cadillac sold for $7,450 to the Pigeon Forge Car Museum. The 138 acres of land were divided into four tracts of 27, 32, 37, and 42 acres, with one tract including the two houses. When the auction closed at four o'clock, the take amounted to $131,085.[3] The Akemans' lake home sold in another auction on March 9. Again administered by the Howells, this sale brought $27,500, the house going to Potter Truck Lines of Nashville.

The Akemans' estate had achieved an important stage in becoming settled, but the fireworks were far from over in sorting out the aftermath of the murders. Those fireworks had begun only four days after the arrests back in January. On Monday, January 21, attorney Howard Butler came to Shriver and the investigators, saying he represented Charlie Brown. A photograph of Butler, who had formerly been an assistant district attorney, presents him as a Lyndon B. Johnson look-alike; certainly, he shared some of that president's audacity. Butler assured the investigators that Charlie had nothing to do with the murders and that Charlie would tell them everything he knew if Shriver and the investigators agreed to drop the charges against him.[4] Nickens asked Butler if Charlie would tell them where to find the murder weapon and will, but Butler would reveal nothing without a deal. While Jacobs objected, the other detectives, especially Green, had known Butler from previous investigations and trusted him.[5]

Shriver agreed to the deal and listened as Butler spoke. "I've talked to Charlie," the lawyer said, "and the only thing he knows about the case is that John and Doug came to him on Saturday night, the 10th of November and wanted to borrow his gun. He wouldn't let them have it, but gave them a $100 bill because they said they were going to pull some kind of job because they didn't have any money."[6] The investigators waited for more, but Butler said that was all Charlie knew. Butler later told the newspapers there actually was not a deal made because there was no evidence against Charlie.[7] Rather, Charlie "took a nolle" on charges of receiving and concealing stolen property, meaning Shriver reserved the right to bring up the charges at a later date if Charlie changed his mind about testifying. Jacobs would forever believe they had made a mistake in letting Charlie go.

Preliminary hearings began the next day, Tuesday, January 22, when Doug, John, and Roy appeared before Judge A. A. Birch.[8] Bond was set and posted for Roy. Joseph Binkley refused to represent *both* Doug and John, citing "possible conflict of interest." John requested a postponement of the hearing until he could obtain private counsel. When the hearing ended at eleven, the detectives obtained permission to put Doug in a lineup where he was identified as the perpetrator of an armed robbery of Hensen's Bi-Rite Food Store in Goodlettsville near Stringbean's home back on August 23.[9] A hearing for this new armed robbery charge was set the next day but was postponed for the Friday Akeman case hearing. That Friday hearing was not to be, as Binkley and Jim Everett announced that their clients, Doug and Roy, respectively, were waiving their right to a preliminary hearing, thus being bound over to the grand jury.[10] John still did not have private counsel, and Hicks asked for a three-week continuance because he had not had ample time to prepare for the hearing. Birch said flatly he did not "want to wait that long" and set the hearing for the next Friday.

The next day, Saturday, January 26, a surprising event occurred that would have a bearing on the developing case. Roy, out on bond, was arrested again. An article buried deep in the *Tennessean* explained that FBI agents saw Roy "leaving a house at 1206 Riverside Drive. Agents had the house, which is rented to James Jenkins, under surveillance in connection with a bank robbery."[11] The FBI called Metro police in to assist in arresting Roy for carrying two weapons in his car. Roy posted a $500 bond and walked free that day. Strange that a man so in the spotlight would brazenly put himself in a position to break the law again. But another dimension of the event would prove more significant and also mysterious. Roy was arrested with another man named Kenneth Wayne McKee, also of Greenbrier, whom police served "old warrants" against, including "writing a worthless check, larceny of an auto, using false credit cards, contempt of court, and failure to appear in court." Though few, if any readers, would have taken note of his name, McKee's heading to the workhouse with the Browns would raise questions later.

Hicks started off the following week by filing a writ of habeas corpus. He argued that John was being illegally held at the courthouse because the warrants for arrest had failed "to comply with at least four sections of the Tennessee Code Annotated."[12] Criminal court judge John Draper ordered that the matter be addressed on Friday, the same day the hearing was to be held. The next day, the papers reported that divers had again been sent to search for Akeman evidence, presumably the .32 and perhaps the will.[13] Neither was found.

Finally, Friday, February 1, arrived, and the case was for the first time brought before the judge who would preside over the Stringbean murders trials, the Honorable Allen R. Cornelius. Born December 27, 1920, Cornelius had graduated from West End High School in 1938 and, after serving as an army medical corpsman during World War II, went on to earn a degree at the Cumberland School of Law at Samford University in 1947.[14] Beginning his career as an insurance agency attorney, he served a two-year term in the Tennessee House of Representatives in the mid-1950s and then was elected as Davidson County general sessions judge. After a decade in that position, he became the first judge to preside over the Division III Criminal Court. A man of Stringbean's generation, he was older and eccentric by the winter of 1974.[15] A portrait painted by Bing T. Gee that hangs in what is now called the A. A. Birch Building in Nashville captures Judge Cornelius's appearance at the time. Swaddled in black robes, his gray hair distinguished, eyes placid yet sharp behind wire-framed glasses, his lips raised in a slight smile, he epitomizes the appearance of a solemn old judge.[16]

Judge Cornelius showed no interest in cutting John a break. He overruled the writ of habeas corpus motion and listened as a new public defender on John's team, James Havron, made another motion to exclude reporters from the hearing.[17] "A closed trial creates more problems than it solves," Judge Cornelius declared. "The news media not only has the right but the responsibility to cover this hearing. I've always found the press to be fair in this county. The public is entitled to know not only that justice is being done but how it is being done." With his motion shut down, Havron waived John's right to a preliminary hearing, binding him to the grand jury along with Doug and Roy. On Monday, March 4, two days after the Stringbean auction, the "Davidson County Grand Jury returned a two-count murder indictment" against both John and Doug and an indictment of "accessory after the fact of murder and for concealing stolen property" against Roy.[18]

As the spring accomplished amid the colors of jonquils, redbuds, and dogwoods, Stringbean continued to be remembered even as country music continued to change. The day after the grand jury indictments, Joe Allison, head of Capitol Records in Nashville, honored String and Tex Ritter at the Nashville Songwriters Association's honorary banquet.[19] But the Songwriter of the Year Award went to Kris Kristofferson for "Why Me," which was released on the *Jesus Was a Capricorn* album, a surely unimaginable title to Uncle Dave or Stringbean. Hank Williams Jr. now took a turn away from the past and to the present's outlaw-country movement being spearheaded by String's old Ridgetop neighbor Willie Nelson, along with Waylon Jennings. The Ides of March saw the final performance of the Opry at the Ryman.[20] The next night, a besieged President Nixon participated in the show on the stage of the new Opry House as part of the dedication ceremonies: he played "Happy Birthday" on the piano while the crowd sang to his wife, who was turning sixty-two that weekend.[21] An era had ended and another had begun. But String, even in death, bridged the gap, alive as ever on television screens in *Hee Haw*.

SANITY TRIAL: MAY–JULY 1974

April passed quietly into May, with Judge Cornelius setting the trial date for July 15.[22] That month *Country Song Roundup* finally ran the article for which Genevieve Waddell had interviewed String before the murders. Still preserved in the present tense in which it was originally written, the article made it seem as if Stringbean were still alive. Also in May, *Detective Files* magazine ran a story, and a special Stringbean memorial version of the Bluegrass Festival was scheduled for the next month in Charlotte, Michigan. On May 10, a hearing was held for Doug's petition for bond. The only witness in the hearing was Bobby Green, who testified that Doug held Stringbean down while John shot him.[23] Green's source was Charlie. Although Shriver objected that Doug had "committed a capital offense," Cornelius ruled that bond would be set at $30,000 because the state failed to carry "the burden of proof to satisfy the constitutional requirements necessary to deny a man his liberty." It was a victory for the defense that would seem to spell trouble for Shriver. In fact, Cornelius and Shriver had locked antlers before, and Cornelius had not exactly endeared himself to Metro police. On the other hand, if the judge could be convinced of someone's guilt, he showed no leniency, and signs had not been in favor of John Brown.[24]

But John now had on his team one of the most dynamic young lawyers in Nashville, Arnold Peebles. The thirty-six-year-old was the son of a judge of the same name in Columbia, Tennessee. Receiving his law degree from the University of Tennessee, Peebles began his career as a clerk to the Tennessee State Supreme Court, then became an assistant under Shriver, serving as a prosecutor with the district attorney's office. At that point, Peebles joined with

Binkley, gaining a formidable reputation as a flamboyantly brilliant young attorney. Then, abruptly, Binkley expelled him. Peebles's drinking had interfered with his work.[25] An intense, addictive personality, Peebles's alcohol problems had first emerged in college. He may have been part of the Nashville establishment as Shriver was, but whereas Shriver (seven years older) represented the staid, stable, genteel order, Peebles came across as a cocky, headstrong scrapper with a chip on his shoulder and given to theatrics. The contrast of Shriver and Peebles would become so compelling that Binkley, great as he was, would be virtually a third wheel in the trial's optics.

Peebles pursued a novel tactic of entering an insanity plea for his client and arguing that case separately from the actual murder trial. John had been undergoing evaluation by psychiatrists at Central State Hospital for months. As May gave way to June, he was being tested for a brain tumor because a scan revealed a shadow.[26] Despite acknowledging that the results of the testing largely hurt John's plea of insanity and a Central State report in the beginning of July confirmed that John was "sane and competent to stand trial," announcement came that a sanity hearing would take place.[27]

Peebles was working another angle also. John was telling him a different story of the murder.[28] In his telling, not only had Charlie set up the deal, but when John and Doug went to his home the night of the murder, Charlie, contrary to his claim, had also given them money not to dissuade them from committing murder but as what John understood to be a kind of advanced payment for executing the crime. Not only that, but Charlie had also given them a carbine and little white pills and told them he would meet them at the Akemans' home that night. They then took off, with John driving initially. But then the pills kicked in, and John passed out. The next thing he knew, Doug woke him saying he, John, had killed Stringbean and Estelle. He had no memory of anything himself. He could only say what Doug had told him. But Doug may have been using John's history of not being conscious of or remembering committing violent acts against him in order to shift blame.

It was one thing for John to claim all of this, but he claimed a witness could confirm it. One evening in the workhouse, when Doug thought John was asleep, John overheard him tell someone that John had indeed been passed out in the car during the murder. The man Doug told this to was none other than Kenneth McKee, the man arrested with Roy back in January. If McKee could corroborate this story, then the entire texture of the case could change. It might implicate Doug, or, more important, someone else.

In fact, Peebles began to build an argument that it was actually Charlie who had committed the murders. He discovered that Charlie had built a brand-new facility for his welding business since the murders and had paid cash for interest in racehorses around the same time. Did these activities, combined with Charlie's paying such high fees for Binkley, indicate a suspicious recent cash influx? Then there was that yellow truck seen on the night of the murder. Could it be that Charlie had actually shown up at the Akemans' home that night and forced them at gunpoint to give him the large amounts of cash they had hidden on the property? If so, then it made sense that, given their knowing him, he would have to kill them to silence them as witnesses. Could Charlie have shot Stringbean with one of his own guns, perhaps one of the .22 rifles, as Doug had claimed in that phone call to the *Tennessean* just after the murders? Dr. Simpkins's autopsy had not confirmed that Stringbean's wound had actually been from a .32 automatic slug, and Peebles was not buying the idea that Doug and John inexplicably swapped weapons that night.

Presenting an alternative murder scenario with Charlie as the triggerman might set his client free, although Peebles faced the daunting problem that Charlie was no longer a charged party in the case and was even a *witness*. Whatever drop Peebles thought he might have on Charlie was essentially moot, but he intended to go after him on the stand anyway.

As scheduled, on July 15, in the very heat of summer (the high reaching ninety degrees), *State of Tennessee v. John A. Brown, Jr.* commenced in the Davidson County Division III Criminal Court, with Judge Cornelius presiding. Shriver represented the state, and Peebles represented John. It took two days to finalize the jury of five women and seven men, whose names were all published in the paper.[29] Shriver took pains to understand the jurors' psychologies, asking if they could find John Brown sane if he "planned the crime and then drank a lot and then claimed no memory of the crime." Peebles too probed, trying to see how the jurors felt about insanity pleas, asking if they saw it as "an attempt to get out of a crime by a trick or something like that." Shriver stressed that the defense sought to convince the jury that John did not know right from wrong, but Peebles explained that the "legal definition of insanity in Tennessee is that a person cannot 'appreciate the nature and quality of his acts,' or that if he does know the consequences of his acts, that he did not know they were wrong."

With the jury picked, the arguments began on the morning of Wednesday, July 17. Because the plea had been entered by the defense, the burden of proof belonged to Peebles. Addressing the jury, Peebles explained that he well knew an "aura of suspicion" surrounded this case and noted that "the course of this trial is very novel, in a lot of respects. One is, that the defendant has entered a special plea of not guilty by reason of insanity." He acknowledged that professional psychiatric evaluators would speak for both sides of the case and that the difference in viewpoint would be clear: "All I can do is attempt to show why the opinions of persons that I will present to you are more valid than those presented from the opposite standpoint," he stated. "I will attempt, as best I can, to show fallacies or weaknesses in the conclusions that have been drawn by those persons employed by the State of Tennessee."[30]

Shriver followed with his opening statement. He, too, noted that there would be conflicted psychiatric evidence and agreed with Peebles that the jury would need to use its own common sense. Predictably, Shriver reminded the jury of the horrible crime that had been committed. He also, however, asserted that "everybody is going to agree" that John Brown "is a man with some emotional disturbance. . . . But, the fact that he is a different kind of fellow doesn't mean that he is insane." Brown might be like someone the jury has known sometime, definitely angry and violent, but none of that necessarily added up to insanity. Shriver closed with the memorable sentence, "What you've got here is a man that's not crazy, he's just mean."[31]

The case consisted of John's family testifying to his troubled past followed by a parade of expert witnesses. By the final day, July 19, Peebles was holding his own and may have succeeded in creating doubts in jurors' minds. But then came Dr. John Kington, a psychiatrist Shriver held for the end who neatly and powerfully dispelled any doubts about evaluations showing John to be sane. Seeing the tide turn against him, John actually accused Kington of lying. Clenching his fists, John responded to Peebles's quieting him by throwing "down a small brown diary, which testimony indicated he had kept during his confinement at Central State" and contradicted Kington's assertion. Despite Peebles's efforts to impeach Dr. Kington, the damage had been done. After less than an hour's deliberation, the jury returned to the courtroom with the verdict of sane at 8:28 pm. Shriver complimented Peebles to reporters, commending him for "'doing an outstanding job' in what Peebles told the jury was probably the hardest case he will ever try in his career." Peebles actually wept after his summation and as John's parents thanked him. He also attacked the state's witnesses to the press: "In my judgment, some Professional people are prostituting their professions so that mental health people can avoid doing their duty. There was borderline perjury committed by some of the Central State Hospital witnesses."[32]

That the handwriting was on the wall for the trial to come surely vexed Peebles. Shriver told the press that "despite virtual admission of John Brown's guilt in the sanity hearing, a guilty plea would be very unlikely." "I don't believe this is a case that is negotiable," he said. "This is one of those classes of cases where the public has the right to see it all aired in a trial."[33] It was a striking statement about the spectacle of public justice and, for many, vengeance the process was becoming.

A CONFESSION AND SHENANIGANS: JULY 21–JULY 26, 1974

Immediately after the decision on John's sanity, a remarkable sequence of events occurred that would play a major role in the murder trial. Sunday, July 21, *Nashville Banner* reporter Larry Brinton received a phone call from Joe Binkley saying that Doug Brown wanted to give him a statement. The reporter went to the Metro Workhouse where, with Binkley present, Doug spoke for more than two hours. Doug essentially gave the story Downey had been telling, although now with new details.[34] He explained that he had been having money problems and so planned for days to rob Stringbean because he had heard there was $25,000 on the property. After driving around smoking and drinking all day, Doug and John went to Charlie's to borrow a gun. Charlie refused, giving them a $100 bill and telling them to forget about the robbery. John and Doug went on anyway, driving up to the house and, seeing the station wagon parked, back out to the road, where they pulled off and put up the hood to make it look as if they were having car trouble.

Doug and John had then walked all around the field to the back door, which they broke in order to unlock it and enter. They ransacked the house but, finding no money, sat down and turned on Stringbean's radio to listen to the Opry in order to know when he might be coming back. After putting the Akemans' guns and other items in a pillowcase, they drank beer from the refrigerator and smoked while they waited and John kept watch at the window. Despite John's watch, Stringbean surprised them when he drove up and came in shooting. Doug knocked him down on his back and was on top of him, holding Stringbean's arm stretched above his head while he kept shooting. Then Stringbean's body went limp, John having shot him. (Doug's narrative accounted for the bullet being stopped by the carpeted floor and later falling from Stringbean's clothing, although it put John in a difficult position to shoot Stringbean in the chest, with Doug on top of him.) Estelle appeared at the front door at that moment, screamed, and ran away. John followed, shooting her once to fell her and then killing her, execution style, as she begged for her life. He came back holding her purse (Doug left out the story Downey had told that John was grinning, saying this was like being back in Vietnam).

With the murders done, John then rolled Stringbean over onto his stomach and searched his back pockets. This detail accounted for Stringbean's lying facedown when Grandpa found him. At the same time, it raised a question why two working-class men, one of whom had grown up on a farm, did not think to check the front bib pocket of String's Liberty overalls, especially in light of the fact that the story around town distinctly mentioned his carrying a wad of money there. At any rate, Doug and John then took the keys to the station wagon, loaded the guns and chain saw inside, and drove it and John's car to the quarry, where they transferred the goods to John's car. They took two handbags that Stringbean had brought home with him and put one inside the other, with its contents, and weighted it down with rocks. They threw the bag into Bloodworth's pond along Ebeneezer Road where they had played as children.

It was a remarkable statement as written by Brinton, quoting Doug periodically. Doug made no mention of a will in this telling. He claimed that he had not made this statement sooner because he was afraid of John. He admitted to calling the *Tennessean* anonymously from a phone booth but made no mention of his having claimed that the murders were committed with Stringbean's own gun. Doug played up his remorse over the whole situation and insisted that it was a mistake and had not been meant to turn into murder. This kind of newspaper confession was a Binkley tactic to get a defendant's story into a trial without having to be cross-examined and in a way designed to create sympathy for Doug.[35] As Hal McDonough, who would participate in the trial as part of Shriver's team, later explained, this approach "depended on the fact that the prosecution would introduce that statement. Had the prosecution chosen not to, then the statement could not have been introduced by Binkley."[36]

Before he went to work writing the article, Brinton hurried off to Bloodworth's pond with photographer Jack Gunter and Sherman Nickens, whom he swore to secrecy so the *Nashville Banner* would not lose the scoop to the *Tennessean*.[37] Brinton, Nickens, and Gunter were not entirely clear as to how to get to the pond. They stopped multiple times so that Brinton could make phone calls to find out the precise directions. Who exactly gave these directions he never revealed on record, but when they finally arrived, Charlie and Roy Brown happened to appear only ten minutes later. This initial foray failed to produce any results, so Brinton and company returned the next morning. It seems that Brinton either made or received more phone calls in order to get a clearer understanding of where to look in the pond. This time they quickly found a satchel floating, which Nickens retrieved (he and Gunter had both donned bathing suits). Brinton put the bag in the trunk and drove to Nickens's home in Goodlettsville where they examined the contents, finding checks from Opryland, a contract with the Wil-Helm Agency, and Stringbean's hat and costume. Gunter snapped a photo of the Stringbean costume laid out on the ground, empty of a person yet eerily and tragically evoking the persona it represented. The bottom of the bag was ripped and papers were bulging out. They finished examining the evidence at two in the afternoon, which was after the *Banner*'s deadline, so it was necessary for Brinton to sit on the article, with photographs taken by Gunter, *and the bag* until the next day.

Later that day, Brinton was informed that another group was going to the pond. Who told him this news remains unclear. In the murder trial, Shriver would imply that John or Peebles had contacted his office, implying that *his* office had contacted Brinton. Shriver would later say on record in the trial (although in the absence of the jury) that "Channel 4 called me and told me that Mr. Peebles wanted me to take John Brown out to this pond and show me where the gun was." Also not clear is how it just so happened that on that same day, John somehow was ready to tell about the location of the satchels and murder weapon. At any rate, Brinton drove back out to the pond, arriving about the same time John and his entourage of Shriver, Dave Roberts, and R. V. Smith did, around three thirty or four. Nickens and Gunter also came, Nickens showing them the bag he had found as well as the contents in it.[38] Brinton told it differently, claiming that the bag remained in *his* possession that day and that the second group did not know about the first discovery. Brinton claimed he stood and watched them search, knowing the whole time the bag was in his trunk. "That's competition," he said on camera later, with a knowing grin.[39] The second group sent a skin diver down to search until dark, finding nothing, but returned the next day to discover another bag floating. This bag contained papers bearing Stringbean's name, including an envelope from the Don Light Talent Agency, and rocks.[40] There was no will or murder weapon. In fact, further searches and even draining the pond failed to produce either. To this day, neither a will nor the murder weapon has been found.

Following this dubious sequence of events, Shriver, Peebles, and Hunter took John back to the workhouse and officially interviewed him. The resulting statement presented John's version of the night of the murders, which he had been telling Peebles.[41] Informing John of Doug's confession appearing in the *Banner* that day, they got John's version. Parts of John's statement appeared on the front page of the *Tennessean* under the incriminating title "Akeman Robbery Plan Laid to Charles Brown." Butler assured the press that Charlie was no killer. In fact, Charlie was "the nicest one of the bunch of them," and if Doug and John "had listened to him (Charles) they wouldn't be in the trouble they are in now." Not only that, but Charlie had no need for money, and he was "friends with many country music stars and several of them called when he was arrested in January and offered to testify in his behalf." John, on the other hand, was a lying lowlife whose claims were uncorroborated. "Doug told it exactly like it was, exactly like Charles told it, exactly like Jack Holt told it," Butler said. "The only one who says differently is John. I'm not surprised at anything he says."[42]

It was everyone else's word against John, who not only was charged as the triggerman but was even acknowledging he believed Doug's account of what he had done. No one seemed to notice that the very legal principles Butler cited could just as easily be turned the other direction. The only validating difference between Doug's and John's differing stories was corroboration, but Doug's corroboration came from dubious sources that led back to Doug himself. Moreover, aspects of Doug's story had changed. Which liar should be believed?

In the wake of these events, on July 24, Roy's lawyer, Everett, requested a meeting with Shriver.[43] A six-hour discussion ensued with Roy that included details implicating Charlie. But the corroboration of Roy's and John's comments did not count for as much as Downey's and Doug's story, although that corroboration may have been responsible for the above-mentioned article published a few days later explaining Charlie's involvement away. The die was cast for John, and despite Binkley's efforts, Doug's hopes looked dim as well. Nevertheless, John, Doug, and Roy entered pleas of not guilty (Binkley appending the term "temporary" for Doug) on July 26.[44]

TRIAL PREPARATIONS AND STRINGBEAN MEMORIES: AUGUST–OCTOBER 1974

Summer plodded on in middle Tennessee. On August 15, one week after President Nixon's resignation, notification appeared that Jim Everett had made a motion for Roy's trial to be severed from John and Doug's.[45] Being charged with accessory after the fact depended on John and Doug being found guilty, Everett argued. Also, since Everett intended to "call John and Doug Brown as witnesses in the defense of his client . . . to try the cases together could jeopardize the rights of all three men." No immediate decision came from Judge Cornelius on this motion. In the midst of these doings, a touching tribute to Stringbean appeared in the Sunday, August 18, *Tennessean*'s "Old Timer's Almanac" section. Editor Elmer Hinton noted that the best fishing of the week would be that day through Tuesday, that the next day would be a good one for destroying weeds, and "so far as we know, one of the most famous persons who followed the fishing information here was the late David (Stringbean) Akeman."[46]

Stringbean's memory found preservation in other ways, as well. Mike Lattimore published *The "Stringbean" Banjo Method*. In this booklet, Lattimore presented Stringbean's A tuning along with an explanation and diagram of what Lattimore called String's "rapping" style and a selection of songs. Lattimore claimed that Stringbean had given him his blessing to write the book before he died. With its rudimentary outline, it does little to bring readers closer to the mysteries of Stringbean's quirks and provides no insights into his two-finger picking technique, but it paid proper respect to String's memory. Another preservation of that memory appeared in September when *Hee Haw*'s new season started up again. Stringbean no longer lived and breathed on this show, but where he had stood in the cornfield now a lifeless scarecrow stood as motionless memorial.

As the trial date approached in October and temperatures slipped into the sixties, Peebles and a new attorney on John's team, David Pack, made a motion for another sanity hearing because the two attorneys had more allegations of incompetence and possible corruption at Central State.[47] Pack asserted that expert witnesses from the sanity trial "may have information that, in fact, John Brown is insane." Cornelius denied the motion as well as one "to have Shriver provide the defense attorneys with any information exculpatory to Brown and any information tending to lessen the credibility of any state witnesses." Shriver claimed he had nothing to exonerate John but would give it to the defense if so. Judge Cornelius called the motion too broad, covering "just about everything from creation to resurrection." Meanwhile, in preparation for the trying of the Stringbean case and the Widner case, extra security measures would be taken, including a metal screener.[48]

TRIAL, DAY 1: JURY SELECTED, PROSECUTION BEGINS, OCTOBER 28–29, 1974

The day the trial began, Binkley complained of a "circus-like atmosphere," opining, "Somebody, apparently the sheriff, is making a spectacle of this trial."[49] Two television stations were covering the case. Behind the scenes, Bill Downey flew in for the trial from Akron on Shriver's dime, his beard shaved and long hair cut.[50] Jacobs picked Downey up and took him to stay at Capitol Park Inn where all expenses would be paid. Downey would run up a $450 bill, mostly ordering six packs of beer. The police found this humorous as they did many things about him, including, strangely, his minor lawbreaking.

At the last minute, Cornelius granted the severance of Roy's trial from John and Doug's, and *State of Tennessee v. John A. Brown, Jr., and Marvin Douglas Brown,* #B-2678, B-2679, in Davidson County Criminal Court Division III, began on October 28, 1974. Judge Cornelius sat between the Tennessee flag, with its three stars representing the west, middle, and east parts of the state, and the flag of the United States of America. Shriver was assisted by McDonough. Doug was represented by Binkley, John by Peebles and Pack.

As to be expected, the jury selection was tedious. John, dressed in a light-blue suit, sat during the process staring at the table, making erratic motions with a ballpoint pen. Doug wore a black shirt, collar open, and a dark sport coat as he leaned back in his chair. The jury questioning signaled the concerns and directions of the case. The lawyers focused on the effect of almost a year's worth of media publicity, with Binkley asking whether "mitigating circumstances" would influence jurors. Shriver asked if a companion in crime is as guilty as the triggerman. Peebles asked, "Would you feel any pressure or embarrassment if you found that the state had not proved that this boy (John Brown) committed this crime?"[51] It took until 2:05 the next afternoon to get the jury of nine men and three women (all unnamed this time, except to note that one was African American) finally settled upon.[52] There then followed a three-hour recess that included lengthy debate over the nature of the indictments, most particularly that the main charge was murder regardless of original intent or other crimes committed by the perpetrators.

It was 5:20 p.m. when the jury was finally brought in and argumentation began. The indictments were read, and Peebles notified the court that John Brown would stand mute in the case, which, Cornelius explained, resulted in pleading not guilty. Binkley stated that Doug Brown pled guilty to second-degree murder of Stringbean but not guilty to the charge of the murder of Estelle. No attorney made an opening statement, seeking instead to get to certain witnesses who had been waiting throughout the day for examination. Shriver called Luddie to the stand to paint her picture of David and Estelle as a loving, quiet couple. Next, Grandpa Jones recounted his experience finding the bodies and identified the guns. Even though it was, by then, past 6:00 in the evening, Judge Cornelius permitted Shriver to call one more witness, Kenneth Tate, who in 1972 had been working at Farmers Supply Company in Smithville and who testified that in October 1972 Stringbean traded the McCullough Mini-Max 6 chain saw Jerry Clower had given him for another that had an automatic oiler.[53] Cornelius called a halt at 6:32.

The first day had been relatively uneventful except for one thing. Kenneth McKee had been released from Central State that morning, and Peebles had no idea where he was.[54] Since McKee's testimony could go a long way toward exonerating John, his disappearance was potentially disastrous for Peebles's argument.

TRIAL, DAY 2: THE PROSECUTION CONTINUES, OCTOBER 30, 1974

Adding to the troubles for John's defense, the next morning's proceedings were delayed an hour because Peebles claimed he had a dizzy spell at home. "I am just tired," he told the press. "I have been working pretty hard on this case, but I feel fine now."[55] The truth was that his blood pressure had skyrocketed due to cocaine abuse.[56] Unbeknownst to the public, Peebles was a mess. John Brown Sr. had noticed the attorney constantly rubbing his nose and putting powder from a salve box on the sides of his nose.[57] Mrs. Brown's niece Joyce Wilharm, acting as a go-between for Mr. and Mrs. Brown with Peebles, observed even wilder behavior. She claimed Peebles constantly went to the bathroom and came out with white powder around his nostrils, acting erratic, his tongue thick. One time he crawled around on his hands and knees and put his head in her lap and cried. Peebles had started acting this way immediately after the sanity hearing with the events surrounding Doug's confession.[58]

When the court finally convened, McDonough questioned Skeeter Willis in order to establish the murder timeline. Next, Shriver called Bobby Green to the stand to go over the crime scene. When Peebles began cross-examination, what seemed mere routine reporting turned complex and combative. Peebles prodded the investigation practices, showing how protocol was not followed and that there were problems in evidence collecting. He made a particular effort to show that there were more than two perpetrators. At every turn, Green claimed not to know answers to Peebles's questions. Finally, Judge Cornelius dismissed the jury and spoke to the attorneys: "Court cannot concede/believe that a Metropolitan Homicide Detective can be the prosecutor in a murder case that has significance and has received the public attention or the attention that this murder case has received . . . would have as many answers that he does not know." Cornelius asked Green directly to clarify whether a certain diagram had been drawn. Green answered promptly.[59] But when the jury returned and Peebles resumed the questioning, Green continued claiming to know and recall nothing, again prompting Cornelius to intervene. Despite the judge's pointing out that Green answered all of Shriver's questions but seemed to lose his memory when Peebles questioned him, Green's pattern did not change. It was surely merciful to all involved when the questioning of Green ended.

McDonough then called witnesses who identified John's light-blue 1966 Buick. After having Sparta store owner Nancy Phifer confirm Stringbean's purchasing the Colt .22 Peacemaker, Shriver called Jack Rohtert, who focused on Stringbean's and Estelle's bullet wounds.[60] Peebles exposed Rohtert's lack of ballistics training and failure to do a thorough examination of the wounds. Dr. Simpkins then went over the autopsy, and Peebles hit *him* over insufficient ballistics training also. If Peebles was to be believed, it was not at all definitive that both or either of the Akemans had been shot by a .32.

Simpkins's questioning ended the day at 5:50. Outside the courtroom, the press seized upon Peebles's attempt to show there were more than just two people involved in the murder. "Every time something big happens in this county, the police screw it up," Peebles told the press.[61] The day had indeed gone poorly for the prosecution. Peebles had blown glaring holes in the investigation procedures while weaving an implied story of other murderers present. "I don't think Bobby realized Cornelius is going to allow hearsay testimony," Shriver told the investigators privately concerning Green's testimony. "He kept saying he didn't know when asked about things he knew but didn't see himself. Y'all go ahead and say whatever you know about and let me worry about the hearsay."[62]

TRIAL, DAY 3: THE PROSECUTION CONTINUES, OCTOBER 31, 1974

The next day was Halloween. Proceedings began at 9:15 before the jury returned, with Judge Cornelius telling Luddie she should remove herself from the room whenever she felt herself becoming emotional, as that was apt to affect the jury. It seems also that Charlie Brown and his wife had a way of not wanting to be in the courtroom, and the judge permitted them to leave and not return until the next morning but also admonished them not to speak of the case. The jury was then brought in, and Shriver questioned Jack Holt, Thomas Birdwell, and others concerning recovery of the Akemans' secreted weapons.

Shriver called Tommy Jacobs to the stand. Jacobs discussed investigating the station wagon and his role in finding the Akemans' stolen guns. Jacobs also affirmed his understanding that Doug was armed with a twelve-gauge shotgun, which effectively took him out of the crime and pointed to John as the killer.[63] Peebles went to work on Jacobs, attacking the procedure of building a case on an informant's story. It was Binkley who finally brought back into play those .22 casings that had been lost in the shuffle, but Jacobs's insistence that Doug was armed with the shotgun and not his own .32 evidently registered powerfully with the jury.

Finishing with Jacobs, Shriver called up Dave Roberts to discuss his role in recovering the sawed-off shotgun as well as the effort to find the .32 and Stringbean's bags back in July. Roberts's testimony served to establish that the shotgun had never been fired and therefore that Doug not only had not done the killing but was also remorseful and had told the true story of the murder night. After Peebles's questioning, court adjourned at 5:50 p.m.

TRIAL, DAY 4: THE PROSECUTION RESTS, NOVEMBER 1, 1974

The court reconvened with McDonough questioning Judith Baucom, who had gone to search Doug's trailer on November 13, 1973. She noted that Doug had signed the search warrant himself, but Binkley asserted it was done so under duress from Shriver (whom Peebles outside of court was calling Sherlock Holmes)[64] and Nickens themselves and motioned to suppress the search, which was sustained. The jury returned to hear W. R. Arnold testify to his having gone to the trailer to collect evidence. Next, James Vaughn testified to his role in the investigation, dispelling concerns over whether a pack of Chesterfield cigarettes signified another killer. Felix Elliott and Jack Williams followed. Then Shriver called Charlie Brown to the stand. Charlie told his usual story that he had told John and Doug not to rob Stringbean and then offered the narrative of the murder he claimed Doug and John had told him, doing so in a blow-by-blow way that so upset Luddie she was told to leave.

Now came Peebles's turn to tee off on the man he believed to be the ringleader and triggerman in the crime. He noted that Charlie had said on the stand that he was in the "steel and iron business," and he asked, "How do you spell that steel?" Peebles peppered Charlie with questions about his own alibi for the night of the murder. Charlie could not prove what time he had gone to bed, claiming to have been awakened by a phone call around eleven but then changing his story to say he actually fell asleep while on the phone. When Charlie asserted his brother did not kill the Akemans, Peebles shot back, "I don't think your brother did either, Mr. Brown. Now, Mr. Brown, where was your yellow truck the night of this murder?" Charlie replied that the truck was broken down. Pressing further and expanding the focus, Peebles labored to expose Charlie's alleged criminal activities and his lying. Again and again, Charlie changed his story from his previous testimony. In an effort to expose Charlie as manipulating events, Peebles asked if he had told Larry Brinton over the telephone how to get to Bloodworth's pond. Wary, Charlie replied, "No, sir. Not . . . if I have I don't remember it. Let's put it that way. But, I'm sure I haven't never told anybody."[65] When Peebles finished at last, the jury must have wondered what to do with his accusations against someone who was not a suspect.

Roy then took the stand, followed by Downey. Jacobs found Downey's appearance humorous because he started out slouching and then sat upright to conceal the fact that he was wearing stolen boots. Also, prior to being called, Downey had asked if he could smoke or chew tobacco and, when told no, took the stand with a big wad of chewing gum.[66] In the midst of the questioning, Binkley pointed out, perhaps with some frustration, that it would be easier to understand him if he took the gum out.[67] Cornelius "chuckled, reached under his bench and picked up a trash can. He put the can on top of the bench and Downey threw in the gum."[68] Such was the kind of witness the prosecution's case depended on. After Downey told his story to Shriver, Peebles pressed him about his own criminal activity. Suddenly, Downey's memory did not work so well.

Charlie Hunter next took the stand to tell of his experience in the July expedition to Bloodworth's pond. Shriver asked Hunter if he had talked to McKee about John's claim that Doug had said he was unconscious during the murder, and he replied that he had and that McKee was no longer in jail. Seeing danger for Doug, Binkley engaged in the most lengthy questioning he had yet done, pointing out that Doug had not passed out from taking the pills, so why had John? Binkley then asked Hunter if he believed John's statement, and Hunter replied he did not.[69] Peebles suggested that Hunter maybe did believe McKee, since he had talked to him only two days before this questioning, literally during the trial.

Shriver then called Brinton to the stand to read his entire *Banner* article with Doug's statement aloud. Pack cross-examined, trying to show that Brinton's interview with Doug had been orchestrated. He also raised the question of whether it seemed strange that the smaller bag managed to get out of the larger bag, and could it suggest that someone had been out to the pond previously and separated the bags? Pack also asked if Brinton found the pond solely on Doug's instructions. At first Brinton said yes, but then corrected that information and revealed that he had stopped to make a phone call for more information. Pack asked who it was, prompting a removal of the jury and a discussion about shielding sources. Brinton not only chose not to answer that question, but also admitted that he may have made and received multiple calls in order to find the pond. This information implied Charlie's playing an active role in July, but the jury may not have understood that or known what to do with such information.

With the conclusion of Brinton's questioning, the state rested its case and tendered the balance of its witnesses to the defense. The jury was dismissed for the evening, but the attorneys remained to speak with Judge Cornelius. Peebles was irate that evidence from Doug's house was being suppressed, but Cornelius had ruled and was not taking it back. Finally, at 9:35 p.m., the court adjourned, with a special Saturday session scheduled for the next day.

TRIAL, DAY 5: THE DEFENSE ARGUES AND RESTS, NOVEMBER 2, 1974

On the morning of November 2, the defense presented what was surely one of the weakest defenses in Nashville legal history. The sharp, bombastic, confident lawyer who had worked so hard in the sanity hearing now seemed lost. Peebles now seemed an incompetent who could not advance a coherent argument. The drugs in his system may have impaired him, or perhaps the pressure weighed too heavily, or maybe both.

He began by noting that John Brown wished to change his plea from insane to not guilty, apparently forgetting that the original plea had been for John to stand mute. The attorney then made a brief opening speech explaining that his case would have two parts: first, "that there are material pieces of evidence not immanent to the nature that you should have before you for your consideration" and, second, "I am going to ask you to examine the proof in this case. . . . Can you leave out the question with a verdict of, what if he didn't go in the house?"[70] It was not the clearest or most eloquent statement.

With that, Peebles called Nickens, taking him through the ballistics, bringing up those .22 casings, asking if they matched Stringbean's guns. Nickens did not know, which suggested that they were never tested. Peebles also asked Nickens if the investigators had inquired as to whether any of the .22 bullet holes had already been in the walls, obviously thinking of the Burdette shooting years earlier.[71] Nickens could not remember if they had asked, but Peebles did not follow up or explain the full significance of the question.

Peebles then prodded the problem of Stringbean's body being found face down, while most of the blood on him was found on his back and no bullet hole had been found in the back of his jacket. But again the lawyer lost the thread of his argument and failed to show why these points were important. Instead, he switched to talking about Bear Burnette's not being given the polygraph test and then James Hamlett's testimony about the yellow truck, still not drawing clear connections among these details. He finally hit upon more useful testimony when Nickens's comments might have implicated Charlie's directing Brinton to Bloodworth's pond. In an unexpected turn, Peebles told the jury five people mentioned having seen parked at Stringbean's house around eight thirty the night of the murder a 1963 brown Ford, which happened to be the exact same car that belonged to the mother of Darlene, Doug's girlfriend.[72] Overall, Nickens's testimony began to tell a different kind of story with larger connections, but jurors surely were confused.

Finally finishing with Nickens, Peebles called Jacobs and began a wandering, aimless line of questioning with the jury absent, prompting Judge Cornelius to burst in saying they were wasting a lot of time and to bring the jury back in.[73] Peebles made no fuss about this, and Jacobs was dismissed. With the jury back in the courtroom, Pack called up Bear Burnett, who told of his learning about the murder from a neighbor seeing all the cars as well as his discovering the Akemans' station wagon at the quarry. He explained that his brother bought String's house at the auction and that his nephew currently lived in the house. He had taken the time to observe the house and the bullet holes in it. The record is not entirely clear if Burnette's map differed from the diagram that had been drawn earlier in the trial.

Next to be called was the hapless and previously missing Kenneth McKee. He was clearly having trouble mentally and was scheduled to enter the Veterans Administration Mental Institution. Peebles asked him point-blank about the incident with Doug, but McKee claimed he had no memory of it. "I was in pretty bad shape, myself, suicidal, I needed help myself," McKee said. "It's hard for me to put together in my mind exactly what did happen or what was said to me. It's really hard for me to put it together."[74] When it looked as if McKee might reveal something, Shriver objected to it as hearsay. Even more remarkable than such a brazen objection, given that the prosecution's case was based on hearsay, was Peebles's giving up the questioning because it would be hearsay. Peebles was unraveling.

That unraveling continued with the testimonies of Darlene Powell, John Brown Sr., and John's current wife, Deborah, who offered the disturbing news that she had lied in a previous statement to protect John because he had told her Doug had told him he had committed the murders.[75] Peebles struggled through his closing argument. "This ain't no lawsuit," he said. "It's a bunch of scrambled slop. I hope and pray some of you who feel like they don't have the guns in this case will sit back and fight as hard as I have for this boy."[76] Peebles explained that John had a history of mental problems and thus believed he had killed the Akemans because "a man he looked on as a brother (Douglas) told him he had." The lawyer reiterated that the .32 had been Doug's, that he "really liked that pistol, he was crazy about it, he even talked a man into giving it to him, . . . so, please just out of curiosity, ask yourself why John would be armed with it that night."[77]

Then Peebles asserted that "Charles Brown—'a picture of evil'—initiated and planned the Akeman robbery and was probably the man who shot and killed the country music couple." Thus, at last, Peebles made his ideas about Charlie explicit, and he insisted that the police ignored evidence that "would have determined who was at the Akeman farm and who fired the shots." In fact, he went on, Charlie would go on leading his "'wild band of rapers in Robertson County' if the jury 'puts these two young men away and ends the worries of Charles Brown. What kind of thing is trying to be rammed down your throats? . . . What kind of thing is trying to be rammed down the throat of John Brown?'"[78] It was all too little, too late. The day had been a disaster.

Binkley's summation was far more measured. He could not help, in light of Brinton's article, that Doug admitted he had done wrong. But, he said, "I hope you can find some way to give this boy a decent break. This man's a young man and maybe there's something about him that can be salvaged. I'm not trying to paint a pretty picture of this boy. He doesn't say he's innocent, but he had no idea Mrs. Akeman was going to get killed."[79] It was an appeal to the heart.

In his closing, Shriver kept the focus on the brutality of the murders Doug had confessed to being present at and John had said he could not deny. "Whatever you think about Charlie Brown," Shriver said, "that is a case for another jury at another time." Shriver left ringing in the ears of the jury an appeal to the city's need to see someone punished for the murders: "We should keep these men locked up just as long as possible." When he finished, John "scribbled the numerals '99' twice on a piece of paper and passed the paper to Douglas Brown."[80]

SENTENCE AND IMPRISONMENT: NOVEMBER 2, 1974

With the argumentation ended, Cornelius charged the jury, which left the courtroom to deliberate at 5:15 p.m. Two and a half hours later, at 8:45, the jurors returned. The jury foreman, William G. Sadler, read the verdict:

> In case B-2679, we the Jury, find the defendant, John A. Brown, guilty of murder in the first degree of David Akeman and fix his punishment at ninety-nine years in the penitentiary. In B-2678, We, the Jury, find the defendant, John A. Brown, guilty of murder in the first degree in the death of Estelle S. Akeman and fix his punishment at ninety-nine degrees . . . ninety-nine years in the penitentiary. We recommend that these two sentences be served concurrently. In case B-2679, We, the Jury, find the defendant, Marvin Douglas Brown, guilty of murder in the first degree in the death of David Akeman and fix his punishment at ninety-nine years in the penitentiary. In B-2678, We, the Jury, find the defendant, Marvin Douglas Brown, guilty of murder in the first degree in the death of Estelle S. Akeman and fix his punishment at ninety-nine years in the penitentiary. We recommend that the sentences be served concurrently.[81]

John and Doug sat quietly, showing no emotion. Darlene cried aloud, while Deborah "placed her hand over her face and wept quietly." Judge Cornelius made one change—instead of concurrent sentences, he made them consecutive, with each man eligible for pardon in thirty years. When court adjourned, Binkley and Doug sat talking, while Peebles stood up with his "arm around John Brown's shoulders and talked to him briefly."[82]

As people made their way out into the pleasant seventy-degree night, some spoke to the press. Luddie believed justice had been served, "but I feel sorry for these boys' families and I feel sorry for the boys themselves." Shriver said, "It is never pleasant to send a man to prison for the rest of his life but with all the proofs in this case I think the verdicts were justified." When reporters asked Peebles about his efforts to find holes in the investigation, he replied, "Obviously there weren't." Binkley commented, "I think the sentence was too harsh, but I wasn't surprised. My client took it well. I had prepared him for this."[83]

The police took John and Doug by the workhouse to get their belongings and then to the Tennessee State Penitentiary. This fortress-like building had been constructed in 1898, back when Uncle Dave was still learning old-time music and long before there had come into existence the Grand Ole Opry, country music, David Akeman, Stringbean. Later, Doug would be installed at Mountain State Penitentiary in East Tennessee, also constructed in the late nineteenth century and harboring Martin Luther King Jr.'s assassin, James Earl Ray, and nearly the fictional Hannibal Lecter in *The Silence of the Lambs*.

Newspapers across the country reported the verdict. On November 5—Guy Fawkes Day in England—the *Tennessean* ran an interview with John from prison in which he claimed it had been part of the plan from the start "for him to take the rap and plead insanity." According to John, this scheme had been in place all along: "Insanity was all planned before we got arrested. We had a meeting out in the field where Charlie's . . . new shop is right now. . . . We planned then that if we got arrested, I would plead insanity and take the rap for everybody. I would have to stay in a mental institution for a while and nobody else would have to do any time. For doing this, I would get some money." John still maintained he could not remember what happened at the Akemans' house and that he wished he could. Again he rehearsed the events of the hours leading up to the murder, stating flat-out that Charlie had lied about his involvement. The article went on, "Brown also said yesterday that he feels there were at least two other persons at the Akeman home the night of the murders, in addition to himself and Doug Brown." "'They never told me,' he said, 'but I have heard them talk about it.'" John said he bore no ill will toward Doug but did have hard feelings against Charlie, although "not a feeling to hurt him." He said he "got weak in the knees" and "almost messed my pants" when the jury read the verdict, and he "wanted to break down and cry like a baby" when he walked into the prison. He did not like prison, but "I'm not going to run because it's not in me. I'm just going to do my time and not give anybody any trouble but I'm not going to take any."[84]

John's comments may have resonated with any readers who harbored doubts that justice had fully been served, given that Charlie had not even been tried. Peebles had succeeded in highlighting gaps in the evidence, and the prosecution's building its case on such a band of ruffians was problematic. One juror commented, "There was a general feeling among the jury that we didn't know half of what the real truth was, a feeling that none of the witnesses could be believed." Another juror explained how a decision was reached anyway: "There was a lot of missing pieces, but it was clear cut that they (the Browns) were there and that they were armed, and that was it."[85]

The next week, November 10, the anniversary of David's and Estelle's deaths, a small article mentioned that the arson charge against Felix Elliott had been dropped. "This is the deal he wanted," Shriver said. "There is no question he had some extremely valuable information to trade with."[86] The trial of Charlie Brown that Shriver had suggested might be held at another time never took place.

In December Stringbean's brother Robert officially donated the Vega No. 9 to the Country Music Hall of Fame.[87] It was a nice closing gesture, the end of a terrible ordeal. The killers had been caught and punished to the limit of the law. Nashville, the country music industry, David's and Estelle's families, and even the Browns could move on.

FORGETTING TO FORGET YOU
1975-2014

The Akeman furor had hardly died down when Nashville exploded with another dramatic investigation when nine-year-old Marsha Trimble went missing in February 1975. The case would remain unsolved for years, but it involved many of the same investigators as the Stringbean case and their charging the wrong person in the crime. In the midst of the early months of this saga, news of Peebles's addiction emerged. In April, as *Master Detective* magazine ran an article on the Stringbean murder and trial, John wrote Peebles a letter informing him he no longer wanted his counsel.[1] By early June, increasing evidence of Peebles's committing conflict-of-interest violations was being brought to light.[2] On the twenty-fifth, the *Tennessean* announced that Peebles, "citing 'mental and emotional difficulties' as extenuating circumstances, has pleaded guilty to charges of professional misconduct and surrendered his law license to the Tennessee Supreme Court."[3]

E. E. "Bo" Edwards stepped in to represent John. Motions for a retrial for Doug and John had been registered within a month of the November 1974 sentencing, and Edwards went to work right away to continue those efforts for John. Delays came with completing the court transcript because the court reporter had resigned. As those delays continued, on September 27, Charlie Monroe passed away.

The next year, Edwards succeeded in getting an audience with Cornelius. John's father and Joyce Wilharm testified to Peebles's drug use and its effects on him, but their accounts failed to impress Judge Cornelius. Edwards kept at it, crystallizing his charges into a list of problems in the trial, including the fact that it was held under such publicity as to make an unbiased jury impossible, that Tommy Jacobs had made a prejudicial but unsubstantiated claim that John and Doug had swapped weapons, that Larry Brinton's article should have been excluded because it was based on hearsay, that the evidence did not support the jury's decision, and that John had received ineffective counsel.[4] In the meantime, Jacobs offered his story beyond the courtroom via his collaboration with *Banner* reporter Warren B. Causey in a book titled *The Stringbean Murders*, published in November. When the coauthors attempted to sell it at Nashville's Fan Fair, the event's organizer prohibited them from doing so, perhaps a sign that at least some in the industry wanted to move on from the murders.[5]

In June 1976, Edwards again argued his case. Dr. W. R. C. Stewart Jr. testified to the effects of cocaine on a person's performance, but Shriver established that Dr. Stewart had not examined Peebles himself.[6] Meanwhile, that year Bobby Land released the single "Banjo Man (a Tribute to Stringbean)," written by Phil Whitehawk and released on Dream Records (DR-076). The year ended with Shriver and Everett striking an agreement to reduce Roy's charge to "attempt to commit a felony," for which he received a suspended sentence of eleven months and twenty-nine days, with charges of receiving and concealing stolen goods dismissed.[7] A few months later, and more than three years after the murders, in April 1977, the reward money was finally awarded. Felix Elliott, James Hamlett, Terr Mingly, Donna Beardsworth, Bill Downey, Jack Holt, and a genealogist named W. A. "Bill" Jones all laid claim to the $17,000. But chancellor Ben Cantrell awarded the full amount to Downey.[8]

Finally, on September 9, 1977, Cornelius denied the motion for a retrial. In yet further appeal argumentation, Edwards added to his long list of Peebles's mistakes the idea that three new Supreme Court decisions should be applied retroactively concerning ineffective assistance, consecutive sentencing, and the standards for insanity.[9] David Raybin argued his case with Thomas Shriver at his side, and Judge Cornelius sided with them, saying:

> The record of the trial . . . reflects a most aggressive defense counsel, assisted by a very able and aggressive co-counsel whose credentials are well known by all courts of this state. . . . Considering the totality of this case, there was very little antagonism between this defendant's lawyers and the co-defendant's abled and experienced counsel. . . . Defense counsel in this case demonstrated an extreme sensitivity to the issues and unquestionably put the prosecution to its proof and pressed relentlessly the question of reasonable doubt. It is tragic that the after-

math saw an aggressive young lawyer retire his license, but in no way did this amount to a violation of this defendant's right to effective assistance of counsel.[10]

Stringbean's sister Nora died on May 23, 1978, as appeals continued into the next decade.[11] In May 1982, with Peebles now reinstated and practicing law again, Edwards made his case for a retrial. On the witness stand, Peebles admitted the poor job he had done and insisted that the trial would have gone differently had cocaine not interfered. "I thought the proof was extremely meager, extremely sloppily presented, to me," Peebles said. "I think if you removed the name 'Stringbean Ackerman' out of the case, make it a normal case, [John Brown] would walk out not guilty, and if it was tried properly by his counsel." Of all his mistakes in performance, Peebles said, the "most glaring example I remember so vividly was, and I even knew at the time it was horrible, was the final argument."[12] The district court judge, L. Clure Morton, was no more impressed than Cornelius had been.

John was faring well enough in prison.[13] However, a bizarre event occurred in 1983 when some Opry performers, including Jan Howard, performed for the inmates and John jumped onstage to introduce them. John may have meant it as a positive gesture, but it angered the performers.[14] Also angry were Stringbean's and Estelle's families, who felt they had not received all of their inheritance.[15] While Larry Westbrook had stated the estate to be $334,238 after taxes and fees, only $150,000 was left to go to the heirs. Ironically, attorneys and the state of Tennessee together received more of Stringbean's money than the killers allegedly came away with.

In 1987 John's wife, Deborah, was making her first appeals to public sympathy on John's behalf in a newspaper article bemoaning her situation at Christmas with her husband being in prison.[16] "Both of us get real depressed during the holidays, and it never gets any better," she said. "You see a lot of children during the holidays, and I know I won't be able to have any." The next year, on March 31, 1988, Stringbean's brother Robert died of a heart attack in Scottsburg, Indiana.[17]

By the start of the next decade, Doug and John shifted their attention to parole. In November 1992, Roy Acuff died, and the next month John asked for parole based "on an old state law commuting any prison term over 65 years as if it were a 30-year sentence."[18] The Correction Department replied that his parole date would be 2028. But several months later, on July 19, 1993, John and Doug appeared before the parole board and were denied.[19] Now bespectacled, John especially sought to appear benign and sympathetic. The warden of the Lois M. DeBerry Special Needs Facility, where John was now incarcerated, spoke well of him. John claimed he still could not recall committing the crime but through research felt he had had flashbacks and was convinced of his guilt. He knew he had changed into a better person after his 1974–76 solitary confinement, and he had been a model inmate, completing his associate degree, becoming active in Alcoholics Anonymous, and not having had a "single 'write-up' or disciplinary action" in nineteen years.

Luddie and District Attorney Torry Johnson spoke against the Browns, but perhaps there was a hint of hope for John.[20] Nashville was changing. It was growing quickly, taking on more outsiders. In 1994 the skyline welcomed the "Batman Building" (currently the AT&T Building), and the country music industry was booming with a new crop of stars led by the pop-crossover phenomenon Garth Brooks. Losses in the older generation piled up in the meantime: Minnie Pearl died in March 1996, and six months later Bill Monroe passed away.

But Stringbean was not to be forgotten. In 1996 a statue of him was unveiled in Jackson County. The event coincided with the inaugural Stringbean Memorial Bluegrass Festival, organized by David's nephew Phillip Akemon. Porter Wagoner unveiled the statue, and Grandpa and Ramona came to the event. It continues to be held every year the week of Stringbean's birthday.

The next year, 1997, sensational news broke that money had been found hidden in the Akemans' house.[21] According to the newspaper, Tommy Jacobs had been at the house to do an interview for the Nashville Network when the home's current owner, whose name Jacobs could not remember and who "could not be located for comment," had told the detective about finding old, deteriorated fragments of money stuck behind the mantle. Taking the mantle off, the owner "found the remnants of probably what was a lot of money," Jacobs said, and then added, "It would stand to reason that nobody is going to stick a couple of bucks in there in the hollowed place behind the mantle. . . . It's just very reasonable that that's all or part of the money that Stringbean had hidden in the cabin all these years." The tentative tone of the story along with its less than clear, dubiously substantiated, and even missing details give it a bit of a suspect air. William Faimon was never contacted about this alleged find.[22] There is no reason not to believe Jacobs saw what he saw, but there is little verification to ensure that the shredded bits of apparently real cash were not planted for the sake of a story. It *is* worth noting that Bobby Anderson, now retired from his newspaper ownership in Sparta, did write that a fellow church member named Jason McCaslin claimed to be the one who found the money while renovating the house ahead of a new family moving in.[23] Whether real or not, the story has become a part of Stringbean lore, lending it an intriguing symmetry.

Also in 1997, *Hee Haw* ended its long run, and more people from String's life, death, and era died. Luddie died on July 30.[24] On October 25, Thomas

Shriver died, and three months later String's beloved friend Grandpa suffered two strokes after an Opry performance and passed away on February 19, 1998. Three months later, Frank Sinatra exited the world's stage.

Stringbean's case made a new appearance on September 14 as part of the first season of A&E's *City Confidential* series. Episode 8, "Nashville: Murder in Music City," featured interviews with String's Opry and *Hee Haw* colleagues as well as Nickens, Jacobs, Brinton, and others involved in the case. Around the same time, the Nashville Network program aired, featuring interviews with Jacobs, Porter Wagoner, and John Brown himself. In the larger cultural saga, young men in the United States were now wearing their pants low around their knees just as Stringbean had. It was not a conscious imitation, and it may be that the practice derived from oversize prison clothing, while precedents could be found in cruel buck-busting acts against enslaved people.[25] At a deeper level discussed earlier, however, the style was part of a tradition of racial performativity of which Stringbean was a part.

The new millennium arrived despite media Y2K hype that the world might end. Nashville was experiencing a renaissance, growing at a breakneck pace, while bluegrass and old-time music returned to WSM with the popularity of the Cohen Brother's film *O Brother, Where Art Thou?* (2000), which featured Ralph Stanley's singing that old Kentucky number Dick Burnett had written not long before David Akeman's birth, "Man of Constant Sorrow." Two years into the millennium, String's brother Alfred passed away in Pleasant Grove, Utah, on August 3, 2002.[26]

On January 8, 2003, Doug died in Brushy Run of natural causes and was buried in the prison cemetery.

John, meanwhile, had committed himself to God, driven by Deborah's encouragement based on her association with Cornerstone Church. This megachurch had been established not far from Ridgetop in 1983 and grew quickly when Maury Davis arrived as pastor in the 1990s. Davis had murdered a woman in 1975 but had turned to God and ministry. A highly controversial figure, he built Cornerstone into a powerhouse, and by 2006 it had a massive building not far from Ridgetop and was growing rapidly in membership. One of Cornerstone's practices was to hire ex-cons into the maintenance department, and Deborah had the assurance that John would have a job there if paroled. Davis's voice of support brought increasing heft to the case.

Voices speaking against John's parole were becoming more and more silenced. Curt Gibson died in September 2006, and Stringbean's sister Sallie Russell died on October 14.[27] Judge Cornelius died in January 2007, and Porter Wagoner passed away later that year. The year 2008 saw John trying for parole again, this time with more people supporting him. "I truly feel that [John] is extremely repentant of his sins, what he did," one of his nurses asserted. "It saddens me that we can all preach forgiveness, yet we can't forgive."[28] Opry stars, family, as well as a thousand people who signed a petition all opposed John's parole, and it was denied. But the atmosphere in Nashville itself was changing still more. Forgiveness now was being seen as more laudable than justice. Amid this proceedings, Verlon Thompson released "The Ballad of Stringbean and Estelle."

In 2011 Deborah—or "Debra" as she now spelled it—led the charge again in the wake of the Great Recession and amid the proliferation of smartphones. Now she was claiming she had gone backstage at the Opry when she was sixteen with her aunt and flirted with String. The article quoting her displayed little awareness of the case or the flavor of the midseventies. In fact, it was an article likely to appeal to the hipsters filling the city, creating a new era signaled by the series *Nashville* that began airing the next year. The reporter presented the standard story of the Stringbean murders, unquestioned, and gave Debra her voice begging forgiveness for John and asking, "How do you overcome public animosity?"[29]

The effort failed again. Parole board member Chuck Taylor told John, "You have turned a corner. But the bigger issue is the crime has not turned a corner with you. . . . Releasing you would depreciate the seriousness of the crime." Jan Howard said, "Stringbean and Estelle were two of the kindest, sweetest people I have ever met. I never want (Brown) to breathe fresh air again. I don't care how much he has accomplished in prison."[30] A photo from the parole hearing presented Debra with hands folded in a beatific attitude and John looking up toward heaven—an image reminiscent of a baroque painting.

After having been reinstated to the bar in 1981 only to be convicted of obtaining money under false pretenses in 1988, Arnold Peebles died on August 31, 2013, aged seventy-five.[31] The next year, Deborah and John made their greatest push yet, with a media blitz that brought equally fierce opposition. Even as Debra marshaled support from Maury Davis, against her stood arrayed Mac Wiseman, Jan Howard, Jean Shepard, and Whispering Bill Anderson. Wiseman said, "I fully believe that the good Lord forgives us for our mistakes," but the parole board members "don't have the authority, spiritually or otherwise, to forgive that man, I don't think."[32]

But there was more support for John. Against the testimony of these outraged friends of the Akemans stood thirty-one letters of support. One was from Kate King, a professor of criminology at Western Kentucky University, who had met Brown while teaching a class in prison. King claimed that every year, on the anniversary of the crime, John prayed and fasted for the Akemans and that "his remorse is deeper than it has ever been." In fact, King went on, "The man who sits before you is not the same person he was 40 years ago. In the community, John will be an enormous resource for good. Indeed, with his wisdom and hard-earned sensitivity, he will benefit us more in the community than he ever can in prison."[33] Another supporter who had met John in a classroom, Tom Hallquist, insisted that John was "scared because he's not sure of what's going to happen," but if "he can help another person not make the same mistake he's made, he's going to make a difference. . . . I think he can do a lot more good on the outside than he can on the inside."[34]

On October 15, John appeared before five of the seven members of the Tennessee Board of Parole. In an arrangement imaginable in the 1970s only in *Star Trek*, two members participated by teleconference. In the hearing, John took full responsibility for the murders but still used language implying he based his understanding of the killings on what he had been told. The board asked him about Charlie and his involvement, and John reiterated that Charlie set up the job as a robbery. In a statement the board permitted John to give, he said, "When I was, back in my early twenties, I didn't know how to live," but now he had changed. "I hold my head up and I'm not that person or that young punk I was back then."[35] The hearing ended with four of the five members voting to grant John parole.

John was set free on Monday, November 3, 2014. Reporter Adam Tamburin described the moment of liberation:

> On Monday, under a clear blue sky, John A. Brown took his first steps as a free man in more than 40 years.
>
> The convicted double murderer climbed into a white van just before 9 am and rode away from the Lois M. DeBerry Special Needs Facility. His blue prison scrubs had been traded for khakis and a white polo.
>
> . . . [H]is release was subdued; no family or protesters were there. A small cluster of news reporters watched quietly from the guard parking lot as the van drove off the property, headed toward an undisclosed family member's home.[36]

Mac Wiseman commented that this result was "a great miscarriage of justice. It makes me question the legal system."[37] It was an ironic statement in light of some of the questions that had surrounded the original investigation and trial. In fact, the story had morphed over the decades just as the world had. John benefited from a changed social and moral climate, a time when many were doubting the police (the Ferguson, Missouri, riots had erupted that August). And in a city that was growing chic, hipster, and with a postmodern sense of flattened time, the kinds of questions that might have been raised of the police, media, and the legal system in the original conviction were not countenanced because the original 1973–74 story had been forgotten. In further irony, the remaining major figure from the murder still living was the convicted triggerman.

Four years later, on November 9, 2018, the Nashville Bar Association presented a Continuing Legal Education program at the Nashville Main Public Library titled "The Stringbean Murders: Death in Baker Holler." Speakers on the program included Steve Gibson, John McLemore (who was a *Banner* reporter during the investigation and trial), and Hal McDonough (the only attorney from the murder trial still living). Video clips from an interview with Sherman Nickens were played, and Torry Johnson, David Raybin, and Ben Cantrell spoke from their experiences throughout the appeals process. Here, along with the immense personae of Grandpa, Stringbean, and John and Doug Brown, the personalities of the lawyers also emerged. Shriver's compelling role in the case came clear, Binkley's history of defending rich widows whose husbands had "accidentally" died was revealed, and Peebles vividly appeared as a tragic figure blessed with great skill that went to waste. The presenters grappled with the differences between 1974 and 2018 in the legal and law enforcement professions, noting that some of the tactics used by both investigators and attorneys then would not be acceptable legally or ethically now. While Raybin believed the same verdict would have been reached if the case were tried now, program director Ed Yarbrough acknowledged, "Many people think Charles Brown had more to do with this than he ever revealed." In the end, presenter Torry Johnson summed up the entire saga:

> Some situations defy a clear answer or easy solution. Two innocent victims were shot down at their own home by two young men careening through life fueled by alcohol, drugs, and greed. What made them commit the crime in the first place, and what made John Brown execute Estelle Akeman in cold blood, are questions that elude an answer. A jury and a judge were appalled by the crime and meted out harsh sentences to the killers. But, unlike so many other young men sent to prison for similar tragedies, John Brown set about making himself into a better person. After four decades in prison, one would hardly recognize the rowdy youth he once was. Remorseful and rehabilitated, he has tried to make amends for what he did to the Akemans and to society. Does that rebalance the scales of justice as all is forgiven, as memories fade?[38]

Whether all is forgiven and memories have faded is not altogether clear, as Nashville and the country music industry have lately entered into another phase of soul-searching. As one of this manuscript's evaluating readers eloquently puts it:

Nashville's popularity as an entertainment destination is changing the character of the city while bringing increased crime, dreadful traffic snarls, and endless construction projects. The southern charm of Broadway and the downtown district is being obliterated by the massive vertical construction of faceless, steel and glass high rises and vast throngs of drunken sports and music fans. Like String's final years, Nashville and country music today are changing to the distress of many of their most avid supporters. What can be learned from Stringbean's latter years that might help Nashville and country music survive a similar era?

Finding answers to that vexed question will be challenging, but it is worth noting that Stringbean's own durability resulted from a personality absolutely rooted while also facing change with dry-witted humor, gentleness, benevolence, and an honesty that never goes out of style. That he arguably stood poised to produce his best music yet and to continue through more decades of change and upheaval just as he had done throughout his life are all testimonies to the balance of not being afraid that change of externals means change of core. Finding an equilibrium between outrageousness and humility requires a special kind of personality, and Stringbean's model might well be heeded.

Despite all the changes of culture and society, what never does quite seem to fade is the old-time music Stringbean loved and played. While such brilliant banjoists as Béla Fleck, Tony Trischka, and Noam Pikelny have carried on Scruggs's legacy and have reached new heights with the melodic style first developed by such pioneers as Bill Keith, many others have embraced clawhammer and two-finger picking as well as Stringbean's style of comedy and entertainment. Dom Flemons has, along with MacArthur Fellowship winner Rhiannon Giddens and other African American musicians, embraced the banjo, playing clawhammer and minstrel style. Old-time banjoist, singer, and comic Leroy Troy carries on those playing and singing styles. In Troy's banjo twirling can be found echoes of Uncle Dave, but his greatest hero is Stringbean. Stringbean's family, from Phillip and his children to Nora St. John's daughter Patti Hastings, as well as more distant relatives and Stringbean and Estelle devotee Angela Hacker, promotes Stringbean's legacy and the music and style it champions.

A single marker indicates Stringbean and Estelle's resting place. On the left side of the attached metal plaque is imprinted the name "David," and with it his death year and his birth year erroneously printed as 1916. Under his name in quotes appears "Stringbean," and under that an embossed banjo slants toward the lower left corner. To the right on the marker, a plaque says "Estelle" with her birth and death years. Under her plaque and symmetrical to the banjo on David's, a fishing rod and reel slants toward the lower right corner. A tiny scroll between the plaques says, "Together forever," and underneath that appears the name AKEMAN. The marker serves as a fitting metaphor for these people's lives and deaths—simple, effective, and clear, yet oddly inaccurate, inexplicable, and provocative.

The Gibson banjo Uncle Dave left String remained at Metro for decades and now is housed at Gruhn Guitars in Nashville. The Vega No. 9 resides in the Country Music Hall of Fame, and sometimes the staff puts it on display to bear mute testimony to the triumphs and terrors it saw. The head is still worn from Stringbean's fingers, and there is pride in the instrument's bearing, a kind of satisfaction that it did its job well and still carries within its ribbony figured wood grains, gleaming brackets, and incandescent mother-of-pearl inlays the spirit of its owner. For those who know, its strings need never be touched again, for its ringing continues on in the imagination and the soul.

ACKNOWLEDGMENTS

I first learned of Stringbean from a book, now long lost to me, on the history of country music. It belonged to my parents, who also took me to the Country Music Hall of Fame in Nashville when I was about twelve years old. Already, I wanted terribly to learn to play the banjo, and they bought me a Harmony from Sears for my birthday. When I saw Stringbean's banjo on display, it opened new vistas for what a banjo could be, with its engraved inlays and delicately shaped neck and peghead. I was fascinated by the white coating on that banjo's head being worn away by intense playing. My father mentioned something about Stringbean having been murdered. The comment planted a seed in my head, and I must begin by thanking my parents for setting me on the road to this book with their patient indulgence in my interest in music. From day one of this project, they have listened, discussed, and encouraged.

So many people help with a project such as this one, and I want to start out by apologizing for anyone I leave out — my doing so is entirely inadvertent and unintentional. I must thank some of the biography and historical nonfiction writers who have inspired me to write this book, showing me the narrative and expository possibilities in the genre. This "education" started with my Ballen-Isles Country Club charity work organized by Carol Karp, Bobbie Lipoff, Arlene Oleson, Vincent and Connie Tamburo, and Jerry and Judy Wycoff. In various events, I met many wonderful writers who inspired me, especially Tom Clavin and Lawrence Leamer. I particularly want to thank Scott Ellsworth, who first encouraged me to do this kind of writing and gave me advice and encouragement all along the way. I cannot begin to express my gratitude to him. Another writer I want to thank is Darden Pyron, whose biographies of Margaret Mitchell and Liberace and kind correspondence particularly inspired me concerning possibilities for a biography about a performer written by an academic seeking to write for broader audiences.

A special thank-you goes to Betsy Lerner. Upon meeting her, I was impressed and moved by her commitment to helping writers find success in publishing. Despite her vast experience and accomplishment as both writer and agent having taught her the realities of publishing, she responds to writers with the alacrity of someone new to the business. She is nobody's fool, yet she has maintained an openness and hopefulness that, I know for a fact, have meant a very great deal to many people. I feel very fortunate to have been the beneficiary of her generosity. I am also deeply grateful to Ayşe Papatya Bucak, who introduced me to Betsy as part of her overall encouraging of my writing. Papatya is a great writer committed to the integrity of writing. She has been far kinder to me than I deserve. Her fingerprints, including her observation that I might do well to write nonfiction, swirl about my consciousness as a writer and are to be found in this book, albeit in less demonstrative ways in its final form as it veered further away from creative nonfiction. I also want to thank Andrew Furman, who has always supported me, first as the department chair who hired me and since as a colleague. He not only has offered guidance on how to proceed writing in new directions, but has also modeled those new directions, and I am very grateful to him.

Along with the writers above, certain scholars have played important indirect roles in my writing about country music. Nolan Porterfield's biography of Jimmie Rodgers has inspired me for many years. The same goes for Barry Mazor, whose *Meeting Jimmie Rodgers* expanded my world and vastly opened my way of thinking and writing about a country music performer. Thomas Goldsmith's book on Earl Scruggs and "The Foggy Mountain Breakdown" inspired me very much. Thomas Alan Holmes and Michael Cody first set me on the road to writing about country music, and I will forever be grateful to them and Roxanne Harde for including my essay in the collection *Walking the Line: Country Lyricists and American Culture*.

Part of the great fun of this project has come in communicating with people about the various people, processes, and places of Stringbean's life. Johnny and Jennifer Burkhart provided information on the experiences and processes of tobacco growing. Terry Flenel at the Bill Monroe Homeplace was helpful. It was a pleasure to talk to the energetic and incredibly knowledgeable Rick Warwick of the Heritage Foundation of Williamson County, Tennessee. Adam Southern of the Maury County Public Library generously provided details regarding Estelle's life and family. James Davidson, of the Clay County Genealogical and Historical Society, kindly helped me with details pertaining to a possible early Stringbean radio appearance. Thank you to Marilyn Jones Boyd, daughter of fiddler Casey Jones; any chance to talk with her is a pure pleasure. I am grateful to Linda Waggener of ColumbiaMagazine.com, Columbia, Kentucky, for posting my project and thereby putting me in touch with Ms. Boyd and others. It has been a particular pleasure to converse with Steve Gibson about his father and Stringbean. His interview with Eddie Stubbs was tremendously helpful, and the information he has shared has been of great assistance. For information on Stringbean's first wife, Blanche, I am grateful to her cousin Bernice Gibson, her son Tom, and her sister Carol Brewer. Mitch Diamond has helped with information about Hatch posters. Thank you to Mark Kelsay Royse, grandson of Clyde Royse, who generously provided the early photograph and poster of Stringbean and for sharing information about the Bar-X-Boys.

People from Stringbean's home in Kentucky have been equally generous and helpful. I cannot say enough to thank Robert "B-Bob" Blanshard, the genealogy specialist and music and ephemera archivist at the Kentucky Room of the Jackson County Public Library in McKee, Kentucky. Thank you also to Phillip Akemon, who kindly provided information and encouragement along the way and generously provided photographs. Sherri George, who handles public relations for the annual Stringbean Bluegrass Festival, is a special jewel, and meeting and working with her has been just divine. Thank you to Avery Bradshaw, manager of the Kentucky Music Hall of Fame at Renfro Valley. Thank you to William C. Chappell, Marty Spence, and Doreen Abner Tuttle. Charles Jackson, son of Amon Jackson, contributed wonderful details. No one has been more helpful, encouraging, and filled with such infectious excitement for String and Estelle and this book than Angela Hacker—thank you so much, Angela!

Innumerable people have offered bits of information, facilitated something, or just encouraged me at different points in the process, and everything from a conversation to a kindly word has meant a very great deal. To mention just a few, I enjoyed a great conversation about Stringbean with Jeremy Stephens, of High Fidelity. I was thrilled to receive a word of excitement about this book from Kyle Cantrell. Thank you to Ebie McFarland, of EBM: Essential Broadcast Media, who was especially wonderful to work with. Thank you to Debra Jean Wagoner, daughter of Porter Wagoner, for kind words about the book and her father's affection for Stringbean.

Some of Stringbean's friends kindly offered their memories. Whispering Bill Anderson generously shared his memories of Stringbean with a graciousness and warmth that have been the hallmarks of his career and personality. I had a great conversation and text exchanges with the late Mark Jones, son of Grandpa; I am very sad that he did not live to see this book published. Sandra Scott Whitmore generously shared memories and photographs about Stringbean and Estelle. Conversation with Roni Stoneman is a delight in every way, and I am grateful to her for her memories, including an account of her talking to Stringbean the night he was murdered. I had the great honor of an interview with Lulu Roman, a bright and lovely soul who, along with Roni, filled so many of my Saturday nights on television when I was a child. Porter Wagoner's daughter Debra Jean gave me wonderful exhortation. A big, big thank-you goes to Loretta Lynn for sharing her memories and thoughts on Stringbean.

Two people I especially want to acknowledge tirelessly research and promote Stringbean. Brian Buchanan, the current owner and resident of the Akemans' home, has generously provided information about the house and environs and has also helped pursue answers to various questions about Stringbean's life. Making his acquaintance has been one of the highlights of this experience. And I absolutely have to say the same for getting to know Leroy Troy, who embodies the great traditions of old-time music and comedy exemplified by Stringbean, Uncle Dave, Grandpa, Minnie, and so many others. I am grateful to his wife, Kendra, for kindly putting us in touch.

This project has benefited greatly from the insights of Dom Flemons. I was already a great admirer of his music and research, and my admiration grew still more when he kindly agreed to talk to me. He helped tremendously in lending nuance to my understanding of banjo and roots music history and Stringbean's place in it. Dom is a treasure, and getting to talk to him has been another great experience. I am exceedingly grateful for his generous time and illuminating conversation.

The staff at the Country Music Hall of Fame have provided much help. I owe mountains of gratitude to Print Collections librarian Kathleen Campbell, who is just plain great. I had the honor to converse also with senior historian Dr. John Rumble, whose deep knowledge helped me see important aspects of the Stringbean story. Thank you to Jack Clutter for the detailed description of the Vega No. 9 and for clarifying a number of elements about the banjo's construction.

Joe Spann, of Gruhn's Guitars, provided the description of the Gibson RB-1 Uncle Dave Macon left to Stringbean. Thank you to Byron Fay for his help with details about the Grand Ole Opry and Stringbean's appearances on it.

Archival administrators have been tremendously helpful. The Center for Popular Music at Middle Tennessee State University is an excellently run resource, and I want to thank Rachel K. Morris, CA, archivist, for all of her wonderful help. Catherine Uecker, head of research and instruction at the University of Chicago Library's Hanna Holborn Gray Special Collections Research Center, helped me to find the 1965 festival Stringbean played there. Although we did not succeed in pinpointing the date of Stringbean's appearance in Las Vegas's Last Frontier Village, I am indebted to library technician Stacy Fott and her assistant Soly-ana Belay at the University of Nevada at Las Vegas's Special Collections and Archives for their help. Thank you to Linda Barnickel of the Nashville Public Library Special Collections for providing me with *Nashville Banner* articles and to Kathleen Feducia and Elizabeth Odle for helping me to locate photographs from the *Banner*'s morgue. Thank you to Cindy Grimmit of the Maury County, Tennessee, Archives Division for her help in getting information about Estelle Stanfill. Thank you to Michelle Weiss, media asset supervisor at Jupiter Enter-tainment for providing me with the link to the *City Confidential* episode "Nash-ville: Murder in Music City." Thank you to Kim Meador of the Appellate Courts of Davidson County and to Diane Gregory and Harvey Owens of the Davidson County Criminal Court for providing me with court transcripts. Thank you to Drew Cuthbertson of IMAGN, the photograph and licensing division of Gannett and the USA Today Network, for help with securing images and permission for photographs from the *Tennessean*.

Thank you to Stacy Harris, who was wonderfully forthcoming and encour-aging, telling her experience of interviewing Stringbean on the final night of his life. The same goes for Tommy Jacobs, who very kindly shared the original photos from the crime scene with me and was patient enough to answer my questions about the investigation. Thank you to Hal McDonough for an en-lightening conversation.

Thank you to Terry and William Faimon for their memories and information. Likewise, thanks to Frances Bell of Nashville, who provided information from her experience living with her musician father in David and Estelle's lake house on Center Hill Lake. A big thank-you to Crystal Lorimor who opened fruitful information about Stringbean's military history as well as his marriages. David Ramm has been a part of so many efforts in my life, and this one is no exception. Thank you to Ashley and her father for a great time in Nashville doing research and even enjoying some snow. Thank you to James, Jan, and Jenna Cossey for having me in their home so many times and for their interest and support of this book.

I have enjoyed every single minute of working with Laurie C. Matheson, director of the University of Illinois Press. She has shown such excitement and appreciation for this project. It was a dream of mine early on for this book to be a part of the Music in American Life series, for I have loved so many volumes in it. Thank you to everyone at the press who has played a role in producing this book. Thank you to the anonymous manuscript readers: both have offered insightful, penetrating, pitch-perfect feedback while also embracing the project's focus and scope. Thank you to Mariah Mendez Schaefer for guiding me through the production and editorial process. Thank you to Jennifer S. Fisher for a fantastic cover design. Thank you to Tad Ringo for guiding this book to fruition. A big thank-you to Annette Wenda for great editing. Thank you to Kevin Cunningham for developing advertising copy.

Some very important people have supported me throughout the time I wrote this book. Thank you to Marianna De Tollis for unflagging belief in me and this project. Thank you to Marky Madeiros, Carly Stewart, and Amanda Amis, who read and listened to "updates" on the book's progress. Hope Goodsite has been more encouraging to me in so many ways than she can possibly know. Thank you to Joe Urgo and John Wharton Lowe for always being so supportive of me and my career. Warren Kelly has been there all along the way, showing great enthusiasm; when he told me his aunt Nancy's response to the idea of this book, I began to think it really could be viable. Thank you to Barbara Dahlem always. I can never hope to thank Laura Cade enough: so much support from her, so many insights, just everything.

The people this book is dedicated to are Helen and Jess McKenzie, two of the finest, sweetest people I have ever known. Jess played the mandolin beautifully, and Helen sang brilliant, plaintive harmony. Their son, Kevin, loves country and bluegrass music as much as they. And the same goes for their daughter, Michelle, and her husband, John. My life was immeasurably enhanced to know these good people. I hope this book does honor to their memory and the music they made.

Finally, thank you to my family. Jack Pence, my brother-in-law, has shared so much enthusiasm for this project. My sister, Libby, has believed in me in so many important ways. Their two precious children, Emory and Everett, have brought the brightest of all light into my life, as has my canine nephew, Hidlebrando. Cousin Bob Tompkins's unflagging enthusiasm inspires me in so many ways. I appreciate so much my cousin Tommy Simms's conversations and unflagging zest for life. Although my grandmother Virginia Azlee Jackson Hagood passed away many years ago, her passion for country music and the Opry as well as my aunt Nancy's have driven this book along the way. And her husband, my grandfather Cleatos Samuel Hagood, stands always just in the shadows in my life, especially in the period during which I have written this book. The same goes for all of the Tennessee side of my family, and I absolutely must thank my aunt Lydia and her husband, Roger Fisher, who went to work for the district attorney in Nashville around the time of the Stringbean trial and who offered insights into that time and place. Although I do not get to interact with him as much, my cousin Matt Morrison's passionate interest in music, history, and art has played a role in inspiring this book. I am grateful for years of encouragement, too, from his parents, Matt and Betty, and to Jimmy and Donna Cox, all of whom have always cherished family. I have been very glad during this process to be literally as well as in memory and imagination in Tennessee.

·

NOTES

Prologue. Short Life and Trouble

1. Weather Underground Report for Nashville, November 11, 1973, wunderground.com. Subsequent weather references for this day taken from the same source. Mark Jones remembered the car being a Lincoln (Mark Jones, Facebook message to author, February 21, 2021).

2. Louis M. "Grandpa" Jones, with Charles K. Wolfe, *Everybody's Grandpa: Fifty Years behind the Mike*, 206. Jones's detail about hunting grouse appears in *State of Tennessee v. John A. Brown, Jr., and Marvin Douglas Brown*, #B-2678, #B-2679, Davidson County Criminal Court, Division III, Nashville, 1974, 37. The latter multivolume, continuously paginated document will be referred to hereafter as "Murder Trial Transcript."

3. Jones discussed the agreed-upon time of departure in court. "Murder Trial Transcript," 37.

4. "Murder Trial Transcript," 40.

5. For the distance estimate from the house, see Jones, *Everybody's Grandpa*, 206; for the estimate from the cattle gate, see "Murder Trial Transcript," 40.

6. "Murder Trial Transcript," 40.

7. Grandpa detailed his war experience of seeing dead bodies in Jones, *Everybody's Grandpa*, 85–87; his account of finding blood on Estelle's back appears in "Murder Trial Transcript," 41; his mention of finding the gunshots in the back and the head appear in Jones, *Everybody's Grandpa*, 206.

8. Grandpa describes rushing and yelling Stringbean's name in Jones, *Everybody's Grandpa*, 206. Like most people who knew him, Grandpa regularly referred

to Stringbean as simply "String," and I am attributing his using that familiar form in that stressful moment.

9. Description in Jones, *Everybody's Grandpa*, 206.

Chapter 1. Way Back in the Hills of Old Kentucky

1. Tom Ewing, *Bill Monroe: The Life and Music of the Blue Grass Man* (Urbana: University of Illinois Press, 2018), 112.

2. Pradyumna P. Karan, *Kentucky: A Regional Geography* (Dubuque, IA: Kendall/Hunt, 1973), 28, 26.

3. 1880 U.S. Census, Crockettsville, Breathitt County, KY, Enumeration District 14, Supervisor's District 13, p. 40, Ancestry.com.

4. A strange claim has arisen among researchers on Ancestry.com that Alice gave birth to a child named Pearl when Alice herself was only six years old. In addition to being physically impossible and worthy of medical recording, no mention is made of a daughter in the 1910 census or beyond.

5. Description of the Akemons' home provided by Susan Moore, Facebook message to author, February 11, 2021.

6. Birth date based on official birth certificate (file no. 116: 1915 29376; 4945172; date filed June 26, 1915). Over the years, there has been much dispute about the year of birth, with Robert Akemon claiming a family Bible recording 1914 (Charles K. Wolfe interview, WOLFE-00836, Charles Wolfe Audio Collection, Center for Popular Music, Middle Tennessee State University, Murfreesboro), and Ben Cantrell ventured a date as late as 1917 ("The Stringbean Murders: Death in Baker Holler, Part 1"; this source hereafter will be referred to as "Stringbean Murders: Part 1"). One writer has strangely suggested July 4 as David's day of birth (Peter Cooper, "1973 Killings Brought Fear to Nashville," *Tennessean*, November, 10, 2017, https://www.tennessean.com/story/entertainment/music/2014/10/15/peter-cooper-1973-killings-brought-fear-to-nashville/17306095/). The latter newspaper, variously known as the *Tennessean* and the *Nashville Tennessean*, is called simply *Tennessean* throughout the notes.

7. Charles K. Wolfe, *Kentucky Country: Folk and Country Music of Kentucky*, 126.

8. T. H. Watkins, *The Great Depression: America in the 1930s* (New York: Little, Brown, 1993), 44.

9. Marty Spence, Facebook post in "Jackson County History and Genealogy," February 10, 2021.

10. Laurent Dubois, *The Banjo: America's African Instrument* (Cambridge, MA: Harvard University Press, 2016), 21. Details in this section are gleaned from the latter source as well as Karen Linn's *That Half-Barbaric Twang: The Banjo in American Popular Culture* (Urbana: University of Illinois Press, 1994), Bob Carlin's *The Birth of the Banjo: Joel Walker Sweeney and Early Minstrelsy* (Jefferson, NC: McFarland, 2007), and my own experiences playing bluegrass and clawhammer banjo as well as hands-on experience in banjo building and alteration.

11. Wolfe, *Kentucky Country*, 14–18, 19–21.

12. Wolfe, *Kentucky Country*, 125.

13. Historical details on WSM taken from Craig Havighurst, *Air Castle of the South: WSM and the Making of Music City* (Urbana: University of Illinois Press, 2007).

14. Stringbean, interview by Reuben Powell and Bob Hyland; Charles Jackson, email to the author, February 14, 2021.

15. Phillip Akemon, email to the author, August 20, 2020.

16. Joseph is listed living with Nora in the 1930 census. 1930 U.S. Census, Pond Creek, Jackson County, KY, Enumeration District 0006, p. 3A, FHL microfilm 2340486, Ancestry.com.

17. Bill M. Cohen, "Stringbean Murders: Part 1."

18. Watkins, *Great Depression*, 44.

19. Watkins, *Great Depression*, 55.

20. Mark Jones (phone conversation with the author, November 17, 2021) and Roni Stoneman remember Stringbean's telling of killing blackbirds. Roni Stoneman (as told to Ellen Wright), *Pressing On: The Roni Stoneman Story* (Urbana: University of Illinois Press, 2007), 144–45.

21. Cover notes, *Way Back in the Hills of Old Kentucky: Stringbean with His 5-String Banjo* (Starday, SLP 260, 1964).

22. Cohen, "Stringbean Murders: Part 1."

23. Genevieve J. Waddell, "Stringbean," 43.

24. Charles Jackson, email to the author, February 13, 2021.

25. Stringbean, interview by Douglas B. Green.

26. Charles Jackson, email to the author, February 14, 2021.

27. William C. Chappell has related this claim (Facebook post in "Jackson County History and Genealogy Group," February 10, 2021).

28. Bob Blanshard asserts that two-finger picking style was known to exist in David's region of Kentucky (conversation with the author, August 2, 2017).

29. Sebastian Schroeder, *2-Finger Banjo: Index Lead Style for 5-String Banjo* (Luebeck, Germany: independently published, 2017), 1:5.

30. Sebastian Schroeder, *2-Finger Banjo: Index Lead Style for 5-String Banjo*, vol. 2 (Luebeck, Germany: independently published, 2018).

31. Bob Baker, interview by John W. Rumble, December 4, 1985, Country Music Foundation Oral History Project, Mount Vernon, KY, Country Music Hall of Fame, Nashville, 34.

32. Watkins, *Great Depression*, 124.

33. Wolfe, *Kentucky Country*, 125.

34. "Camp Roosevelt Beginnings," Civilian Conservation Corps Legacy, 2018, http://www.ccclegacy.org/Camp_Roosevelt_68B9.php.

35. *Youth Jobs Program during Great Depression: The March of Time*, 1933, YouTube, July 31, 2007, https://www.youtube.com/watch?v=qolPqXNGW3I.

36. "CCC Camps Kentucky," Civilian Conservation Corps Legacy, 2018, http://www.ccclegacy.org/CCC_Camps_Kentucky.html.

37. Cohen, "Stringbean Murders: Part 1."

38. Thank you to Angela Hacker for this information.

39. Genevieve Waddell, "A Serious Look at a Funny Man: Stringbean," 45; Angela Hacker, Facebook message to the author, February 13, 2021; "Banjo Brings Shots," *Lexington Leader*, March 1, 1935, 22.

40. "Banjo Brings Shots," 22.

41. John A. Salmond, *The Civilian Conservation Corps, 1933–1942: A New Deal Case Study* (Durham, NC: Duke University Press, 1967).

42. Ralph Brockman, Facebook post, February 13, 2021.

43. Waddell, "Serious Look at a Funny Man," 14.

44. "Crowd at Old Fiddlers' Contest," *Stanford (KY) Interior Journal*, October 29, 1935, 4.

45. "Perryville: Wins Contest," *Danville (KY) Advocate-Messenger*, March 18, 1935, 2.

46. On Martin, see Tony Russell, *Country Music Originals: The Legends and the Lost* (Oxford: Oxford University Press, 2007), 90–92; and Charles K. Wolfe, *Classic Country: Legends of Country Music* (New York: Routledge, 2001), 249.

47. Wolfe, *Kentucky Country*, 29–31.

48. Standard comment has been that Stringbean would join Martin's *Morning Round Up* program, but it does not seem to have been created in 1935. Programming did regularly begin the day with a slot titled *Good Morning*, so it may be that Asa was regularly presenting music and musicians with his band at that time.

49. Asa Martin, transcribed from *The Stringbean Memorial Bluegrass Festival* album (Old Homestead Record Company, OHM 80005, 1975). Asa was apparently mixing up the *Renfro Valley Barn Dance* (which did not come into being until 1937) with the *WLS Barn Dance*, although it *was* Kentuckian John Lair, the creator of *Renfro Valley* in his home state not far from David's home, who signed Ledford to a five-year contract on WLS where he then worked.

50. Martin, *Stringbean Memorial Bluegrass Festival*.

51. Wolfe, *Kentucky Country*, 80.

52. Baker, interview, 6.

53. Baker mentions Uncle Henry's Kentucky Mountaineers playing in Livingston (Baker, interview, 7).

54. Baker discusses playing on the courthouse steps (Baker, interview, 6–7). Charles Wolfe asserts that the contest was held in the courtroom in "String," *Bluegrass Unlimited*, June 1982, 47, although the article does have inaccuracies.

55. Baker explains a contest in Livingston being judged by applause (Baker, interview, 8).

56. Quote transcribed from Martin, *Stringbean Memorial Bluegrass Festival*.

57. Wolfe, *Kentucky Country*, 125.

Chapter 2. Stringbean and His Banjo

1. Waddell, "Serious Look at a Funny Man," 14.

2. No one has suggested this mix-up outright, but it may be that the details about Amon Jackson's driving David to Manchester became mixed up with driving him to Lexington and his later living in Winchester.

3. Charles Jackson, email to the author, February 14, 2021.

4. James Davidson, email to the author, February 24, 2021.

5. Descriptions of Lexington in Stringbean's time are taken from Workers of Federal Writers' Project of the Works Progress Administration for the State of Kentucky, *Lexington and the Bluegrass Country,* American Guide Series (Lexington: Commercial Printing, 1938).

6. 1930 U.S. Census, *Population: Volume 1, Number and Distribution of Inhabitants*, 432, U.S. Census Bureau, https://www.census.gov.https://www2.census.gov/library/publications/decennial/1930/population volume 1/03815512v1ch05.pdf; Waddell, "Serious Look at a Funny Man," 14, 4, 25.

7. Spengler sign information taken from photograph posted on Kentucky Photo Archive: photos from the *Lexington Herald-Leader* archives, https://kyphotoarchive.com/page/8/.

8. Workers of Federal Writers' Project of the Works Progress Administration for the State of Kentucky, *Lexington and the Bluegrass Country*, 51. Further details about WLAP history taken from Lewis M. Owens, "WLAP through Sixty Years, 1922–1980," 1983, Scott Wills Broadcast Consulting, http://engineerscott.com/?q=node/12.

9. Owens, "WLAP through Sixty Years."

10. "Today's Programs: WLAP," *Lexington Herald*, November 2, 1935, sec. 2, p. 5.

11. Martin, *Stringbean Memorial Bluegrass Festival*.

12. Charles K. Wolfe offers the following account: "When Asa got ready to introduce his new band member on stage, he couldn't remember David's real name, but he looked over at the long, skinny young man and announced him as 'String Beans.' The name stuck, and within a few weeks the new banjo player was known by this name; later, on the Grand Ole Opry, the name was to be changed to the singular form, 'Stringbean.'" Wolfe, *Kentucky Country*, 125–26. It is possible that Wolfe's account is more accurate and that either time altered David's memory of the event or he was simply retelling it this way as a variation.

13. The quote is taken from Stringbean's own words in the final interview he gave the night he died, printed in Stacy Harris, "Stringbean 'Went a Lot Further . . . '," *Nashville Banner*, November 12, 1973, 1. David used the singular form in Waddell's article "Serious Look at a Funny Man" also, although he told the story as happening "one night" when the "emcee couldn't think of my name," not mentioning Asa's name at all (14).

14. David later made a point of saying, "I won't named for a bean. And it won't cause I'm skinny as a bean pole" (Waddell, "Serious Look at a Funny Man," 14), proceeding then to tell the story of Asa's naming him. But, of course, it was his physique that caused Asa to apply the name.

15. For details on the nuts and bolts of the music industry in this era, see Neil V. Rosenberg, *Bluegrass: A History* (Urban: University of Illinois Press, 2005), 24–27.

16. Wolfe, *Kentucky Country*, 126.

17. Wolfe, *Kentucky Country*, 126.

18. Ben Cantrell, "Stringbean Murders: Part 1."

19. Little is published on Silas Rogers's Lonesome Pine Fiddlers (in fact, the shortened "Si" has often been written as "Cy"). The band members' names are based on a 1937 photo posted by Thornton McCord's grandson on Reddit at https://www.reddit.com/r/TheWayWeWere/comments/k9vyz7/my_great_grandfather_and_the_band_he_was_in_silas/?utm_source=BD&utm_medium=Search&utm_name=Bing&utm_content=PSR1. Also posting on Facebook, Barry Warfield mentions McCord's being an electrician.

20. "Marty Roberts Biography," Home of Old-Time Country Music, http://www.hillbilly-music.com/artists/story/index.php?id=12951.

21. Marty Roberts, "Roberts' Roundup of Country and Western Music," *Tarheel Wheels*, December 1973.

22. Roberts, "Roberts' Roundup"; Waddell, "Serious Look at a Funny Man," 14.

23. Waddell, "Serious Look at a Funny Man," 14–15.

24. Information about the RB-11 based on details posted on Earnest Banjo: Prewar Gibson Mastertone Banjos, http://www.earnestbanjo.com/gibson_banjos_by_style.htm. A copy of the 1930–31 Gibson catalog is available online at https://acousticmusic.org/wp-content/uploads/2016/02/Gibson-1930-31-Catalog.pdf.

25. Earnest Banjo, http://www.earnestbanjo.com/gibson_banjo_RB-11_9938.htm.

26. Earnest Banjo, http://www.earnestbanjo.com/gibson_banjo_TB-11_127.htm.

27. The 1930–31 Gibson catalog lists the RB-1 at $60 with case (https://acousticmusic.org/wp-content/uploads/2016/02/Gibson-1930-31-Catalog.pdf). A 1937 Gibson price list includes the RB-11 at $55 alone and $69.50 with the case (http://www.gibson-prewar.com/gibson-prewar-price-lists/).

28. https://www.infoplease.com/business/poverty-income/capita-personal-income, sourced from U.S. Department of Commerce, Bureau of Economic Analysis, Survey of Current Business.

29. Quote taken from the X Bar X Boys Series (seriesbooks.info). This series had begun in 1926, so these young men would have grown up following the adventures of Roy and Teddy Manley. David Baumann, "The X Bar X Boys: The Sons of the Golden West," xbarxboys.com.

30. "Favorite Old Photo: The Bar-X-Boys, 1938, Columbia, KY," *Columbia Magazine* posted August 24, 2017, http://www.columbiamagazine.com/photoarchive.php?photo_id=74404. Mark Kelsay Royse provided the alternative name of the group (Facebook message to the author, December 17, 2021).

31. Royse, Facebook message.

32. *Stanford (KY) Interior Journal*, April 25, 1939, 1.

33. Charles K. Wolfe, *Stringbean: Barn Yard Banjo Picking*, CD liner notes, 6.

34. George D. Hay offers the information about Akeman's working with Silas Rogers and learning these songs in *A Story of the Grand Ole Opry* (n.p.: n.p., 1953), 61.

35. This detail was mentioned by Waddell in "Serious Look at a Funny Man" and in Waddell, "Stringbean," 41–44.

36. Waddell, "Stringbean," 43.

37. Searches were made in StatsCrew (statscrew.com) and Baseball Reference (baseball-reference.com) using multiple spellings of David's last name. Also, a search was made of the rosters of each team in the Mountain State League.

38. Baseball Reference, https://www.baseball-reference.com/register/player.fcgi?id=aikenso01jam.

39. For an essay that captures town and CCC-camp baseball, see "The Great Depression and Baseball in Mendocino County," *Matthew Reed Online* (blog), https://reedhistorian.blogspot.com.

40. The 1940 census reveals that his parents had moved away from Jackson County (Graham, Jefferson County, Indiana, Enumeration District 39-1, p. 6B, Ancestry.com). Susan Moore, granddaughter of Alfred Moore, confirms that her grandfather bought the farm from the Akemons (Susan Moore, Facebook message to the author, February 11, 2021).

41. Blanche's cousin Bernice Gibson claims that Dan made big money working in the Grady Oil fields (phone conversation with the author, February 10, 2021). The 1940 census confirms his working in the oil industry (1940 U.S. Census, Clark, Kentucky, Enumeration District 25-3, p. 8A, Ancestry.com).

42. Thank you to Mrs. Gibson, her son Tom, and Carol Brewer for sharing these memories via phone conversations in the winter of 2021.

43. The biographical details in this paragraph are taken from Tom Ewing, *Bill Monroe: The Life and Music of the Blue Grass Man* (Urbana: University of Illinois Press, 2018); Rosenberg, *Bluegrass: A History*; and Richard D. Smith, *Can't You Hear Me Callin': The Life of Bill Monroe, Father of Bluegrass* (Cambridge, MA: Da Capo Press, 2001).

44. Smith, *Can't You Hear Me Callin'*, 61.

45. Quoted in Ed Davis, "Stringbean: Image Lives On." *Greensboro Daily News*, November 19, 1973.

46. "Doc" Tommy Scott with Shirley Noe Swiesz and Randall Franks, *Snake Oil, Superstars and Me: The Story of Ramblin "Doc" Tommy Scott*, 56.

47. Scott with Swiesz and Franks, *Snake Oil*, 33, 17, 35.

48. Scott with Swiesz and Franks, *Snake Oil*, 57.

49. Scott with Swiesz and Franks, *Snake Oil*, 57.

50. Quoted in Davis, "Stringbean: Image Lives On."

51. The 1940 population count is recorded in *Hill's Greensboro (Guilford County, N.C.) City Directory* (Richmond, VA: Hill Directory, 1955).

52. Penny Parsons, *Foggy Mountain Troubadour: The Life and Music of Curly Seckler* (Urbana: University of Illinois Press, 2016), 25.

53. Scott with Swiesz and Franks, *Snake Oil*, 59.

54. Parsons, *Foggy Mountain Troubadour*, 25–26, 21.

55. Scott with Swiesz and Franks, *Snake Oil*, 59.

56. There may also have been a band member named Jim Porter during this time.

57. Parsons quotes Scott's mention of the rehearsal sessions. Parsons, *Foggy Mountain Troubadour*, 21.

58. Parsons, *Foggy Mountain Troubadour*, 57.

59. Michael D. Doubler, *The Dixie Dewdrop: The Uncle Dave Macon Story* (Urbana: University of Illinois Press, 2018), 31.

60. Leslie Gourse, *The Billie Holiday Companion: Seven Decades of Commentary* (New York: Schirmer Trade Books, 2000), 103–4.

61. David Akeman, draft card, serial #3962, order #2448, October 16, 1940.

62. Parsons, *Foggy Mountain Troubadour*, 26.

63. Cantrell, "Stringbean Murders: Part 1."

64. 1940 U.S. Census, Graham, Jefferson County, Indiana, Enumeration District 39-1, p. 6B, Ancestry.com; Alfred Akemon, draft card, serial #999, order #1562, October 16, 1940.

Chapter 3. Goin' to the Grand Ole Opry to Make Myself a Name

1. Bill Monroe, interview by John W. Rumble, November 18, 1992, Country Music Hall of Fame, Nashville.

2. Charles Wolfe, "String," *Bluegrass Unlimited* 16, no. 11 (1982): 48.

3. Richard D. Smith, *Can't You Hear Me Callin': The Life of Bill Monroe, Father of Bluegrass* (Cambridge, MA: Da Capo Press, 2001), 72.

4. Smith, *Can't You Hear Me Callin'*, 62, 67.

5. In *Kentucky Country*, Wolfe attributes the following story to Doc Roberts: "Bill come up here and got him when he was playing on WLAP and living at Winchester. Bill went up there to get him to play baseball for his team. He first hired him as a baseball pitcher. As far as I know, Bill didn't even know he played banjo when he hired him. After he found out he could play, he went to playin' a little with Bill's band" (127). In his earlier published article, however, Wolfe attributed it to David's brother Robert, which seems to be the more likely source. Wolfe trusted Robert a little too much (Robert also claimed David had been born in 1914), which he may have realized later, for in the *Kentucky Country* version, Wolfe omitted a sentence Robert added: "Then he left Bill to go with Charlie [Monroe] and then went into the service, and then he came back and went with Bill again" ("String," 48), which clearly jumbles the chronology of Stringbean's life, as will be further shown.

6. Neil V. Rosenberg, *Bluegrass: A History* (Urbana: University of Illinois Press, 2005), 57; Tom Ewing, *Bill Monroe: The Life and Music of the Blue Grass Man* (Urbana: University of Illinois Press, 2018), 123.

7. Rosenberg, *Bluegrass: A History*, 56.

8. Smith, in *Can't You Hear Me Callin'*, notes Bill's practice, pointing out that he kept the radio on constantly, "listening attentively and discerningly, quietly filing away in his mind pickers, fiddler, and singers, their names and locations, their styles, strengths, and weaknesses. When he needed a new band member, he would simply call a station, introduce himself, and get the appropriate musician's home phone number" (81).

9. Surviving recordings of the Blue Grass Boys on the Grand Ole Opry do not seem to include any banjo playing. The first of these that does is December 12.

10. Ewing, *Bill Monroe*, 116.

11. Rosenberg, *Bluegrass: A History*, 56.

12. Wolfe, *Stringbean: Barn Yard Banjo Picking*, CD liner notes, 4.

13. David Akeman, "Goin' to the Opry," lyrics transcribed from recording.

14. Wolfe, *Stringbean: Barn Yard Banjo Picking*, CD liner notes, 10.

15. Quoted in Wolfe, *Stringbean: Barn Yard Banjo Picking*, CD liner notes, 8.

16. Karen Linn, *That Half Barbaric Twang: The Banjo in American Popular Culture* (Urbana: University of Illinois Press, 1994), 141.

17. Dom Flemons, interview by the author, March 31, 2021.

18. Flemons, interview.

19. The following details about David's purchasing the instrument are taken from his interview with Green. I am indebted to Jack Clutter of the Country Music Hall of Fame for the information and description regarding Stringbean's banjo. Additional information on Tubaphones gleaned from George Gruhn, "Technical Reference Manual," *Pickin': For People into Music* 9 (1979): 46–48.

20. Jack Clutter suggests, "Mike Holmes has been researching Vega Fairbanks banjos for a number of years, and has also received aid from George Gruhn. His thoroughness leads me to believe that his research is most likely as accurate as anyone could hope. Following his list, he would place this banjo as having been built sometime between 1925–1930" (email to the author, February 2, 2021).

21. "Deering Banjo Tone Ring Comparisons," Deering: The Great American Banjo Company, https://www.deeringbanjos.com/blogs/banjo-buying-tips/10319001-deering-banjo-tone-ring-comparisons .

22. "Old Time Open Back Banjos and Tone Rings," Bucks County Folk Music Shop, https://www.buckscountyfolkmusic.com/blogs/news/102225665-old-time-open-back-banjos-and-tone-rings.

23. Ewing, *Bill Monroe*, 120.

24. Frank Buchanan, interview by Douglas B. Green, June 5, 1975, Country Music Hall of Fame, Nashville.

25. William U. Eiland, *Nashville's Mother Church: The History of the Ryman Auditorium* (Nashville: Grand Ole Opry, 2014), 56.

26. George R. Stuart, *Sam P. Jones, the Preacher* (Siloam Springs, AR: International Federation, 1900), 35

27. Eiland, *Nashville's Mother Church*, 56–57.

28. Ewing, *Bill Monroe*, 121.

29. The diagnosis is withheld by the National Archives and Records Administration on the hospital admission card, service number 34738550.

30. Wolfe, *Kentucky Country*, 126.

31. Waddell, "Stringbean," 43, 188; *Grinder's Switch Gazette* 1, no. 4 (December 1944): 2.

32. Eiland, *Nashville's Mother Church*, 58, 59.

33. A 1954 ad reproduced in *Snake Oil* makes mention of his having performed on the segment for ten years. Scott with Swiesz and Franks, *Snake Oil*, 304.

34. Scott with Swiesz and Franks, *Snake Oil*, 139.

35. Quoted in Jay Feldman, "Bluegrass Baseball: Barnstorming Band and Ball Club," Baseball Research Journal Archives, http://research.sabr.org/journals/bluegrass -baseball-barnstorming-band-and-ball-club.

36. Ewing, *Bill Monroe*, 123.

37. Details of the tent show are taken from Smith, *Can't You Hear Me Callin'*, 69–70.

38. Ewing, *Bill Monroe*, 124.

39. String would later comment that when he was with Bill, he would at times wear a costume of tennis shoes and a big hat pinned up. Stringbean, interview by Powell and Hyland.

40. Stringbean, interview by Powell and Hyland; Getahn Ward, "Historic Former East Nashville Boarding House to Country Stars Up for Sale," *Tennessean*, March 5, 2017, https://www.tennessean.com/story/money/real-estate/2017/03/05/historic -former-east-nashville-boarding-house-country-stars-up-sale/98776042/; "Mom Upchurch's Boarding House in East Nashville Is for Sale," ACRE of Benchmark Realty, March 8, 2017, https://www.acrestate.com/blog/mom-upchurchs-boarding-house-in -east-nashville-is-for-sale/.

41. Photograph published on the jacket of the album *Stringbean: More of That Rare Old Time Banjo Pickin' and Singin'* (Starday, SLP 179, 1962).

42. I am indebted to Joe Spann of Gruhn's Guitars for information on the unusual make of the Uncle Dave Gibson (email to the author, February 5, 2021).

43. Stringbean, interview by Powell and Hyland.

44. Smith, *Can't You Hear Me Callin'*, 80.

45. Blanch Gibson, phone conversation with the author, February 10, 2021.

46. "Official Weather Forecast" (state of weather on February 13, 1945, at 7:30 p.m.), *Chicago Tribune*, February 14, 1945, 13.

47. Ewing, *Bill Monroe* 126.

48. Penny Parsons, *Foggy Mountain Troubadour: The Life and Music of Curly Seckler* (Urbana: University of Illinois Press, 2016), lists this lineup (61).

49. Ewing, *Bill Monroe*, 26.

50. Wolfe, *Stringbean: Barn Yard Banjo Picking*, CD liner notes, 7.

51. The record was released on two different 78 pressings: the Bridgeport, Connecticut, pressing with catalog number 37151, and the Kings Mills, Ohio, pressing with catalog number 20080.

Chapter 4. Big Ball in Nashville

1. Richard D. Smith, *Can't You Hear Me Callin': The Life of Bill Monroe, Father of Bluegrass* (Cambridge, MA: Da Capo Press, 2001), 82.

2. Don Rhodes, "Lester Flatt: Talking with a Bluegrass Giant," *Pickin': For People into Music* 6, no. 1 (1979): 26.

3. There is some dispute about the 1945 date because Flatt often cited 1944 as the year he joined Bill (and, in fact, he inaccurately remembered being with Charlie in 1940–41). Smith cites the dates above, and Parsons also acknowledges that Flatt's not

being in the Chicago session strongly suggests he had not yet joined the Blue Grass Boys. Smith, *Can't You Hear Me Callin'*; Penny Parsons, *Foggy Mountain Troubadour: The Life and Music of Curly Seckler* (Urbana: University of Illinois Press, 2016).

4. Smith, *Can't You Hear Me Callin'*, 84, 83.

5. Rhodes, "Lester Flatt," 26.

6. John Bush, "Lew Childre," All Music, https://www.allmusic.com/artist/lew-childre -mn0000256985.

7. Wayne Erbsen, *Rural Roots of Bluegrass: Songs, Stories, and History* (Asheville, NC: Native Ground Music, 2003), 143.

8. Erbsen, *Rural Roots*, 143.

9. Rhodes, "Lester Flatt," 26.

10. Rhodes, "Lester Flatt," 26.

11. Charles Wolfe, "Uncle Dave Macon," in *Stars of Country Music: Uncle Dave Macon to Johnny Rodriguez*, ed. Bill C. Malone and Judith McCulloh (Cambridge, MA: Da Capo Press, 1975), 50.

12. Dom Flemons, interview by the author, March 31, 2021.

13. Wolfe, *Stringbean: Barn Yard Banjo Picking*, CD liner notes, 8.

14. Jones with Wolfe, *Everybody's Grandpa*, 205.

15. 1910 U.S. Census, Civil District 14, Giles County, TN, Enumeration District 0029, p. 10B, Ancestry.com; 1920 U.S. Census, Fly, Maury County, TN, Enumeration District 105, p. 2B, Ancestry.com; 1930 U.S. Census, District 2, Maury County, TN, Enumeration District 0003, p. 1B, Ancestry.com.

16. Information on Estelle and her family generously provided by Rick Warwick.

17. Decree of Divorce, Maury County Genealogy Society.

18. *Polk's Nashville City Directory* (St. Louis: R. L. Polk, 1942), 671.

19. Address information for Luddie and Ennis both taken from *Nashville City Directory*. Dalton's and Ennis's occupations are listed on their draft cards.

20. Quoted in Warren B. Causey, *The Stringbean Murders*, 35. I have not been able to locate the article. No title or information is supplied; the information may not be accurate, especially because the article states that String was with Tommy Scott several years ago but in fact was with him in 1954–55.

21. Joe Denton, "Stringbean's Killer Wants a Second Chance" (letter to the editor), *Tennessean*, August 5, 2008, A7.

22. *Grinder's Switch Gazette* 2, no. 6 (1946): 4; "Grand Ole Opry," *Barn Dance Magazine*, September 1947, 16.

23. Country Music Hall of Fame Digital Archive, Nashville. This listing adds inches to David's height as recorded in his draft card. Throughout his life, he was variously listed as being between six-foot-one and six-foot-three.

24. Wolfe, *Kentucky Country*, 8.

25. Jones with Wolfe, *Everybody's Grandpa*, 198.

26. Jones with Wolfe, *Everybody's Grandpa*, 198.

27. Jones with Wolfe, *Everybody's Grandpa*, 198–99.

28. Jones with Wolfe, *Everybody's Grandpa*, 198.

29. "Ramona Jones remembers her late husband, Country Music Hall of Famer Grandpa Jones," YouTube, https://www.youtube.com/watch?v=CmRoSnCajkM.

30. Jones with Wolfe, *Everybody's Grandpa*, 112.

31. David made these comments in response to Bob Hyland mentioning having some Opry tapes from 1947 that featured Uncle Dave (Stringbean, interview by Powell and Hyland).

32. Tom Ewing, *Bill Monroe: The Life and Music of the Blue Grass Man* (Urbana: University of Illinois Press, 2018), 148.

33. Jones with Wolfe, *Everybody's Grandpa*, 123, 124, 203.

34. Concerning Stringbean's performing and coaching with Bill, see Ewing, *Bill Monroe*, 151.

35. *Fayfare's Opry Blog*, June 9, 2014, http://fayfare.blogspot.com/2014/06/june-11-1949-hank-williams-opry-debut.html?m=1.

36. *Polk's Nashville City Directory* (St. Louis: R. L. Polk, 1949), 35.

37. Armed Forces Radio Service, #130, June 1950, Country Music Hall of Fame Digital Archive, RS.2018.1260; Armed Forces Radio Service, #151, November 11, 1950, Country Music Hall of Fame Digital Archive, RS.2018.1265.

38. Roy Clark with Marc Eliot, *My Life: In Spite of Myself!* (New York: Simon and Schuster, 1994), 41, 42, 43.

39. Information about the Last Frontier Village gleaned from Stefan Al, *The Strip: Las Vegas and the Architecture of the American Dream* (Cambridge, MA: MIT Press, 2017), 18–26; Jeff Burbank, *Lost Las Vegas* (London: Pavilion, 2014), 112–17; and the University of Nevada–Las Vegas Special Collections.

40. University of Nevada–Las Vegas Special Collections Digital Collection, https://d.library.unlv.edu/digital/collection/menus/id/2004/rec/53.

41. Recording information available at Bluegrass Discography, http://www.ibiblio.org/hillwilliam/BGdiscography/?v=fullrecord&albumid=6750.

42. Stringbean, interview by Powell and Hyland.

43. Joe Spann, email to the author, February 5, 2021. This banjo is currently on display at Gruhn's Guitars.

44. Thank you to Carol Brewer and Bernice Gibson for the family story.

45. "Mrs. Blanche McQueen," *Owensboro (KY) Messenger-Inquirer*, July 16, 1952, 12.

46. Jones with Wolfe, *Everybody's Grandpa*, 199 .

47. Jones with Wolfe, *Everybody's Grandpa*, 199.

48. I am indebted to Brian Buchanan as well as to Grandpa Jones's book for descriptions of the cave. Buchanan speculates that Stringbean himself may have installed the piping, but it may have been there before he bought the property.

49. Again, I thank Brian Buchanan for this local lore.

50. Jones with Wolfe, *Everybody's Grandpa*, 199.

51. Venues based on original Hatch posters in the Country Music Hall of Fame Digital Archive.

52. *Kansas City Times*, October 20, 1952, 4.

Chapter 5. Herdin' Cattle in a Cadillac Coupe de Ville

1. These prints are included on the Country Music Hall of Fame Digital Archive, Nashville.

2. Jones with Wolfe, *Everybody's Grandpa*, 199, 201–2.

3. Jones with Wolfe, *Everybody's Grandpa*, 204, 201.

4. Steve Gibson, "Interview with Steven Gibson Regarding His Memories of Stringbean," 7.

5. Angela Hacker confirms Estelle's calling him by his real name, and a letter written from the Sunset Motel in Winchester, Illinois, by Estelle to her family demonstrates this practice.

6. Jones with Wolfe, *Everybody's Grandpa*, 201.

7. A photograph of Lizzie's tombstone is posted on Find a Grave, https://www.findagrave.com/memorial/166539102/elizabeth-a-smith.

8. Recording of interviews with Jimmy C. Newman (performer), Clyde Moody (performer/songwriter), Bill Carlisle (performer), and Jimmy Riddle (performer), conducted by Biff Collie on September 12, 1974. Country Music Hall of Fame, Nashville, RT-7-03988_1. Hereafter referred to as "Biff Collie interview."

9. Concerning television in Nashville and insight into the Kate Smith show's Opry performance, see Colin Escott with George Merritt and William MacEwan, *Hank Williams: The Biography* (Boston: Back Bay Books, 2004), 217.

10. Gary Gannaway, "Country Legend Grand Ole Opry Stars of the 50s," YouTube, November 11, 2019, https://www.youtube.com/watch?v=gpGAxNp1-m8. Originally broadcast for RFD-TV.

11. Jones with Wolfe, *Everybody's Grandpa*, 201.

12. "Prince Albert Grand Ole Opry," WSM Radio, Country Music Hall of Fame Digital Archive, RS.2002.83.0467.

13. "Noontime Neighbors Radio Show," WSM Radio, December 12, 1953, Country Music Hall of Fame, Digital Archive, RS.2002.83.0471.

14. Dates and venues based on Hatch show prints in Country Music Hall of Fame Digital Archive.

15. Scott with Swiesz and Franks, *Snake Oil*, 79.

16. Scott with Swiesz and Franks, *Snake Oil*, 264.

17. Scott with Swiesz and Franks, *Snake Oil*, 303.

18. Scott with Swiesz and Franks, *Snake Oil*, 305.

19. Quoted by John McLemore, "Stringbean Murders, Part 1."

20. Scott with Swiesz and Franks, *Snake Oil*, 305–6.

21. Scott with Swiesz and Franks, *Snake Oil*, 307.

22. Sandra Scott Whitmore, phone conversation with the author, January 25, 2022.

23. Scott with Swiesz and Franks, *Snake Oil*, 309.

24. Scott with Swiesz and Franks, *Snake Oil*, 315.

25. Whitmore, phone conversation with the author.

26. Scott with Swiesz and Franks, *Snake Oil*, 308.

27. Chet Atkins, "Tips on Pickin'," *Country and Western Jamboree*, April 1955, 33.

28. Tyler Mahan Coe offers particularly engaging details about Denny's checkered Opry tenure in "Ernest Tubb: The Texas Defense" (CR001) and "The Louvin Brothers: Running Wild" (CR006) episodes of the *Cocaine and Rhinestones* podcast. See also Craig Havighurst, *Air Castle of the South: WSM and the Making of Music City* (Urbana: University of Illinois Press, 2007).

29. The following quotes are taken from Bobby Anderson, "Stringbean's Friend Relates Fond Memories 35 Years Later," *Kentucky Explorer* (November 2008): 29–30.

30. Scott with Swiesz and Franks, *Snake Oil*, 308.

31. Waddell, "Serious Look at a Funny Man," 15.

32. Scott with Swiesz and Franks, *Snake Oil*, 307.

33. "Biff Collie interview."

34. Scott with Swiesz and Franks, *Snake Oil*, 307, 309, 307.

35. Certificate of Death, Commonwealth of Kentucky, file no. 116 56-27053, December 29, 1956.

36. Jones with Wolfe, *Everybody's Grandpa*, 202.

37. Jones with Wolfe, *Everybody's Grandpa*, 199.

38. Letter courtesy of Angela Hacker.

39. This clip has been posted on YouTube at https://www.youtube.com/watch?v=8uOy3WdT3mY&t=21s.

40. Quoted in Alec Wilkinson, *The Protest Singer: An Intimate Portrait of Pete Seeger* (New York: Random House, 2009), 50.

41. Pete Seeger, *How to Play the 5-String Banjo: A Manual for Beginners*, 3rd ed. (Beacon: published by the author, 1952), 33.

42. Details of this story taken from "4 Shot Here in Family Feud," *Tennessean*, December 12, 1958, 1, 16.

43. Jones with Wolfe, *Everybody's Grandpa*, 203; "Biff Collie interview."

44. "Biff Collie interview."

45. Gibson, "Interview with Gibson," 1.

46. Alan Lomax, "Bluegrass Background: Folk Music with Overdrive," *Esquire*, October 1959, 108.

Chapter 6. Pretty Polly

1. Weather Underground, https://www.wunderground.com/history/monthly/us/tn/nashville/KBNA/date/1960-2.

2. This episode has been posted on YouTube at https://www.youtube.com/watch?v=n0rTIfeOIkA.

3. Scott with Swiesz and Franks, *Snake Oil*, 308.

4. Loretta Lynn, email to the author, February 10, 2021.

5. Steve Eng, *A Satisfied Mind: The Country Music Life of Porter Wagoner* (Nashville: Rutledge Hill Press, 1992), 232.

6. "The Porter Wagoner Show w/ Stringbean, September 19th, 1961," Country Music Hall of Fame Digital Archive, https://digi.countrymusichalloffame.org/digital/collection/movingimage/id/750/rec/1.

7. "The Porter Wagoner Show #22 w/ Stringbean, 1961," Country Music Hall of Fame Digital Archive, https://digi.countrymusichalloffame.org/digital/collection/movingimage/id/4381/rec/2.

8. This history of Starday draws from Neil V. Rosenberg, *Bluegrass: A History* (Urban: University of Illinois Press, 2005); and Nathan D. Gibson with Don Pierce, *The Starday Story: The House That Country Music Built* (Jackson: University Press of Mississippi, 2011).

9. Gibson with Pierce, *Starday Story*, 124.

10. Gibson with Pierce, *Starday Story*, 125.

11. "Sessions Mount at Starday Studios," *Music Reporter* 5, no. 10 (1960): 26.

12. Don Pierce interview by Douglas B. Green, September 25, 1974, Country Music Hall of Fame, Nashville, 5.

13. Bill Anderson, email to the author, June 27, 2022.

14. An advertisement from the agency titled "Presenting. . . . . Stringbean" is in the archives of the Country Music Hall of Fame.

15. Phil Sullivan, "More than a Name," *Tennessean*, April 1, 1962, F4.

16. Pierce, interview by Green, 5.

17. Sullivan, "More than a Name," F4.

18. This story appears in John Roger Simon's *Cowboy Copas and the Golden Age of Country Music* (Ashland, KY: Jesse Stuart Foundation, 2008), 302. Bill Anderson affirms the story as his first offstage memory of Stringbean (Anderson, email to the author).

19. Anderson, email to the author.

20. Pierce, interview by Green, 6.

21. Lynn, email to the author.

22. *Those Stonemans* television show excerpt, YouTube, https://www.youtube.com/watch?v=blrqDHzg1ac.

23. Pierce, interview by Green, 5.

24. *University of Chicago Magazine* 57, no. 6 (1965): 9.

25. *Those Stonemans* television show excerpt.

26. *University of Chicago Magazine*, 9.

27. Richard D. Smith, *Can't You Hear Me Callin': The Life of Bill Monroe, Father of Bluegrass* (Cambridge, MA: Da Capo Press, 2001), 173, 171.

28. Smith, *Can't You Hear Me Callin'*, 202.

29. The original recording from this event has been posted online at "Bluegrass Story—Part 1," Fincastle 1965: The First Multi-day Bluegrass Festival, http://frobbi.org/audio/fincastle65/.

Chapter 7. Me and My Old Crow (Got a Good Thing Going)

1. Stringbean's appearance on the show can be found on YouTube at https://www.youtube.com/watch?v=blrqDHzg1ac&t=223s.

2. *City Confidential*, "Nashville: Murder in Music City."

3. "The Stoneman Family," All Music, https://www.allmusic.com/artist/the-stoneman-family-mn0000475313/biography.

4. Jones with Wolfe, *Everybody's Grandpa*, 143–44.

5. Bill Anderson, email to the author, June 27, 2022.

6. Recording of interviews with Jimmy C. Newman (performer), Clyde Moody (performer/songwriter), Bill Carlisle (performer), and Jimmy Riddle (performer), conducted by Biff Collie on September 12, 1974, Country Music Hall of Fame, Nashville, RT-7-03988_1. Hereafter referred to as "Biff Collie interview."

7. *City Confidential*, "Nashville: Murder in Music City."

8. Grandpa confirmed the Bank of Goodlettsville checking account that drew interest ("Murder Trial Transcript," 68). Terry Faimon confirms that the Akemans kept money in a bank strongbox.

9. Bobby Anderson, "Stringbean's Friend Relates Fond Memories 35 Years Later," *Kentucky Explorer*, November 2008, 29–30.

10. Mark Jones, phone conversation with the author.

11. Lulu Roman, interview with the author, February 24, 2021.

12. Quoted in John Aylesworth, *The Corn Was Green: The Inside Story of "Hee Haw"* (Jefferson, NC: McFarland, 2010), 55.

13. Aylesworth, *Corn Was Green*, 72.

14. This episode can be viewed on YouTube at https://www.youtube.com/watch?v=eYOf38Z8UrM&t=2684s.

15. Jones with Wolfe, *Everybody's Grandpa*, 174.

16. Sam Lovullo and Marc Eliot, *Life in the Kornfield: My 25 Years at "Hee Haw"* (New York: Boulevard Books, 1996), 80.

17. Lovullo, *Life in the Kornfield*, 80.

18. Steve Eng, *A Satisfied Mind: The Country Music Life of Porter Wagoner* (Nashville: Rutledge Hill Press, 1992), 232.

19. Jones with Wolfe, *Everybody's Grandpa*, 197.

20. Jones with Wolfe, *Everybody's Grandpa*, 197, 204.

21. Paul Hemphill, *The Nashville Sound: Bright Lights and Country Music* (1970; reprint, Athens: University of Georgia Press, 2015), 269–70.

22. A clip from this video, circa 1970, can be viewed on YouTube at https://www.youtube.com/watch?v=qzloBAtkiOA&t=137s.

23. Story told by Mark Jones, phone interview, February 2021.

24. Jones with Wolfe, *Everybody's Grandpa*, 204–5.

25. Jones with Wolfe, *Everybody's Grandpa*, 204.

26. This photograph hangs in the Jackson County Library and is marked as being from the collection of Gary D. Bailey.

27. https://automotivemileposts.com/cadillac/cadi1974interiortrim.html.

28. Roni Stoneman, as told to Ellen Wright, *Pressing On: The Roni Stoneman Story* (Urbana: University of Illinois Press, 2007), 145.

29. Roni Stoneman, phone interview with the author, March 17, 2021.

30. Stoneman, *Pressing On*, 146.

31. Scott with Swiesz and Franks, *Snake Oil*, 307.

32. Scott with Swiesz and Franks, *Snake Oil*, 308.

33. Information on Harry Wright is scarce. Ted Shred owns one of these Stringbean figures and has kindly posted and shared information on Facebook. On Harry Wright's being from Cave City, Kentucky, see "Hand Made Roy Acuff Figurine," Everything but the House, https://www.ebth.com/items/2113884-hand-made-roy-acuff-figurine.

34. Waddell, "Serious Look at a Funny Man," 15.

35. Anderson, email to the author.

36. Scott with Swiesz and Franks, *Snake Oil*, 307–8.

37. The following information taken from Oscar Sullivan's sworn statement reproduced in "Murder Trial Transcript," 1204–6.

38. *State of Tennessee v. John A. Brown, Jr.*, #B-2678, #B-2679, Davidson County Criminal Court, Nashville, Division III, 1974, 411. This multivolume document will hereafter be referred to as "Sanity Trial Transcript."

39. "Murder Trial Transcript," 896.

40. "Sanity Trial Transcript," 411.

41. "Murder Trial Transcript," 896.

42. Gibson, "Interview with Gibson," 1.

43. Gibson, "Interview with Gibson," 2–3.

44. Gibson, "Interview with Gibson," 2.

45. Gibson, "Interview with Gibson," 2.

46. Gibson, "Stringbean Murders: Part 2."

Interlude. Goodbye Sweet Thing

1. I have put this dramatization of the final day of Stringbean's life in a different typeface and present tense in order to create a sense of immediacy and to signal the transitional function of this segment of the book. The goal herein is to narrate Stringbean's final day of life. Whereas previous chapters deal with multiple years, the final two chapters present events that transpired in slightly less than a single year. Furthermore, the novelistic style of this section hopefully will heighten the emotional register of the moment of Stringbean's murder. No less fidelity is being given to the truth of Stringbean and his world and moment and to the facts of the day, as best they can be determined. The movements and conversations in sections one and two are based on Stringbean's environment and style of conversation as evidenced in sources already cited. The details in section three simply bring to life information as presented in Causey, *The Stringbean Murders*, and court records. Dialogue and details from the remaining sections are cited.

2. Causey, *The Stringbean Murders*, 11.

3. "Murder Trial Transcript," 37.

4. Jerry Thompson, "Opry Colleagues, Fans Pay Akeman, Wife Tribute," *Tennessean*, November 17, 1973, 17.

5. Charles Wolfe, "String," *Bluegrass Unlimited* 16, no. 11 (1982): 46.

6. Stacy Harris, phone conversation with the author, August 28, 2018.

7. Wolfe, "String," 46.

8. Wolfe, "String," 46.

9. Details from the following exchange from Roni Stoneman, phone interview with the author, March 17, 2021.

10. David Raybin, "The Stringbean Murders: Death in Baker Holler, Part 2."

11. "Murder Trial Transcript," 88–89.

12. Causey, *The Stringbean Murders*, 18.

13. "Murder Trial Transcript," 91.

Chapter 8. Sinner Man, Where You Gonna Hide

1. "Murder Trial Transcript," 41.

2. Causey, *The Stringbean Murders*, 24–25, 26.

3. Tommy Jacobs, email to the author, October 4, 2018.

4. Causey, *The Stringbean Murders*, 34.

5. Causey, *The Stringbean Murders*, 110, 63.

6. "Murder Trial Transcript," 123.

7. Causey, *The Stringbean Murders*, 45–46.

8. Causey, *The Stringbean Murders*, 143.

9. "Murder Trial Transcript," 827.

10. Causey, *The Stringbean Murders*, 52.

11. Sandra Scott Whitmore, phone conversation with the author, January 25, 2022; Gibson, "Interview with Gibson," 4–5.

12. Causey, *The Stringbean Murders*, 51.

13. Causey, *The Stringbean Murders*, 47.

14. "Murder Trial Transcript," 340–62, 344–46.

15. Causey, *The Stringbean Murders*, 46.

16. A letter from Lillies Ohlsson, with *Kountry Korral Magazine*, is in the Stringbean file at the Country Music Hall of Fame, Nashville.

17. Nancy Varley and Frank Gibson, "Killers Missed $5,700," *Tennessean*, November 12, 1973, 10.

18. *City Confidential*, "Nashville: Murder in Music City."

19. Causey, *The Stringbean Murders*, 64.

20. Causey, *The Stringbean Murders*, 54, 56, 57.

21. Causey, *The Stringbean Murders*, 63, 65–66.

22. Causey, *The Stringbean Murders*, 69, 75.

23. Jerry Bailey, "Those He Made Smile Saddened," *Tennessean*, November 14, 1973, 1, 20.

24. Causey, *The Stringbean Murders*, 71.

25. Causey, *The Stringbean Murders*, 71.

26. Bailey, "Those He Made Smile," 20.

27. Frank Gibson and Nancy Varley, "Old House Center of Slaying Probe," *Tennessean*, November 14, 1973, 1.

28. Causey, *The Stringbean Murders*, 20, 76.

29. *City Confidential*, "Nashville: Murder in Music City."

30. Causey, *The Stringbean Murders*, 76.

31. "Shriver Seeks Seat in Legislature," *Nashville Banner*, June 8, 1960, 4.

32. "Nashville Lawyer to Be Named US Attorney," *Knoxville Journal*, January 25, 1964, 3; "Shriver Delivers Blow to City Bachelor Club," *Tennessean*, January 1, 1964, 1.

33. "Shriver Jaycee's 'Young Man of the Year,'" *Tennessean*, January 11, 1967, 33.

34. Causey, *The Stringbean Murders*, 77.

35. Causey, *The Stringbean Murders*, 76–77.

36. "Murder Trial Transcript," 838.

37. Causey, *The Stringbean Murders*, 77.

38. Hal McDonough, "Stringbean Murders: Part 1."

39. Causey, *The Stringbean Murders*, 83, 81–82, 83.

40. "Pair Intensively Quizzed, Let Go in Akeman Case," *Tennessean*, November 15, 1973, 1, 14.

41. Roy was born on February 21, 1948, Doug on August 4, 1950.

42. Memorandum, State of Tennessee Division of Probation and Paroles, April 15, 1977.

43. Larry Brinton, "Doug Brown Relives Agonizing Moments," *Nashville Banner*, July 23, 1974, 1, 12.

44. "Pair Intensively Quizzed," 14.

45. "Police Checking Every Lead," *Tennessean*, November 16, 1973, 1, 11.

46. "Murder Trial Transcript," 1206.

47. "Murder Trial Transcript," 90.

48. *State of Tennessee v. John A. Brown, Jr.*, #B-2678, #B-2679, Davidson County Criminal Court, Nashville, Division III, 1974, 6–8. This multivolume document will hereafter be referred to as "Sanity Trial Transcript." Incidentally, John Brown Sr. remembers his son's birth year as 1949.

49. "John A. Brown, Parole Hearing," transcript, October 15, 2014, 3.

50. "Sanity Trial Transcript," 10, 12, 59. In the summer of 1974, Thomas was four years old and John was three.

51. "Brown, Parole Hearing," 4, 14, 59, 15.

52. Jerry Thompson, "Opry Colleagues, Fans Pay Akeman, Wife Tribute," *Tennessean*, November 17, 1973, 17.

53. Thompson, "Opry Colleagues," 17.

54. Causey, *The Stringbean Murders*, 91.

55. Causey, *The Stringbean Murders*, 87–88, 91, 95, 96.

56. Causey, *The Stringbean Murders*, 97.

57. Jerry Thompson, "Opry Family Honors String," *Tennessean*, November 18, 1973, 24, 1, 24.

58. Thompson, "Opry Family Honors String," 24. ·

59. Byron Fay, email to the author, March 20, 2021.

60. Causey, *The Stringbean Murders*, 103.

61. *Charleston (WV) Sunday Gazette-Mail,* November 18, 1973; Causey, *The Stringbean Murders*, 71–72; Marc A. Zolotar, "'Stringbean Akeman' Recalled by Singer," *Kansas City Times*, November 19, 1973; Bill Preston Jr., "Dogwood Saved to Serve as Tribute to Akemans," *Tennessean*, November 27, 1973, 1, 4.

62. Jerry Thompson, "Couple Dined Together Minutes before Death," *Tennessean*, November 29, 1973, 1, 12.

63. Gibson, "Interview with Gibson," 4.

64. Frank Gibson, "Opry Stars Taking More Precautions," *Tennessean*, December 3, 1973, 1, 5.

65. Gibson, "Opry Stars Taking More Precautions," 5.

66. Causey, *The Stringbean Murders*, 114, 121.

67. Causey, *The Stringbean Murders*, 123.

68. "David 'Stringbean' Akeman," *Bluegrass Unlimited* 8, no. 6 (1973): 5; Mark Jones, phone conversation with the author, February 21, 2021.

69. Causey, *The Stringbean Murders*, 122.

70. Jerry Thompson, "Akemans Left at Least $500,000," *Tennessean*, December 11, 1973, 1, 3.

71. Faimon maintains that he never knew of a will. William Faimon, phone conversation with the author, October 4, 2019.

72. Faimon, phone conversation with the author.

73. Jerry Thompson, "Farm Death Scene Yields Shell Casings," *Tennessean*, December 19, 1973, 1, 19.

74. Causey, *The Stringbean Murders*, 128, 131.

75. The diver's name was Jim Gaddis, and it seems that he charged Metro a premium price. Causey, *The Stringbean Murders*, 132–33.

76. Causey, *The Stringbean Murders*, 143, 145.

77. Causey, *The Stringbean Murders*, 147, 149.

78. Causey, *The Stringbean Murders*, 153.

79. David Raybin explains this law in "Stringbean Murders, Part 2."

80. Causey, *The Stringbean Murders*, 154.

81. Causey, *The Stringbean Murders*, 155, 156, 157.

82. Jerry Thompson, "Akeman 'Star Witness' under Guard," *Tennessean*, January 17, 1974, 1, 2.

Chapter 9. You Can't Do Wrong and Get By

1. The description of the auction of the Akemans' effects is gleaned from Tom Gillem, "Akeman Estate, Minus Banjo, Goes on Auction Block Today," *Tennessean*, March 2, 1974, 1, 13; Tom Gillem, "Stringbean's Land, Items to Be Sold," *Tennessean*, February 14, 1974, 21; Jerry Thompson, "Auction Shows Stringbean's Memory Valued," *Tennes-*

sean, March 3, 1974, 14; and Hubert D. Songer, "Estate of Grand Ole Opry and Hee Haw Television Star Sold at Auction" (publication information unknown, article in private collection of Leroy Troy), 25–34.

2. Thompson, "Auction Shows," 4.

3. Thompson, "Auction Shows," 4. Songer claims the auctioned ended at six.

4. Causey, *The Stringbean Murders*, 161.

5. Ed Yarbrough states that "it seems that Bobby Green and perhaps other detectives were predisposed to favor Butler because of their past relationship when he was a prosecutor." "Stringbean Murders, Part 1."

6. Causey, *The Stringbean Murders*, 162–63.

7. Jerry Thompson, "1 of 4 Akeman Suspects Freed," *Tennessean*, January 22, 1974, 8.

8. Thompson, "1 of 4 Akeman Suspects Freed," 8.

9. "Murder Hearing Postponed," *Kingsport (TN) Times*, January 23, 1974, 2.

10. "Two Bound over in Akeman Case," *Tennessean*, January 26, 1974, 13.

11. "Akeman Defendant Draws New Charge," *Tennessean*, January 27, 1974, C23.

12. Jerry Thompson, "Akeman Case Defendant Asks Release," *Tennessean*, January 29, 1974, 2.

13. "Police Use Divers in Akeman Search," *Tennessean*, January 30, 1974, 39.

14. Biographical information on Judge Cornelius based on obituary, *Tennessean*, January 24, 2007, B4; and "Judge Cornelius's Court, 1969 May 2," Digital Library of Tennessee, https://tn.dp.la/item/da7461854a26f75c53365594c56e43ca?subject=%22 Lawyers—Tennessee—Nashville%22&type=%22image%22&page=1.

15. Causey, *The Stringbean Murders*, 166.

16. "Judge Allen Cornelius," Tennessee Portrait Project, https://tnportraits.org/portrait/cornelius-judge-allen/.

17. "Akeman Hearing Ruled Open," *Tennessean*, February 2, 1974, 14.

18. "2 Indicted for Murder of Akemans," *Tennessean*, March 5, 1974, 19.

19. Jerry Bailey, "'Janitor' Kristofferson Gets Second 'Songwriter of the Year' Award," *Tennessean*, March 8, 1974, 30.

20. Pat Welch and Frank Gibson, "3 Generations Sing Goodbye to the Ryman," *Tennessean*, March 17, 1974, 12.

21. Jerry Thompson and Pat Welch, "Nixon Dedicated New Grand Ole Opry House," *Tennessean*, March 17, 1974, 1, 13.

22. "Stringbean's Murder Trial Set for July 15," *Tennessean*, April 10, 1974, 25.

23. Nancy Varley, "Defendant in Stringbean Slayings Allowed Bond," *Tennessean*, May 11, 1974, 1.

24. Causey, *The Stringbean Murders*, 166.

25. Kenneth Jost, "Law License Surrendered by Peebles," *Tennessean*, June 25, 1975, 1–14.

26. Jerry Thompson, "Akeman Suspected Tested for Tumor," *Tennessean*, June 5, 1974, 19.

27. "Accused Akeman Murderer's Sanity Hearing Slated July 15," *Tennessean*, July 3, 1974, 41.

28. John later presented his version of the murder night in a statement to Shriver, Peebles, and Charles Hunter. "Statement of John A. Brown, Jr.," taken at the Metropolitan Workhouse, Nashville, July 23, 1974.

29. Pat Welch, "Hearing Starts Today on Brown's Sanity," *Tennessean*, July 17, 1974, 9.

30. *State of Tennessee v. John A. Brown, Jr.*, #B-2678, #B-2679, Davidson County Criminal Court, Nashville, Division III, 1974, 1, 2. This multivolume document will hereafter be referred to as "Sanity Trial Transcript."

31. "Sanity Trial Transcript," 3, 4.

32. Pat Welch, "Brown 'Sane,' Trial Slated," *Tennessean*, July 20, 1974, 12.

33. Welch, "Brown 'Sane,' Trial Slated," 12.

34. Larry Brinton, "Doug Brown Relives Agonizing Moments," *Nashville Banner*, July 23, 1974, 1, 12.

35. Hal McDonough discusses Binkley's motivations and also addresses the legal problems with using the statements of codefendants against one another ("Stringbean Murders: Part 1").

36. McDonough, "Stringbean Murders: Part 1."

37. "Murder Trial Transcript," 1109.

38. "Murder Trial Transcript," 1100, 672, 685, 692.

39. *City Confidential*, "Nashville: Murder in Music City."

40. "Murder Trial Transcript," 685, 686.

41. "Statement of John A. Brown, Jr.," 1.

42. Doug Hall, "Akeman Robbery Plan Laid to Charles Brown," *Tennessean*, July 28, 1974, 12.

43. George Watson Jr. and Doug Hall, "Roy Brown's Lawyer Asks Charge Drop," *Tennessean*, July 25, 1974, 1, 2.

44. "Akeman Case Suspects Enter Innocent Pleas," *Tennessean*, July 27, 1974, 8.

45. Frank Gibson, "Roy Brown Asks Separate Akeman Trial," *Tennessean*, August 15, 1974, 55.

46. "Old Timer's Almanac," *Tennessean*, August 18, 1974, 146.

47. Doug Hall, "Akeman Suspect's Motion for Sanity Hearing Denied," *Tennessean*, October 23, 1974, 13.

48. Doug Hall, "Special Security Planned for Two Murder Trials," *Tennessean*, October 26, 1974, 28.

49. Doug Hall, "11 Sit Tentatively on Akeman Trial," *Tennessean*, October 29, 1974, 1. Elsewhere, police interrogated Roger Dale Keith of Springfield, who had claimed he had the infamous .32 murder weapon, but now said he had just been joking.

50. Causey, *The Stringbean Murders*, 167.

51. Hall, "11 Sit Tentatively on Akeman Trial," 7.

52. Doug Hall, "Opry Star Recounts Discovery of Bodies," *Tennessean*, October 30, 1974, 10.

53. "Murder Trial Transcript," 17–18, 27, 75.

54. Hall, "Opry Star Recounts Discovery of Bodies," 10.

55. Hall, "Opry Star Recounts," 10.

56. *John A. Brown, Jr., v. James H. Rose and William Leach*, Evidentiary Hearing, 1982, 10.

57. *State of Tennessee v. John A. Brown, Jr., et al.: Bill of Exceptions, Motion for a New Trial Hearing*, 1976, 110–11.

58. Susan Thomas, "Stringbean Case Lawyer 'Addicted'?," *Tennessean*, July 28, 1979, 1.

59. "Murder Trial Transcript," 223–26, 228.

60. "Murder Trial Transcript," 280, 290.

61. Doug Hall, "Others Involved in Akeman Case," *Tennessean*, October 31, 1974, 1, 18.

62. Causey, *The Stringbean Murders*, 168.

63. "Murder Trial Transcript," 646.

64. Doug Hall, "Coworker Helped Build Akeman Case," *Tennessean*, November 1, 1974, 26.

65. "Murder Trial Transcript," 879, 896, 937.

66. Causey, *The Stringbean Murders*, 168–69, 109.

67. "Murder Trial Transcript," 993.

68. Causey, *The Stringbean Murders*, 169.

69. "Murder Trial Transcript," 1060, 1076.

70. "Murder Trial Transcript," 1155.

71. "Murder Trial Transcript," 1176, 1177.

72. "Murder Trial Transcript," 1184, 1207.

73. "Murder Trial Transcript," 1220.

74. "Murder Trial Transcript," 1249–51.

75. "Murder Trial Transcript," 1291.

76. Doug Hall, "Browns Guilty, Get 99-Year Terms," *Tennessean*, November 3, 1974, 1.

77. Hall, "Browns Guilty," 13.

78. Hall, "Browns Guilty," 13.

79. Hall, "Browns Guilty," 8.

80. Hall, "Browns Guilty," 13, 1.

81. "Murder Trial Transcript," 1332–33.

82. Hall, "Browns Guilty," 1.

83. Hall, "Browns Guilty," 1.

84. Dwight Lewis, "John Brown Discusses Slayings, 'I Was Picked to Take Rap,'" *Tennessean*, November 5, 1974, 1, 5.

85. Kirk Loggins, "2 Begin Terms in Murder of Akemans," *Tennessean*, November 4, 1974, 2.

86. "Arson Charge Dropped," *Clarksville (TN) Leaf-Chronicle*, November 10, 1974, 13.

87. "Stringbean's Banjo Donated to Hall," *Nashville Banner*, December 24, 1974, 9.

Epilogue. Forgetting to Forget You

1. Malcolm Burdsall, "Swan Song for the Country Music Killers," *Master Detective* 90, no. 1 (1975): 33–35, 66–70; Kenneth Jost, "'Stringbean' Triggerman Fires Peebles," *Tennessean*, May 1, 1975, 91.

2. Doug Hall, "More Misconduct Allegations Added to Peebles Suit," *Tennessean*, June 5, 1975, 17.

3. Kenneth Jost, "Law License Surrendered by Peebles," *Tennessean*, June 25, 1975, 1,14.

4. *State of Tennessee v. John A. Brown, Jr., et al.*, Bill of Exceptions Motion for a New Trial, #B-2678, #B-2679, Criminal Courts of Metropolitan Davidson County, Nashville, Division III, May 7, 1976.

5. Tommy Jacobs, email to the author, October 4, 2018.

6. Deposition of Dr. W. R. C Stewart Jr., June 8, 1976, *State of Tennessee v. John A. Brown, Jr., et al.*, Bill of Exceptions Motion for a New Trial.

7. Kirk Loggins, "Final Stringbean Suspect to Plead a Lesser Charge," *Tennessean*, December 15, 1976, 21.

8. Kirk Loggins, "Reward Given in Stringbean Murder Case," *Tennessean*, November 23, 1977, 1; Kirk Loggins, "Stringbean Case Reward Division Eyed," *Tennessean*, April 13, 1977, 43; Nancy Varley, "Nashvillian Files Claim for Stringbean Reward," *Tennessean*, June 5, 1977, 20. Jones had written police chief Joe Casey early in December 1973, during the investigation, saying that "an acquaintance had convinced him that Doug Brown and Elliott had committed the crime" and had spent the blood money. Jones had also suspected another acquaintance of the Browns, Mitchell Payne, as being involved. Jones was discredited. Kirk Loggins, "Nashville Heir Finder Proves Hard to Find," *Tennessean*, December 20, 1977, 1, 22.

9. David Raybin, "Stringbean Murders, Part 2."

10. Kenneth Jost, "John A. Brown Jr. Denied Trial," *Tennessean*, September 10, 1976, 18.

11. Nora St. John Death Certificate, No. 10846.

12. *John A. Brown, Jr., v. James H. Rose and William Leach*, Evidentiary Hearing, United States District Court for the Middle District of Tennessee, No. 82-3124, May 5, 1982, 12–13, 11.

13. Dwight Lewis, "Inmate Wants Prison Editor Returned to Custodial Duties," *Tennessean*, October 1, 1982, 2.

14. "Stringbean Killer Opens Show, Jolts Opry Stars," *Nashville Banner*, May 27, 1983.

15. Kirk Loggins, "Slow Action Irks Akemans' Heirs," *Tennessean*, September 6, 1984, B2, B6.

16. Renee Elder, "Christmas Lonely for Some," *Tennessean*, December 25, 1987, 28.

17. "Robert Akeman," Indiana State Board of Health Certificate of Death, No. 83-011697.

18. "Killer of Opry Star Asks Parole," *Tennessean*, December 1, 1992.

19. Randy Barlow, "Killer Says He's Changed," *Tennessean*, July 19, 1993, 11.

20. Jim East, "Browns Denied Parole," *Tennessean*, July 20, 1993, B1, B2.

21. Linda A. Moore, "Stringbean's Cash Stash a Mouse Nest?," *Tennessean*, January 28, 1997, B6.

22. William Faimon, phone conversation with the author, October 4, 2019.

23. Bobby Anderson, "Stringbean's Friend Relates Fond Memories 35 Years Later," *Kentucky Explorer*, November 2008, 30.

24. "Ludy Frances Sparkman," obituary, *Tennessean*, August 1, 1997, B5.

25. Cheryl E. Preston, "Sagging Pants Have a Dark History Rooted in American Slavery and Rape," Styled, 2020, https://vocal.media/styled/sagging-pants-have-a-dark-history-rooted-in-american-slavery-and-rape.

26. "Alfred Akemon," obituary, *Orem-Geneva (UT) Times*, August 8, 2002, A4.

27. "Sallie Russell," obituary, *Richmond (IN) Palladium-Item*, October 17, 2006, A5.

28. Kate Howard, "Stringbean's Killer Denied," *Tennessean*, August 9, 2008, B6.

29. Erin Quinn, "Wife of Stringbean's Killer Says He Deserves Freedom," *Tennessean*, July 17, 2011, B1, B5.

30. Erin Quinn, "Stringbean Killer's Plea Resisted," *Tennessean*, July 20, 2011, B1, B8.

31. Kirk Loggins, "Peebles Guilty, Faces Term of 3 to 6 Years," *Tennessean*, April 30, 1988, 1, 2.

32. Adam Tamburin, "Brown 'Cold-Bloodedly Killed Two Friends of Ours,'" *Tennessean*, October 16, 2014, A16.

33. Adam Tamburin, "Freedom May Meet Anniversary of Killings," *Tennessean*, November 3, 2014, A13.

34. Adam Tamburin, "Man Who Murdered Stringbean Akeman Set Free," *Tennessean*, November 4, 2014, A6.

35. "John A. Brown, Parole Hearing," transcript, October 15, 2014.

36. Tamburin, "Man Who Murdered Stringbean Akeman Set Free," A3.

37. Tamburin, "Brown 'Cold-Bloodedly Killed Two Friends of Ours,'" A13.

38. Torry Johnson, "Stringbean Murders: Part 2."

SELECTED BIBLIOGRAPHY

Causey, Warren B. *The Stringbean Murders*. Nashville: Quest, 1975.

Gibson, Steve. "Interview with Steve Gibson Regarding His Memories of Stringbean." Unpublished manuscript, 2013.

Jones, Louis M. "Grandpa," with Charles K. Wolfe. *Everybody's Grandpa: Fifty Years behind the Mike*. Knoxville: University of Tennessee Press, 1984.

Scott, "Doc" Tommy, with Shirley Noe Swiesz and Randall Franks. *Snake Oil, Superstars and Me: The Story of Ramblin "Doc" Tommy Scott*. Toccoa, GA: Katona Productions, 2007.

State of Tennessee v. John A. Brown, Jr., and Marvin Douglas Brown. #B-2678, #B-2679, Davidson County Criminal Court, Division III, Nashville, 1974. Abbreviated in the notes as "Murder Trial Transcript."

Stringbean. Interview by Douglas B. Green, OH533, August 12, 1972. Country Music Foundation, Nashville.

———. Interview by Reuben Powell and Bob Hyland. WOLFE-00231. Charles K. Wolfe Audio Collection, Center for Popular Music, Middle Tennessee State University, Murfreesboro.

"The Stringbean Murders: Death in Baker Holler, Part 1." Nashville Bar Association Continuing Legal Education Program and the Nashville Bar Association Historical Committee, Nashville Main Public Library, November 8, 2018. https://www.youtube.com/watch?v=8-lAR_lHeGo&t=4931s. Abbreviated in the notes as "Stringbean Murders: Part 1."

"The Stringbean Murders: Death in Baker Holler, Part 2." Nashville Bar Association Continuing Legal Education Program and the Nashville Bar Association Historical

Committee, Nashville Main Public Library, November 8, 2018. https://www.youtube.com/watch?v=QK9JVZdm1_M&t=291s. Abbreviated in the notes as "Stringbean Murders: Part 2.

Waddell, Genevieve J. "A Serious Look at a Funny Man: Stringbean," *Country Song Roundup*, May 1974, 14–16, 45.

———. "Stringbean." *Country Music World*, January–February 1974, 40–44.

Wolfe, Charles K. *Kentucky Country: Folk and Country Music of Kentucky*. Lexington: University Press of Kentucky, 1982.

———. *Stringbean: Barn Yard Banjo Picking*. CD liner notes. Gusto, B000LC4ZGM, 2006.

INDEX

TAYLOR HAGOOD is a professor in the department of English at Florida Atlantic University. His books include *Faulkner, Writer of Disability* and *Secrecy, Magic, and the One-Act Plays of Harlem Renaissance Women Writers*.

MUSIC IN AMERICAN LIFE

The University of Illinois Press
is a founding member of the
Association of University Presses.

Composed in 10.25/13 Marat Pro
with ITC Franklin Gothic STD display
by Lisa Connery
at the University of Illinois Press
Manufactured by Sheridan Books, Inc.
University of Illinois Press

1325 South Oak Street
Champaign, IL 61820-6903
www.press.uillinois.edu